Chapter 1

I'm going to start at the beginning. Not that I don't appreciate a clever framing device, but so few stories seem to start at the beginning anymore. I won't be able to end this tale, because it's my own, and I can't write when I'm dead. I don't want to start the story where I am now. Now, I'm in the middle of a dark, lonely, and terrible place, and as I think you will see throughout this narrative, terrible places are best viewed in hindsight.

I apologize if I boast and flatter myself. My intent is to be honest, but of course, we all honestly think of ourselves as great people. Besides, the higher a tower is built up, the more entertaining it is to watch fall.

In my earliest memories, my parents are still together. They divorced when I was three, which serves as a convenient time stamp. My father is a wise and kind man, but a father's anger is hard to forget, as is his sadness. No doubt my own children will never forget mine.

My father and mother were sleeping in the same bed while I slept in my crib. I woke up from a nightmare and crawled into bed with them. I remember my father didn't want me there. A sentiment I fully sympathize with now that I am a parent. They argued and I ended up back in the crib. Tough love is something every boy needs. Momma won't be there to coddle you forever. I think this is my first memory.

I only remember my father disciplining me once. I couldn't find my sisters and asked my mom where they were.

"They went to Chris's house," she answered.

Chris was a boy their age who lived on the other side of the creek. Normally they would take me with them. I was hurt and feeling left out, a feeling the youngest of five becomes familiar with. My sisters had walked with me to his house before and I was sure I could get there on my own. Mom would never let me go that far without my sisters, but three year old me reasoned that once I got there I would be with my sisters. *No harm, no fowl, right?* I reached Chris's house and was quite proud of my accomplishment until his parents got a phone call.

"Yes he is here and he is ok.........I'll tell them."

It was a long terrifying walk back home with my sisters. My father took me to the laundry room and tanned my hide with the paddle. Which paddle, I can't remember. We had two: the Big Bad Butt Bopper and Sting. Mom handled discipline after the divorce. There is no way I can recall how many times she had to spank me.

My father's sadness stands out the most. He had to tell me about the divorce. My father had to explain to me why my mother was making him leave. Remember this, it will become important later. He was living out in the detached garage he used for a cabinet shop. Three year old me didn't think it strange that he was living out in the garage. It was a fun fort and I wanted one of my own. We were eating his fried eggs that were never as good as the ones mom cooked. He always managed to crack the yolk, like I do now. I can't remember his words. I can only remember he had a hard time saying them. I was crushed and couldn't understand why he had to leave, especially when he wanted to stay. I knew he loved me. I ran inside the house to my mother.

"Mommy, I need my Daddy," I told her.

She remembers me saying this. I went back outside and stopped him while he was mowing the lawn, wanting him to make sense of it. I wouldn't understand until much later. I never felt like it was my fault. I don't know why that's such a common concern. Maybe I didn't feel that way because I was so young. I did, however, blame my mother as I grew older and came to understand. It will break her heart to read this, but it's the truth. I've asked a few times growing up and still don't understand why, just as I don't understand why the mother of my children left me. My mother never denied my father the right to see his children though, so it's easy to forgive her.

The memory marking the rest of my life came after the divorce when my brother was still around. We were looking at one of his knife magazines and there was a picture of two guys dressed as ninjas. I, of course, was obsessed with ninjas due to my brother's influence. He explained that the men in the picture were Navy SEALs. I decided I wanted to be a Navy SEAL and never changed my mind. I don't think I was even in kindergarten yet. The divorce was much harder on my brother. He ran away when he was fourteen or fifteen, I think, living in the hills behind the house. He eventually moved in with Pop, just as we all eventually did.

Kindergarten is my next set of memories. I got an unusual hernia above my belly button. The doctor couldn't understand how someone so young could have such a high abdominal hernia. Then he learned about tickle torture. My sisters would take turns holding me down and tickling me until I couldn't breathe. They thought it was cute, but I would genuinely panic because I couldn't breathe. They would stop for a second and say, "Breathe, breathe." Then start again. Whether or not tickle torture was the cause of the hernia is still debated at family gatherings. In truth, being introduced at such a young age to the panic caused when you can't breathe probably helped with my chosen profession.

I have several memories from doctors' offices and being in the surgery room. The large cut in my stomach was covered with clear plastic so I could show it off to my friends. I showed it to a girl I had a crush on at school, her name was Mary. The most vivid memory was after my surgery, I think, it might have been before. I suddenly had trouble breathing. Hernias don't affect your breathing, but I didn't know that then. All I knew was something serious was wrong with my stomach and suddenly I couldn't breathe. It was probably nothing, but I was not the man I am now. I panicked, which made it worse. My aunt was holding me and my mother was crying as she talked to the doctor on the phone. I must have calmed down because I can't remember the resolution, but the fear of that moment etched it into my memory.

I have started out very gloomy, but I had a great childhood. My father and mother are good people and loved me. I was also blessed with a great stepfather, though I treated him like shit. Money was tight while I was growing up, but we had enough. Pop's cabinet shop struggled, and mom received welfare for a bit. She worked cleaning houses and for a short time as a lunch lady. My siblings and I had what we needed and our divorced parents were always civil with each other. Mom was at her best as a homemaker. She married another carpenter. I was six and he proposed at my birthday. This always angered me, but I was just being a little punk. I didn't find out until after and it was one of the best birthdays I can remember. I got a shit ton of GI Joes. A handful of new ones from friends and family, but the kicker was a giant box of old GI Joes from my brother's friend.

I became interested in girls earlier than most boys. With four older siblings I matured faster than most kids. Hell, I had my career picked out before kindergarten. My first crush was Mary. We were picked as ring bearer and flower girl for the wedding of a family friend. I never really even talked to this girl, but my siblings made fun of me for years afterward. In third grade I had my first girlfriend. Her name was Alex. I was not allowed to have a girl-friend. I wrote her a Valentine saying, *I love you baby*, something I must have gotten from my sister's music. Mom found it, but I can't remember the punishment. We stayed girlfriend and boyfriend for the rest of third grade anyway. From an early age I understood commit-ment. I assumed we would still be girlfriend and boyfriend at the start of fourth grade, but she had other ideas. After a year of going steady, she dumped me at the start of the next school year.

The more important part of third grade was my best friend Zebb. I ended up in the awkward geeky crowd with Zebb. This kid had glasses with a geek strap, a blond penis-head haircut, and a rat tail hanging to his mid back. He couldn't give a fuck, though. Zebb was his own person. The teachers hated him because he always asked questions.

"Why do platypuses lay eggs if they are mammals?" He would blurt out while the teacher was talking.

"Zebb! If you have a question you need to raise your hand first!" they would scold.

Zebb would not just raise his hand. He would shoot it up in the air, wiggle his fingers and wave it back and forth as he bounced in his seat. Zebb would not be ignored. This never ended. In junior high a teacher assigned a kid to sit behind Zebb and smack the back of his head every time he had a question. Teachers could get away with a lot more back then.

Zebb and I were as close as friends get. His mom divorced his old man too, and we both developed a strong sense of commitment. The greatest summer of my life we spent every moment together. During the day we would be at my house, playing outside in the woods, wandering far and wide to build forts. His mother was from Canada and thought America was full of child abductors or "weirdos" as she called them. She would never let him roam, but my mother grew up in SoCal so she was fine with us roaming the hills and streets of a small town in Oregon. In the evenings, his mom would pick us up and we would watch movies and play video games all night. My mom would have killed me if she knew what movies I was watching and the games I was playing. Satanic stuff like Doom, Diablo, and Dumb and Dumber.

The trio was complete when my cousin Joe moved to Oregon in '97 or '96. I was going to be a Navy SEAL, Joe was going to be Marine Recon and Zebb took Green Berets by default. I don't think Zebb ever really wanted to be in the military. Nevertheless, we began our training. During the day we learned the hills behind my house front to back. At night we would dress in black and tie t-shirts around our faces like ninjas. We snuck into people's yards to see how close we could get without getting caught. We spent hours on our bellies crawling up to evening parties and BBQs. Hundreds of people in my small town had grade school kids spying on them from their bushes and never knew. This of course sounds terribly creepy, but we just thought we were training for our future.

We devised manhood tests we all had to pass, many of which were first pioneered by my brother. One was a crawl through a two-foot by two-foot drain pipe that was a good fifty yards long. The pipe curved under the road, so it was dark for most of it. All you could do was slither as fast as you could, trying not think about the things slithering with you in the dark. At the end you could stand up, wipe the cobwebs from your face and call yourself a man; all while trying not to wiggle like a girl as the bugs crawled under your pants.

Killing a rattle snake was the one thing my brother did that we just had to measure up to. Of course we weren't paying attention to the part where he used a .410 shotgun. We headed up into the hills with sticks in our hands and knives on our thighs. The first was a mess. We were all amped up and beat it to death with the sticks. Maybe five inches of good skin was left. We proudly paraded our five inches of rattle snake skin in front of our fifth-grade class. Eventually we realized you could just pin the snake with a stick and cut its head off. The new technique improved the quality of our trophies.

Our trio's antics reached new heights when we found a treasure trove. I'm going to break my mom's heart, and I'll probably tell her not to read this. While up in the woods, we discovered a camper that had rolled off the side of a mountain road. I'm guessing a vengeful woman took everything her man loved into the mountains and dumped it off a cliff. Inside the camper was gunpowder, moonshine, and porn.

We spent the summer in our various forts in the hills looking at naked women while making pipe bombs and Molotov Cocktails. I know most boys would drink the moonshine, but we preferred pyrotechnics. I think Joe might have tried some of it. We designed all kinds of missions to employ our explosives. The town reservoir was a prime target. A strategic installation surrounded by a barbwire topped fence. Zebb held security while Joe and I scaled the fence. The corner post extended to the highest point of barbwire and provided a point of entry. Getting on top of the low roof was easy. Low-crawling across the flat top, we reached the solar equipment. In our imaginary world it was a communications array. I slid our poorly made explosive into a gap in the equipment. My demolition skills were not what they would later become, so we had no way of knowing how long the fuse would last. Joe lit the fuse and we bolted. I dropped down from the roof and started to climb the fence. Joe leapt from the roof, cleared the fence, and landed in a messy dive roll on the other side. He was always the ballsiest of us. Cops and service trucks showed up and started to drive around looking for us, but we knew those hills too well by that point.

We completed several missions until a local cop started dating the mom of one of our school friends. Our friend overheard a conversation about all the damage someone had done to the reservoir. Thousands of dollars worth of damage to government property. To a grade school kid thousands of dollars is a fortune. This wasn't cherry bombs in mailboxes. We were into some serious shit. We wanted to be soldiers, but we were being the bad guys. We realized the gravity of our shenanigans and limited our demolition to imaginary installations.

I still saw my father, of course. We spent every other weekend at his house. Going to the pizza parlor after church on Sundays is one of my fondest childhood memories. He took us on camping trips in the summer and we saw The Sandlot in the theater. It wasn't enough. A boy needs his father. As good a guy as my stepfather was, I would never let him fill that role. My brother was independent from a very young age, so he wasn't around much either. This left room for some very bad influences, namely, my sister's boyfriends. My middle sister was our black sheep and until recently was probably responsible for shaving the most years off my mother's life. She was the very essence of rebellious teenage daughter. She had a thing for bad boys. I remember one of her birthday parties before she had lost all of her privileges. It couldn't have been later than my third grade year and she had a boyfriend named Donnel. Joe and I were playing ninja and Donnel started making fun of us. Maybe he wasn't, but I felt like he was at the time. He got in a fighting stance. It was more playful and condescending than threatening. Nevertheless, I kicked him square in the balls. The kid dropped, spending the rest of the party whining on the couch. He was much older and bigger than me so I felt quite proud of myself.

Donnel probably wasn't a bad guy and he certainly wasn't around for long. My sister eventually got into so much trouble she couldn't be around boys unless she brought me along. Using me as a chaperone was ultimately a bad tactic used by my mother. We children had already developed a code of conduct. Like the mob, we didn't allow rats. My being a terrible chaperone was the least harmful consequence. The main problem was the influence her boyfriends had on me. Young boys need mentors and they will latch on to most older males. We are crafting the man we are going to be by taking the bits we like from the men around us. That phase I went through is the one I am most embarrassed of. The things and boys that I tried to emulate were foolish. One of her boyfriends had been to juvie and I thought it made him tough and strong. I still had my goals, so I never went too far down that road. Unfortunately for my sister, but good for me, she ran off with her boyfriend and got married at a very young age. This went very poorly for her, but removed a very bad influence from my life. I must warn all parents to be vigilant about the men you allow to spend time around your son. He is always looking to emulate someone until he becomes his own man.

Chapter 2

Grade school ended and things started to change. Joe was a few years older than me, so he was in high school when I entered junior high. He was always a personality and started to roll with a bad crowd. He looked out for me, so he didn't include me when his adventures turned from mischief to full on crime, though we had admittedly already crossed that line. As a result, we spent less time together, but we were still close. I discovered contact sports and as a result Zebb and I spent less time together. I had not been into sports, having come from a "sports are for dumb jocks" kind of family. I needed to continue my training and sneaking around the neighborhood was no longer adequate or acceptable for a boy my age. Sports became the new way I prepared to become a SEAL.

Football was first. I was tall, lean and strong for my age. At tryouts the various coaches pitched their chosen fields and we separated into skill players (guys who handle the ball) and linemen (guys who protect or tackle the guy with the ball). The skills coaches didn't make a very good pitch, they didn't need to. All the boys were football fans and they knew what positions got the glory. Skills positions are the quarterback, running backs and receivers, along with their defensive counterparts. The linemen coach, however, made a strong argument. He talked about how only the biggest and strongest could be linemen. He wanted guys to play smash mouth football and bang heads with the opponent every play. His hogs and dogs he called them. I didn't realize he was trying to convince the uncoordinated fat kids to voluntarily become linemen. I signed right up. I made the 7th grade varsity team and started on both offense and defense. I became good friends with our fullback, a guy named Mike. Our very first game, Mike ran the opening kickoff back for a touchdown. The adrenaline rush made me decide I was a jock.

My true passion came next. Wrestling. In the first practice, kids quit and cried. I had found my home. My siblings poked harmless fun at me for playing football, but had a field day when I started wearing spandex and rolling around with other dudes. I didn't care though, wrestling was pain, wrestling was brothers, and wrestling was something I was good at. Of all the families I have, the one most like the SEAL teams is wrestling. I won't belabor the point. Those who wrestle already understand, and those who don't, never will.

In seventh grade I was winning matches. I didn't have a lot of experience, but I learned quickly and was more developed than most kids. That was, until Lee. Lee was a kid from a wrestling lineage who started his training out of the womb. I had been doing well and some of my family came to watch. I had heard about Lee's prowess, but across the mat from me was a very harmless looking Asian kid. That kid spanked me. That wasn't my first loss in life and certainly wasn't my last, It had an impact. My team didn't lose, I lost, and in a very decisive fashion. Lee would go on to be my driving force for the next few years, though he probably never spared me a thought. At the district tournament I beat the other kid I lost to during the season and made it into the finals with Lee, where I was promptly spanked again. Still... making it to the district finals my first year cemented me as a wrestler.

That summer I spent more time with Zebb. His mother would take us to the coast when she got jobs painting murals. We would set up in camp sites after the manager had made his rounds and leave before the sun came up so Zebb's mom wouldn't have to pay the fee. She was a sweet, wonderful lady. These sites were not what I would call camp sites, but manicured lawns next to a beach parking lot. During a particularly cold and windy trip, Zebb and I spotted a cute, much older girl in the site next to us. The weather was terrible and all the full grown men in the sites around us couldn't get a fire going. Zebb and I took our shirts off and hiked down the beach to gather driftwood. We knew what we were doing, so we had a fire going in no time, while people in the surrounding sites shivered and looked miserable. We left his mother to watch the fire and headed down the beach for a log that would burn all night and make us look manly carrying it back. When we got back, Zebb's mom had invited the pretty girl and her family by the fire. Zebb and I were flying high, but didn't know what to do about it. We were far too young to do much more than feel good about ourselves, so the pretty girl went back to her site at the end of the night without Zebb or I saying a word to her.

Not every coast trip was so enjoyable. The summer before 8th grade I fell from a sea cliff while climbing. When my head cleared, I noticed my once strait forearm now had a distinct S curve to it. Both bones had broken clean through and the muscles pulled my hand on top of my forearm. Zebb had taken the proper trail up the other side. I yelled for him until his face peered over the cliff edge.

"What did you do now, dummy?" he yelled.

Zebb helped me walk off the beach and flagged someone down to call an ambulance. My ankle and lower back hurt more than the my arm so I laid down on a log to wait for the ambulance. The ambulance arrived and the EMTs prepped a stretcher. I asked one of them if I was going to be able to play football. The season was starting in a month and I had been looking forward to it all summer. He took one look at my arm and told me I wasn't going to be playing that year. He said it nonchalantly, not knowing he had just crushed a 13-year-old kid. I banged my head against the log repeatedly and stood up while they were getting the stretcher ready. The EMTs started yelling at me, but I ignored them and walked to the ambulance. First I tried to get in the passenger side, but the EMT yelled for me to get in the back. I sat down in the back and fumed while the EMT scolded me for being a dumb kid.

Missing a junior high football season seems so trivial now, but it meant the world to me then.

I refused any painkillers, because that's what a man does, right? If I was going to be a SEAL then I could handle a broken bone or two. To be honest, it didn't hurt that bad at the time, however, Zebb's mom decided she wanted to drive me back home so my mom could take me to the hospital. It's a three hour drive on the windiest back road you have ever seen. I did the whole thing with my forearm in an S shape and a splint that wouldn't give when my arm started swelling and because I wanted to be tough, no pain meds.

By the time I got to the hospital I was crying for morphine. My poor mother watched and cried those tears only a parent watching their child suffer understands. Thankfully they put me out to set the bone. Waking up was one of the most pleasant experiences I've had. I think it's the only time I've been high or intoxicated. The bed was the most comfortable bed I've ever been in, and the nurse was one of the prettiest things to wake up to. I have no idea who she was, but somewhere out there is a woman who made a very lasting impression on a young boy.

I missed the football season that year. At the time I thought it was one of the worst things to happen to me. Most people don't understand why something so trivial could do so much damage to a young man's emotions. It's loyalty and brotherhood. My teammates needed me to storm the beach with them, and I was stuck back in England with a broken arm. I probably wouldn't have made a difference to the season. Hell, I can't even remember how the season ended up going.

I spent the fall in a cast from hand to armpit. By the time I got it off I was chomping at the bit. Football wasn't quite over and wrestling was just around the corner. The high school football team had early bird weight lifting classes before the school day officially began. A few other wrestlers and I mentioned this to our wrestling coach who was more than happy to come to school and open the weight room for us an hour before regular classes started. I already had a weight lifting class each day and probably didn't need it. The feeling that I was doing something extra was comforting. That year I wrestled up a weight class so I could face Lee. Off course, he thoroughly kicked my ass every time we faced each other. Wrestling up also introduced me to some tougher opponents and my 8th grade season was not as successful as my 7th. Our team however, went undefeated and solidified the core group of guys I would be spending the next four years sweating and suffering with. I was made team captain that year and would remain so until we graduated high school.

The junior high season ended, but I was not happy with how I performed personally. I signed up for track and ended up being a long distance runner. Track seemed more like a social hour than a sport. I figured distance running would help my wrestling, and track was coed, after all. I had not had much success in the girlfriend department during junior high. Distance running isn't very conducive to chatting up girls, so track didn't help much. Overall I didn't take track very seriously. The high school had a Freestyle and Greco wrestling club during the spring. After track practice I would go straight to the high school and wrestle. I got in some of the best shape I've ever been in. I was getting to school before 7:00 am to lift weights, lifting again during regular classes, running distance at track practice then going to wrestling practice until 7:00 pm. I ran a 5:49 mile that year. In BUDS they don't ever time anything less than a mile and a half so 8th grade year still stands as the fastest mile I've ever run.

Wrestling at the high school as an 8th grader also introduced me to dickheads. Most were alright guys, but of course the assholes stand out. My town's high school did not have a wrestling pedigree and only 7 or 8 kids made up the team. They were a pretty tight group of bad boys who drank, smoked, had sex and thought they were much cooler than they were. All of them would be seniors the next year and they wanted to be sure all the fresh meat earned their keep. Rite of passage is common among elite groups and I was no stranger. I would show up to practice and stand out in the middle of the room waiting for any of the high schoolers to wrestle with me. Freestyle season is more laid back than the folk style season. The high schoolers would talk and joke, sitting against the wall when they weren't wrestling. I would always be pacing out in the middle waiting for another opponent. Paying the man while I was in 8th grade helped me earn their respect and made it much easier to assert myself as a leader freshman year, at least of my age group. The seniors respected me and I count the ones who stuck the year out as good friends.

8th grade year was not over yet and one of the worst times of my life was yet to come. I had already been clashing with my mother for years. The Swift boys grow up too fast and become very independent. Unfortunately, society doesn't really let you strike out on your own until you're 18. In grade school I ran away to the hills once or twice only to come back crying to my mother in a few hours. If I hadn't told her I'd run away she wouldn't have known. Disappearing for most of the day was perfectly acceptable back then. My rebelliousness came to a head 8th grade year.

I got in trouble for something stupid. I wouldn't have gotten in that much trouble for the act itself, but I lied about it, one of the few times I ever lied to my mother, or anyone for that matter. As punishment, she said I couldn't go to wrestling practice. I don't think she could understand how severe a punishment that was. Wrestling is how I was preparing to be a SEAL. Every practice, every drop of sweat was preparing me for what I would face. She just saw it as a practice, I went to them all the time, *what's one practice*? Practice was sacred to me and she crossed a line. She could come up with any punishment, but affecting my goals was too much. I snapped.

"I fucking hate you," I growled at her. Words I wish I could take back. My stepdad pointed to the door.

"Get out!" I don't think he was kicking me out for good, but that's how I took it. I started to storm out and he grabbed me by the shoulders. I thought I was a strong kid, but his hands were vices. He was angry that I was hurting my mother.

"Do you think hurting your mother makes you a man!" I struggled a bit, but could not move an inch. I had never felt that kind of strength. I just glared back until he let me go.

In the middle of the night I started the seven mile walk to my dad's house. About two miles out, my stepdad pulled up beside me in the car and told me to get in. He told me I was hurting my mother but I didn't care. I was an angry punk. I ignored him until he gave up and drove back home. I got to my dad's house and didn't want to knock on the door. I hopped the fence and laid down on a bench in the backyard. It was cold and I left in a T-shirt, so I covered up with a floor mat from the back patio. I was out there for a miserable bit until my stepmom came out and found me. I think my mom called to make sure I had gotten there safely. For the first time in my life I would no longer be living with my mother.

The next day I went to school and struggled to hold it together. The feeling I had then is the closest thing to the feelings I'm experiencing now. We had some kind of study time in English class and the teacher let the radio play in the background. That terrible, sappy Creed song, "With Arms Wide Open" was playing and I needed every ounce of willpower to keep from bursting into tears. I felt like I had lost my mother. Of course it wasn't the case, just a bad argument, but the result was living with Pop for the next few years.

That same year the seed of my greatest pain was also planted. Zebb had a class with a pretty girl named Maegan. For some reason they had to drink orange juice with pulp for a lesson in class. Maegan didn't want to drink hers, so Zebb drank it for her. By that point I had only managed to fumble through two bad make-out sessions and an embarrassing hand job from a high school girl. Zebb managed to call Maegan his girlfriend for a whole two weeks. Maegan had an identical twin that I hoped I might get set up with. Her name was Amanda.

Chapter 3

8th grade wrapped up with me single, living at Pops, and looking forward to high school football and wrestling. I worked on and off at Pop's cabinet shop when I wanted cash and went to the river with Zebb and Joe. My brother took us shooting when he could afford the rounds and I mended things with my mother, though I continued to live at Pop's.

Daily doubles came around and it was time to play high school ball. As freshmen we could only play freshmen ball, so making first string was the goal. My friend the full back talked me into going out for linebacker. My body type was suited for it. I was still one of the biggest and strongest, but lean. It was looking as though I would start as linebacker but I learned that backfield positions don't get to hit someone every play. Most of the time you're just shadowing somebody and only making the tackle if your man gets the ball. I looked over at the linemen. Every play they banged heads with the man across from them. Even when you tackle someone as a linebacker, they aren't fighting back, they're trying to get away. As a linemen you face off with the man across from you and fight for the advantage, like wrestling. After practice one day I asked the coaches if I could go back to being a line-men; a decision I would pay for when kids started getting bigger than me. I enjoyed fresh-men football and the season was good if memory serves me. I was gaining a reputation as a leader, mainly because I knew all the plays and not just my own position. Many of the knuckle draggers on the line would consistently ask me what they were doing for the current play. I played nose guard, defensive end, and because I was the only guy who could reliably shotgun snap, center.

Football ended and the real work began. The school hired a new wrestling coach, a man who would have a huge impact on my life. Coach Thompson was an experience few kids have, but one that would prepare me for the cruelty of BUDS instructors. During one of his frequent explosions of rage he once screamed, "I am fucking Adolf Hitler!" Then he proceeded to prove it. He once got kicked out of a duel meet for arguing with the ref over a JV match. We proceeded to win the varsity meet without a head coach.

For his first season at the school, he got a handful of decent seniors who wanted their old coach back and a solid lineup of talented freshmen coming off an undefeated 8th grade year. A bunch of new kids tried out, but like the next three years and BUDS, most didn't make it past the first few days. A lot of the seniors left because Thompson actually had rules and standards. A handful of solid dudes and good friends stayed to see the season through. Coach made sure they had the best senior year they could manage. The group that came over with me from junior high was as hungry as ever and becoming my first brotherhood. Our first tournament I wrestled two weight classes up so I could face Lee. I was weighing about 145 lbs and wrestled at 160 lbs for that tournament. I beat a couple opponents but was once again thoroughly trounced by Lee. That was the last time I wrestled Lee. He kept getting bigger and bigger and I kind of leveled out. Coach put a stop to my stupid vision quest. The team needed me at 140 lbs where I could score more team points. Freshmen year was brutal. We all wrested varsity against seniors and juniors. I earned a lot of bronze medals that year. We had one of the toughest districts in the state and I managed to place at district, but not qualify for state.

The season ended and we started Freestyle and Greco. I qualified for the Oregon cadet team, but the training camp required a handsome sum so I didn't end up going to the national tournament. One of our guys scraped together the cash to go. The improvement he showed from when he left for the training camp and when he got back from the tournament made us all regret not going.

Sophomore year was a great year for me now that I think back on it, even if it did eventually lead to the greatest pain of my life. I have to start with the summer before school started. I was hanging out at Zebb's place. For some reason he always enjoyed cleaning his room and wanted me to help. I was picking up trash and came across a piece of paper with a phone number. I asked Zebb about it and he said it was from his two week stint being Maegan's boyfriend in 8th grade. I figured, fuck it, and dialed it up. I debated asking for Amanda, but remembered Maegan was the hotter one. She answered in her shy voice and because women can't just say *no I'm not interested in you* she agreed to go to the movie with me. We saw Signs. I kissed her because that's what you do in high school. I learned from my two previous make-out sessions at the movies and toned it back a bit, not that it blew her mind, but it didn't scare her off, and like that we were boyfriend and girlfriend. I took her to the homecoming dance and she came to my football games.

We lost a game to our cross-town rivals. I took sports way too seriously and losses always made me feel ashamed. Maegan tried to comfort me afterward, but losing in front of her made it all the worse. A man being defeated in front of his woman strikes at something primal. She was waiting for me in the parking lot and I walked right past her. She tried to catch up, but I wouldn't let her. I wanted to find a place to be alone and lick my wounds. She got angry and left.

"Fine, just ignore me!" she said to my back.

I went home and realized the damage I had done. I had been interested in girls since kindergarten and horny not long after. This was my first real girlfriend and I was going to lose her because I threw a fit. I convinced her to come over so I could apologize. She was angry and finally had a reason to get rid of me. She stood in the entry way, arms crossed. This time I was the one being ignored.

"Please. I'm sorry," I pleaded. She was unmoved. I got down on my knees and begged. I'm so ashamed of it now, but I begged for her to take me back. For the moment she did. She took me back because she couldn't tell me no while I looked so pathetic, but she didn't like me. A few days later she wanted to "talk." It wasn't to break up with me; that would be too direct.

"I was with some friends at Brian's house while you were at practice." Brian was a bad boy skater type who was much better looking than me. "We were hanging out and ended up kissing." This was her way of saying you should break up with me. Breaking up with me then kissing Brian was too hard for her. Instead, she allowed me to think she liked me and kissed another boy while I was at practice. It was the easy way for her, but it hurt like hell for me. I never really showed her how much that hurt. Right next to the shame of being defeated in front of your woman is finding out your woman prefers another man. We were only fifteen and hadn't been going out for long. I'd seen the movies. I just needed to win her back. I can't believe how foolish I was back then.

First I needed to get rid of Brian. I did that my way, direct, no going behind someone's back. I found him in the breezeway.

"Brian!" I called as if hailing a friend. He stopped and I could see the nervousness in his stance. This kid was not a fighter. "Is there something you want to tell me?" It took him a minute, but I finally got it out of him.

"We were all hanging out and she sat on my lap. One thing led to another and we kissed. I'm sorry man." He couldn't make eye contact. I realized he hadn't put the moves on Maegan. She had made it happen. Not a lot of men can resist a woman coming on to him. If you have your own woman to be loyal to it makes it easier, but not many single men are going to pass on a wanting woman, especially if the other guy is a stranger. Brian was scared and it was obvious. I was starting to feel like a bully. I also might not have been able to play football if I'd crushed the dude.

"Now you understand that is not going to happen again," I said in a matter of fact tone. He nodded. I put my hand out for a handshake to show we were finished. He reached out tentatively. I grasped his withering hand and felt the sweat dripping from it. "We are not going to have this conversation again." Brian wasn't a problem after that. He messaged her on Facebook years later when he'd turned his life around and Maegan and I had a laugh about it.

I thought she had learned to love me over time. In truth, she realized I was the best provider she would ever have a chance with. The few girls who showed an interest in me before Maegan were girls I rode the bus with. Girls who were exposed to me every day and got to know me over time. Of course in my over-eager youth I fucked up all those opportunities once I found out a girl actually liked me. I learned that I do not make a great first impression. My face puts off a very serious "fuck you" vibe that I do not intend. Maegan got over the initial nervousness I tend to give women and my world narrowed to her and wrestling. Zebb starting putting his hair in dreadlocks, listening to Bob Marley and smoking weed. Joe was getting into more and more trouble. We were still brothers, but we definitely grew distant during high school. Now Maegan's gone and those two are still there if I need them. Men learned long ago to find another man who could watch your back. Trust and loyalty make for a strong tribe and a strong tribe helps everyone be successful.

Sophomore year was when I lost my virginity. It's really not a great story and I'm not very proud of it. I'm pretty sure she thought she would have to have sex with me if she wanted to keep me. I told her we didn't have to, but she knew I wanted to. I was so obsessed with her I would have stayed either way. I am ashamed to have pressured her to have sex and as a result my first time was not memorable. I can't even pin down when it actually happened. We just stepped up our fondling every time we could steal a moment together and eventually we were having sex.

We spent a lot of time at her parent's house because, well…. they were terrible parents. They let us hang out in her bedroom, on her bed, with a blanket over us! We would cover our lower halves with a blanket so it looked like we were just watching a movie. Her father would come back and check on us and I would simply stop thrusting until he left. I was a teenage boy having sex with his daughter, in his house, while he was home! This is the kind of non-confrontational weakness she was raised by. Her mother and father didn't like each other. Her mom had run off all her father's friends and was a bitter woman who blamed everyone else for her problems, especially her husband. Like Maegan's sister they never liked me. I didn't care though. I would only have to put up with them for a few years.

The year passed with me going to classes, grinding on Maegan between classes, then going to wrestling practice, something I was doing year round now. I used to look forward to going to school every morning just to see what Maegan was wearing and how she did her hair. After practice I would throw on my plastic suit and run to Maegan's house to cut weight. I did some of the hardest cuts that year. I cut from 170 to 140 in three days once. Now, I was naturally around 160 but was bloated from a previous cut, so the first ten was all water weight. I wrestled poorly that week and coach bumped me up to 145 where I had more success. I won my first tournament that year. We lost most of our older guys and were a team of sophomores. We had one senior who was my wrestling partner most of the time. We called him Papa Oshea because he had knocked a girl up. We were the only team with offspring in the stands, prison tattoos, and guys missing tournaments for court dates.

Our stat girls were terrible at their jobs and spent more time in the back of the van with wrestlers then recording matches. I had set up a teammate with Maegan's sister and once coach learned we had two wholesome girlfriends he convinced them to become stat girls. This meant that my girlfriend got to come on trips and coach only had to worry about two dicks instead of the whole team's.

I put in a little time at Pop's cabinet shop to pay for gas and insurance so I could take Maegan to the lake and movies. My truck had a bench seat so she could sit next to me. There are few things greater than driving a truck to the lake with the windows down, one hand on the wheel and the other around a pretty girl. I wish I had appreciated it more because it was nothing but minivans and family wagons in my future.

I'll count that summer with my sophomore year since it was so pleasant. I made the Oregon National Team in Freestyle and Greco that year. I worked at the cabinet shop to make the money for the training camp and trip. The other guys from my team worked at a job my coach set up for them. Once I realized that job paid a lot more than my Pop did, I joined them. It was an event service that provided supplies for weddings, concerts and even the super bowl. We would wash wedding chairs for a few hours then spend the rest of the time racing golf carts around the warehouse. One of the coaches at the training camp would always yell, "Your parents didn't pay for you to come here and slack off!" That was until we informed him the kids from South Medford were not spoiled rich kids and we all paid our own way. I spent most of the national tournament watching instead of wrestling, but it was still a good experience. I came back in excellent shape and decided I wasn't going to play football anymore. I played football because it was fun and wrestled because I was good at it. Football had become less fun. The head coach was a big fan of the passing game so most practices would be spent going through the motions for hours. We would only dress down in full pads for two or three practices. For the rest of the week the linemen would stand in place so the skill players could run their routes over and over again. It was a winning strategy because the team eventually made it to the state finals, but I wouldn't be there. I found a second family with my wrestling team, one Maegan was a part of.

Junior year was decidedly worse. I had issues with my step mother and they came to a head. I take the blame for issues with my stepfather, but with my stepmother they are shared. She had already raised two sons and I was nothing like them. I don't think she could understand why that was. Things came to a head and I had to leave Pop's house. Luckily, I had patched things up with my mom and stepdad so I had a place to go. Not more than a day or two after I left my Pop's house my stepmom came by and dumped all my stuff in the front yard of my mom's house. Then I found out she had kicked my Pop out of the house, too. Until recent days I have never hated a woman more than I did then. My sister said Pop was living at a friend's empty house only a mile away. I bolted out the front door crying and ran full speed to where he was staying. I wish I had timed that mile. I can't remember why I didn't have my truck at the time. I hope that my son would do the same for me if he could right now. What was said, I don't recall, but once again I can remember my father's sadness and strength. I crashed on the couch a few days and thought now I would get to live with my father as my other siblings had, just me and him. He told me it was only temporary and my stepmom just needed time to cool off. Sure enough she did. My father moved back in and I finished out high school at mom's house.

Maegan didn't come over to my house often. My mother wouldn't even allow her in my room. We could get away with far more right under her parents' noses. One day my mom sat us down and explained to Maegan she wasn't allowed to wear the shirt she was wearing in her house. It was a T-shirt but the whole back was lace. By modern standards it was a modest shirt, but my mom didn't give a shit about modern standards. In her house, only her standards mattered. This wasn't the first time my mother embarrassed one of her kids' friends. Zebb still calls her Mrs. xxxxx. Many of my sisters' friends had similar conversations about acceptable apparel at our house. I stress "conversations". My mother had a way of laying down the law very calmly and respectfully.

"I understand that is the way girls dress today, but it is not appropriate for my house, so I'm going to have to ask you not to wear that shirt here." Maegan was looking very embarrassed and it was making me angry. "When you come over, I would appreciate it if you covered your midriff and...."

"Ok, she gets the point!" I interrupted. I took Maegan's hand and left in a rage. I started walking to the park and Maegan struggled to keep up until I realized I was using my full stride.

"Your mom thinks I'm a slut!" I was angry at my mom, but I knew she didn't think Maegan was a slut and had said nothing to imply it. At first I sympathized with Maegan, but she wasn't being honest about what happened. It was like we had witnessed two different events. Maegan was acting like she had been shamed and called a harlot. I saw my mom explaining her rules like she always did. I thought she should have told me so I could explain to Maegan in a less embarrassing way. Maegan played the victim card so much I ended up straddling the line between defending my mother and being sympathetic to Maegan's embarrassment.

Maegan would eventually become very close to my mother, confiding things in her mother-in-law instead of her own mother or husband. Maegan tried to make everyone happy and was often controlled and manipulated by the people around her. I think my mother was the same growing up. She had an understanding of Maegan that I could never possess. I always thought it a good thing she and my mother talked. Mom had grown into a woman who never let anyone manipulate her. My mother had a hardness Maegan did not, along with willpower and wisdom. Mom was raised in a pack of wolves, where Maegan has always been protected from any true hardship. This will all become important later.

Playing the victim was an art form in Maegan's family. To be fair, Maegan was the least adept at it. Her mother was the master, her sister a journeymen, and Maegan a novice. Victimhood and passive aggression was their go-to tactic. The fact that my mother would sit someone down and be straightforward, honest and god forbid, confrontational, was a shock. This difference in values would be a recurring issue mostly between me and the rest of her family. They liked to manipulate Maegan and they couldn't do that with me around. There was a small but revealing event of what would become a bane in my future. Maegan and her sister Amanda always shared a car. Amanda left a library book on the floorboards of the car and it got damaged while Maegan and I used the car for the day. Amanda blamed Maegan because she didn't have the guts to blame me. I defended Maegan.

"Things thrown on the floorboards get damaged. No one tried to ruin the book and Maegan isn't responsible for making sure your valuables are put away properly."

The next day it came up again and Amanda recounted the previous day's confrontation saying I yelled, screamed and cussed at her. If I recall it was still just us kids present and she had no reason to lie about an event we all witnessed. The fact that she could outright lie with such conviction made me question whether she truly believed herself. This small event has stuck with me through the years and I have always remembered it when dealing with Amanda. The ability to dedicate so much to the victim role you can warp reality in your own mind has always popped up as a problem through the years. Whether it be their mother, Amanda, or even my own wife. Only recently has it cost me so much.

Junior year started and I wrecked my truck driving too fast down a rainy hill. I was pretty stupid and naive, so I called the cops first thing. That's what you do in an emergency, right? Of course the cop showed up and didn't do anything to help. He slapped me with a hefty fine and said tough luck. He did call a tow truck for me. What I didn't realize in my own lack of experience is that I would be paying for the tow truck. I called him, after all, so I could have called a tow truck myself. I thought his offer to call a tow truck was an actual offer. It was the last day before thanksgiving break so the tow yard would also be closed until the following week. In hind sight, I should have just had it towed to my house, but I really didn't know what was going on. In the end I had to pay over $400 in storage fees on top of the ticket. I showed up in court to contest the ticket, or at least get it reduced, and achieved neither. This event really wouldn't be worth mentioning except it would affect decisions made far in the future. I got the truck from the yard and spent hours replacing the tie rods in the dead of winter only to have it still pull too hard to the right. The frame was bent. Luckily my stepdad had a friend with a body shop who was able to fix it and the truck saw me through to graduation.

The biggest blow of junior year was when I tore the meniscus in my knee. I didn't play football that year but worked harder than any fall season before. I was finally one of the older wrestlers and it was going to be my year. I went to school early, well before the early bird weight lifting class, and ran around the school until the coach opened the weight room. At lunch I would go up to the mat room and practice my shots. After school we would meet up and wrestle even though the season had not started yet. All the abuse caught up with me when I tore the bursa sack on my knee. It filled up with fluid and I walked around with a DD boob hanging off my knee for a while. When I got it drained, the bowl filled up to the 8 ounce mark, and that didn't count what spurted all over the floor. The torn bursa was a minor thing, but the knee started to lock up.

I saw a sports specialist and he had X-rays taken. My meniscus was torn clean through. A meniscus tear is probably one of the most minor knee injuries that requires surgery. Usually they just shave off the torn part and smooth it over. Mine was a bad tear right in the middle, and the doctor wanted to try and repair it rather than smooth it out. My coach and mother made the responsible decision to try and have it repaired. In hind sight, it was the wrong decision. The tear would open up my senior year and give me problems until I ground it down with my own bones in BUDS. I only feel it now if I run over five miles.

My mother had coach break the news and tell me I would not be wrestling the rest of the season. I had wrestled my first match of the season and won in overtime. My offense had been severely diminished by the injury. It was a major blow that again seems trivial now, but crushed my soul at the time. I still went to practice and all the tournaments, but could only watch.

A bum leg didn't stop my hormones. Parking out in the woods was still a nightly occurrence. I don't know how car sex appeals to anyone. I suppose when you did it as much as I did it loses its novelty. It's made especially difficult in a small cab pick-up with one leg in a brace. When Maegan's dad bought his daughters a Chevy Trailblazer it made things better. A word of advice to all fathers. Get your daughter the smallest, most uncomfortable car you can find. Get her a Jeep Wrangler, that way she's got a roll cage when she wrecks it and she'll think you got her a cool car.

We got Maegan on the pill. I went to Planned Parenthood with her like a gentleman and sat in the waiting room. She had such great parents that they put her on the pill once they found out we were having sex. When we would go on family camping trips they would let me sleep in her tent with her. I was grateful, shocked, and had no respect for her father. When my family went camping I at least had to sneak into her tent and sneak out before morning. As a result, we had far less premarital teen sex around my family than hers. You be the judge.

We spent a lot of time at her house. So much so that her parents got sick of me, and that's entirely fair. Her parents were not the sort to sit you down and explain they wanted you around less. No, that would be confrontational, and good people aren't confrontational. Instead, they went about it in their passive-aggressive way. I came over after school as I often did, and found out the girls couldn't do anything until their long list of chores were done. These chores included mowing the lawn, trimming the bushes and all kinds of things their dad should have been doing. This was to encourage me to go home. Naturally, I said I would take care of the outdoor stuff so we could finish early and I could spend time with Maegan. It took several hours to get things done and when we finished her parents announced they were taking the girls out to dinner and their boyfriends could not come along. I spent several hours doing their yard work only to be sent home. I politely asked her parents if we could talk in private.

"I understand XXXX and I are here a lot, and you want to spend an evening with your daughters. I would appreciate it next time if you tell us beforehand that the girls are not going to be able to spend the evening with us."

Her parents were so anti-confrontation they acted like they totally understood and everything was fine, just a misunderstanding. I left that night feeling like the air had been cleared and it was overall a positive experience. Maegan called me when I got home.

"My parents yelled at me!" She was crying. They said all the things they didn't have the guts to say to a teenage boy standing in front of them in their own house. I was taken back by such cowardice and deception. That kind of passive aggressiveness was never used in my family. When we had something to say we came out and said it. For the rest of our relationship, I would hear from Maegan how much her parents didn't like me. When I was there in person it was like we were all old friends. I eventually just took to ignoring them and they have yet to find the courage to ever confront me.

So let's chalk junior year up as a bad year. Comparatively speaking, I would call all my years good years. My life has been blessed for the most part, but of course some years are better than others. That summer I was finally able to enlist in the Delayed Entry Program (DEP) for the Navy. I got my SEAL contract and just had to wait for senior year to get out of the way. Being in the DEP program didn't require anything, but we did meet at the recruiters' office once or twice a week to do "Navy" things. Mostly memorize regulation and military drill. I would skip out and go to the Marine office because all they did was PT. I had very little school by that time. I had already knocked out most of my requirements, so I only had to go to school for half a day. Even then I skipped class most of the time because it was easy enough to just show up and take the test. I put in more time at the cabinet shop until I screwed up a job. It was a whole order of face frames. I sanded them down too low so they didn't match up with the drawer fronts. Pop was rightly pissed. He wasn't that harsh on me, but disappointing him got to me. I always made him proud and to do the opposite crushed me. I was childish and couldn't hold it together. I ran home like a baby and cried to mom. I think in any other situation I would have acted like a man and soldiered on, but it was not often I disappointed my father. Pop didn't pay well anyway, and mom offered to pay me to finish the trim inside the house. After that I started finding teachers and rich people willing to pay a kid for yard work. The best job was for a guy who paid me ten bucks an hour under the table. I could show up, work a full day, and walk away with enough cash for the month's car insurance. The next day would be enough to keep my gas tank filled for the month. The rest would be spending money.

Wrestling kicked off and it was time to make our mark. We had a solid lineup of veteran seniors. We did well, winning most duels, a couple tournaments, and losing by a small margin to the school that won state every year. We were still a small team and our conference had schools that could field multiple champions in each weight class. I did well, but my offense had been diminished by the injury. My knee still locked up and I had to learn how to rely on my left leg more. Being so close to finally becoming a SEAL made wrestling less important, I'm afraid to say. Especially when I should have been at my most driven. My first match after the injury was Colby Covington. I lost to Colby, but fell back into my stride.

Freshman year I won so many bronze medals. I was not excited to earn them my senior year. Twice I lost before making it to the finals and didn't think it was worth it to wrestle back for third. I leaned on my injury and asked coach to withdraw me from the tournament. This may be the most shameful thing I have done and it sticks with me through the years. If you gave me a time machine and let me go back to fix a mistake this would probably be my second choice. I did all right that year. Out of 40 or so matches I didn't lose more than 9 and never by more than a couple points.

Once the season ended, I didn't continue with Freestyle or Greco. It was time to pre-pare for BUDS, and the best thing to do was relax a bit for the rest of the year. I got an in-vite to be on the Oregon duel team, but I turned it down. I only had two classes a day and Maegan was my world. I think she came close to loving me then. Affection would never come from her end, but I came to terms with it. I didn't come from a hugging family. I wished she couldn't keep her hands off me. I had never experienced that kind of affection, so I thought it was just a Hollywood fantasy and this was a real relationship. She let me put my hands all over her, after all, and that was good enough for me. I worried about knocking her up and made plans for such an event. I discussed my plans with her and assured her she would be taken care of. It was a simple matter of me putting in regular hours at the shop until I could join the Navy and earn a steady paycheck. She was working at the time and with both of our earnings, we wouldn't have to ask our parents for help.

God was looking out for us during those years and I didn't have to prove I was ready to be a man. I proposed to her on one of our trips to the river our senior year. My plan was to stay engaged during the four months of boot camp and A school. If she still wanted to marry me after that, we would get hitched before I went to BUDS. I broke the news to my parents and hers at a dinner before prom. My mother was overjoyed. She had grown quite close to Maegan by that point. Maegan's parents were angry, though they didn't have the balls to show it. I heard about it from Maegan later, of course. Neither of her parents hid the fact that they resented each other and blamed their unhappiness on getting married too young and their twin daughters. Maegan's mother Shelly was substantially worse about this. I, of course, couldn't give a fuck. Soon enough they would no longer have any bearing on our lives. We made a token appearance at prom and I quickly took Meagan to our usual spot to get her out of the form fitting black dress that had been driving me crazy all night. I left the heels on along with the pink ribbons winding up her calf. God she was beautiful. I loved her as much as a man can love.

Graduation day came. I always got A's with the occasional B in high school. Apparently my GPA meant I could wear some special gold ribbon at graduation. Maegan said I shouldn't wear it because I didn't have to work for my good grades. I don't remember her exact wording, because it didn't bother me. It bothered my mother. I have learned a lot of things made my mother uneasy about Maegan that she kept to herself. Maegan always struggled with academics and only passed math because she was a sweet girl with a male teacher who let her take tests over and over. She got cut from the volleyball team as well, so she always resented my ability to succeed. I didn't care weather she thought I deserved it or not. I wasn't going to wear a gold ribbon. High school was easy and useless. It bothered my mom enough to remember it over a decade later. I only put it in here because she recently reminded me about it and it illustrates a trait I have always just accepted in Maegan. We all have our flaws, and you learn to accept them.

Chapter 4

I shipped out two weeks after graduating. The day before, my sister did a photo shoot of Maegan and I. I can still see the sadness of the moment in the pictures. She is as beautiful as ever, but she is worried. I was leaving her for the first of many times. The war was in full swing in those years and I was headed straight for it.

I got off the bus at boot camp on June 28, 2005. The same day the SEALs from Operation Red Wings were fighting for their lives. I had no idea. I was starting boot camp. My head was already shaved, but they shaved it some more. PT was never a challenge, but lack of sleep definitely sucked. The worst was the first two weeks while the showers didn't work and we were all too scared to tell the instructors. We just thought it was part of boot camp. We took turns pressing our bodies against the wall trying to catch some of the trickle coming from the faucet.

I was put in an all male division. At that time they didn't have specialized divisions for SEAL candidates, so only one other guy was trying to be a SEAL. He eventually made it after getting eye surgery. I bunked under a good old boy who read westerns and fantasy. He was a bit of a nerd and would pop his zits while his balls rested on the bathroom sink, so a lot of people didn't like him. He was a good person and I like me some *Lord of the Rings*, so we had enough to talk about when we had the time.

Most of Navy boot camp was shining shoes and marching. A division leader was called an ARPOC. I can't remember what the acronym stands for or if that's even how you write it. Ours was a total douche. He had some ROTC time, so he was picked to be our leader. He clearly wanted to be the leader and thought he should be, something I've found to be a sure sign of a bad leader. He was constantly fucking up marching commands and the instructors were looking to replace him.

During the first part of boot camp everyone has to be taught how to fold their clothes and make their bed. My mother's standards for such tasks far surpass the Navy's, so my stack of underwear looked better than the example the instructors made. I was also able to teach the division a better technique for hospital corners on the sheets. Because I knew how to fold laundry, the Navy decided to make me a leader of men. I was 18 with dudes over 30 in my division. My first act as leader was to tell the instructors about the showers. They said we were all idiots and had them fixed right away. Most ARPOCs get fired after a few weeks so others get a chance, but I stayed ARPOC until we graduated. My second in charge was an Irish guy with a voice like an angel who sang cadence while we marched. I shit you not, we were the only division with two white guys in charge the whole time we were there. Every division with females had a female in charge and a black dude singing. Make of that what you will. Rhythm and a good voice definitely justified one appointment but the other was pure gender politics. My Irishmen was the best singer in my opinion. We lived the farthest away from any classrooms or the galley, so marching took up most of our day. The only thing about boot camp I remember fondly was the evening march as the sun went down and the Irishman sang his tune. Guys got Dear John letters, but my woman stayed loyal. My sister sent me letters that were so funny I would pass them around so guys could get a laugh. The Swifts have a dark humor that fits with the military.

Back then if you wanted to get enough PT to prepare for BUDs you had to run down to the pool before the day started. Instructors from the various elite special programs would run workouts. I remember a recruit from another division showed up snacking on a dough-nut he stole. I thought he would be ripped a new one. The kid had balls and the instructors got a kick out of it. I was beginning to learn most of my future teammates would not be as straight-laced as myself. I ended up going through BUDS and SQT with that guy and he never lost his *I don't give a fuck* outlook on life. One of our best performers.

Boot camp continued and I got out of shape. The instructors did little to help you on your way to BUDS, you were on your own. That's all changed now. Candidates are groomed before they ever ship out for boot. Its better overall in my opinion. I spent two months learning nothing useful and graduation finally came. We would get two days liberty. Maegan was coming and I was getting laid. Girls at boot camp are not attractive when you first arrive. Every day those girls look better and better. By the end they look like super-models through your boot camp goggles. Maegan looked like an absolute goddess. I felt bad for my parents because we only left our hotel room to have short meals with them.

What was the best weekend of my life to that point ended, and I got ready to head down to Pensacola Florida for my A school. Back then we were all required to learn a regular Navy skill before going to BUDs since we probably wouldn't make it. I picked Aviation Ordinance because it was the shortest school. That decision bit me in the ass when Katrina hit. I was still in Chicago so I had to wait in boot camp until the school house could get its shit together.

Our plane tickets finally got booked and I went to the muggiest place I had ever been. I would spend a lot of time in Florida over my career and it would eventually grow on me. The next couple months are not remembered fondly, however. The school house was backed up and I would be waiting a while for my class to start. In the meantime, I was put on barracks support. Barracks support consisted of standing the worst and most pointless watches. When you were not on watch, you mustered every hour to mop the same hallways over and over. The floors were a petri dish because they never really dried. There is a hierarchy in A school and people fresh from boot camp are at the bottom. This would be fine if the hierarchy was based on merit, but in A school shit bags rule. Some people come into the Navy without a good contract, so they go to the fleet right after boot as undesignated seamen. They chip paint until they can finally get a spot at an A school. When they show up they are the big dicks. They spent time in the fleet. Doesn't matter if they spent that time being useless.

My school house was more backed up than the rest. I found out later my rate was the one everyone who failed other rates went to. It mostly consisted of lifting heavy things. I had a revolving door of roommates. My first, and most normal, was a white trash Georgia boy who listened to hardcore gangster rap. I remember thinking some of it actually sounded good, but have never heard any of it since because it was so underground. He had a DVD collection of South Park we would watch. My next roommate was a super nerd. I leaned on my own nerd cred and we were able to have conversations. He even gave me a few tips that improved my drawing. He would wear a dress. He called it a kilt, but it hung down to his ankles. It was black with the chains and metal rings the goth kids like. He had the balls to wear this when he left the barracks and of course everyone wanted to know more about the weirdo I was rooming with. He was a nice kid. We got a third roommate who was a wrestler from Iowa. I thought, finally, someone with as little eccentricities as myself. Then I found out about his obsession with John Wayne. He wore a cowboy hat and duster coat, in Florida, in the summertime. No South Park collection, but he did have every John Wayne movie on DVD.

After a period of time longer than the actual course I was there for, I finally classed up. Aviation Ordinance school consisted of 10 minutes of instruction then a 15 minute smoke break, then 10 more minutes of instruction. This cycle would continue until clean up at the end of the day. The military can't have a class without a class leader, so the instructors picked one. The one black guy. Just like all the other class leaders. Within the first week our class leader was fired and I was put in his place. I had tried to avoid it. I did not like what the regular Navy called leadership.

I got fired for a matter of seconds in A school. My instructor tasked me with making sure the next door classroom got cleaned. It only needed a few people from the class and I took a handful over to clean. When I got back the instructor was furious. He wanted me to delegate the task and stay behind in case he had more tasks for me. Of course he didn't and I was right next door if he needed me. He fired me and when I didn't look broken up about it he asked me why not. I said I never wanted to be class leader and he promptly made me class leader again.

I met a guy trying to be EOD (Explosive Ordinance Disposal) and we went to the pool to train together. I never found out if he made it. Overall, A school was a terrible and useless experience. I got two weeks of leave after graduation but of course the Navy lost my paperwork. I ran around the base trying to get a leave chit approved by a bunch of *not my problem* kind of people. I needed to get back to Oregon for my wedding. I finally got it done and dressed in my blues to fly home. Like a dumb ass I thought I was required to travel in dress uniform. My connecting flight got cancelled and I ended up sleeping in the terminal wearing my dress blues. When I got home Maegan had the wedding all planned. It was simple and cheap. My uncle married us, my mom baked a cup cake platter and made Maegan's dress. My brother DJ'd and my sister performed an acoustic version of Metallica's "Nothing Else Matters." For a wedding gift, my cousin put us up in a decent hotel for our honeymoon. We spent most of those two weeks in the hotel room and I flew back to Florida just to turn around and head to San Diego. I had a bit of time before classing up and I moved Maegan down into a one bedroom apartment.

Chapter 5

There is a bell in BUDS hanging over the grinder. When you decide you've had enough, as most men do, all you have to do is ring the bell three times. Three rings and the suffering will stop. You sign some paperwork and go back to the fleet. The youngest guy in each BUDS class shines the bell every night. The idea is the youngest guy will most likely quit and has more years than the rest to come back and give it another go. I shared the title of youngest with another guy. Neither of us knew what time we were born so we split bell shining duty between the two of us. It is considered bad luck to be anywhere near the bell. My roommates hated when it was my night to shine the bell. Some of my early roommates quit during the first few days. One even slit his wrists. My other roommate found him in the shower. He was processed out of the Navy and last I heard he was doing well. He had been in my A school class and come from Florida with me. As guys quit, roommates got shuffled around and consolidated. I headed into hell week with two roommates like every-one else. At the other end I think we were the only room with all three guys still intact. My fellow youngster made it through as well.

After the initial kick in the nuts, you start to get time off and I was able to see Maegan and sleep in my own bed sometimes. The second phase of training is the dive phase. My class was Andy Stumpf's first class as an instructor if you know who that is. After learning basic SCUBA you start diving on a re-breather with pure oxygen(O2). It was during second phase, when my little combat swimmers were hopped up on pure O2 that I knocked Mae-gan up. I have always told the story of Maegan being on birth control but my supercharged sperm were too much for modern medicine. For the longest time I did believe my oldest was a birth control baby. Years later Maegan finally revealed to me she had purposely stopped taking birth control and not told me. By that time we had two children I loved more than anything so I wasn't mad. I did feel a little betrayed. I continued to tell the story of our first two babies being birth control failures because changing it would expose Maegan's character to friends and family. I'm still under the impression our second was in fact a birth control baby. I can't be sure anymore.

Maegan was there for me through BUDS. She helped me shine my boots and changed the sheets when my night sweats soaked them through. After hell week, she brought my roommates and I Ensures. We only had a short time as a married couple and never really got to enjoy it with me in BUDS. We had a Blockbuster video down the street from the apartment. Walking a few blocks with her to pick out a movie for the night will always be a memory I treasure. I made it through BUDS and I won't say much more about it. Above all, I think BUDS is the start of a brotherhood. Even the guys I haven't seen since graduating I can still trust more than the woman I provided everything for since she was 18.

I always told my buddies, marriage doesn't change much. Having children is when the real shit begins. Maegan gave birth to our oldest when I was in the follow on course to BUDS called SEAL Qualification Training (SQT). Her water broke late in the night, but she had not started contractions. We called my mother who started the 12 hour drive from Oregon and headed to the Naval Hospital. They gave Maegan Pitocin to help push labor along, which intensifies contractions, making the whole painful experience even more painful. She made it 16 hours before asking for the epidural. The baby came seven hours later. I had older sisters, so I was no stranger to babies. I had been an uncle since I was eight. I was expecting the smashed head, goopy monstrosity that is a newborn baby. While the goop was certainly there, my boy came out with the battle ready skull of the Swifts and looked me right in the eye. That's what I remember the most, his blue eyes looking straight at me with focus, even with half his body still inside my wife. All the newborns I had experienced kept their eyes closed and didn't focus very well when they finally opened them. I won't go on about the joys and emotions of fatherhood. Those who have children understand it, those who don't, won't until they do.

I left the next morning to spend three weeks in the desert. Had I been a SEAL at a team, they would have given me time off. The teams look out for their boys for the most part. SQT was still part of the initial pipeline though, and you couldn't afford to miss a day of it. By that point Maegan had my parents, her parents and her sister with her, but it was still hard on her. I always thought of my eldest as the second to easiest baby, but Maegan always assured me he wasn't. I suppose she's right. I missed a lot of his first months and she was left to do a lot of it alone.

I'm going to try and leave the teams out of this as much as possible, but my life is inseparable from them so I need to explain a little. There are three places you can go for your first team: Virginia Beach, San Diego and Hawaii. Now there is little difference between the teams in Virginia and San Diego as far as operations go. At the time, both coasts were sending everyone to Iraq. Hawaii had a specialized team that focused on the diving part of the job. Every team guy develops a hatred of diving during BUDS. Most of us want to kick in doors and shoot bad guys. I was no different. The team in Hawaii, which you can just Google so I don't know why I'm being vague, is not somewhere team guys want to go. The operations there are very high level and super secret squirrel, but the amount of diving you do sucks your soul. I didn't want to go there, but being the youngest fucked me over again. The idea, once again, was being the youngest meant I had more time to go to another team. You still got chances to augment in Afghanistan and Iraq, so I wasn't completely crushed. The guys from Lone Survivor were from the team in HI. 2007 was a big year for me. I became a Navy SEAL and a father. I kind of glossed over 2006 but it was all BUDS. Finally, I had achieved the goal I had since before grade school.

Chapter 6

Day one at the team did not go well. For the command's morning PT we were driven a mile off shore and dropped in the water. I had never seen the Hawaii shoreline and had no idea where I was going. I asked one of the older guys and he said, "Do you see that life-guard tower?"

I said, "No."

He said, "Swim towards it."

After zigzagging my way through the ocean, the current washed me over a reef that created a surf zone well off shore. Needless to say I was one of the last guys out of the water and that's not good for a new guy. I was only able to make up so much ground on the run, so my first impression was pretty much blown.

Luckily my first platoon did their own thing for PT, so they were not there to see. Some guys have good first platoons and others have bad experiences. My first platoon was one of the best I worked with. Right as I entered the door to the platoon space I was told to drop my pants. I found out this is how they greeted every new guy, just to see how he would react. I've never been a shy guy, so I dropped them as casually as if I was at the doctors, despite the fact I had gone commando since hell week. They all had a laugh and my nonchalant demeanor helped my first impression.

"Swift doesn't give a fuck," one of the older guys said. That's a compliment in our community. The platoon chief is the guy who runs the platoon. Our chief was a ripped, bald, 70's porn star looking dude. Chief pointed me out to Matt Leathers and said, "He's yours. If he fucks up, I'm coming to you."

Matt was a natural grease monkey so he was in charge of the boats, outboard motors and vehicles. We call this job 1st LT. I don't know why. Matt taught me outboard motors along with how to drive 10k forklifts and line hauls. I say taught in the loosest sense of the word. He sat me down in the 10k and wiggled the plethora of controls telling me what each one did. After a max of 30 seconds he pointed to a 20 foot shipping container and told me to load it on a flatbed, then walked off. When it was time to learn the line haul he gave a similar lesson and told me to back it into the high bay and left me to it.

Matt took more time to teach me the proper foreplay to get an outboard to start. His tutelage has gotten me out of many a bad spot. Every time you're in a rubber dingy, with a two stroke outboard motor, you're in a bad spot. Whether you're just training or someone got the bright idea to use one on a real op. Maybe they worked well on the rivers of Vietnam, but on the open oceans and in the plethora of surf zones I've taken them through they always go to shit. Matt was one of those guys who would have been a normal team guy during Vietnam, but in the modern era he was prone to disciplinary action. Matt was the kind of guy I missed during my short stint in law enforcement. Guys like Matt don't make it past the hiring process and the modern law enforcement community is decidedly neutered because of it. We'll get to that rant later in the story.

Liking every guy you work with is rare in the real world, but it's the norm in the teams. I made a good impression in my first platoon. Unlike a regular team, we dove almost every day. While the dive profiles changed, the required prep work remained fairly consistent. It was easy to learn all the tasks needed to get men in the water and make sure they were done before the older guys had a chance to ask about them. Where a lot of new guys fuck up is simply not knowing a task needed to be completed. At that team there were so many things needing to be done a new guy could always be working on something: surface support boats needed to be loaded and prepped, the Sub needed to be prepped and loaded, calls needed to be made to harbor control for deconfliction, dive rigs needed to be built and checked, dives needed to be planned and so on. The older guys wouldn't care if something still wasn't done because they'd seen all the other things you'd been working on. At a regular team you can make your new guys do all the shit work, but at my first team there was too much shit work for the older guys not to chip in. The LPO (leading petty officer) makes sure the platoon runs smoothly. He is the head sled dog. Before the morning meeting, I would make sure the surface support boats were loaded with all the necessary equipment.

"Make sure the boats get loaded," my LPO would say.

"Already done," was my answer.

At this point I had already decided drinking wasn't for me. I was still under age so I had an excuse, but that didn't excuse me from going out with the guys. My first platoon is still the best drinking platoon I've had. They were all very mature and manageable when drunk. This is very important to a 19-year-old new guy who has to round them up at the end of the night and get them home safely. Matt was the exception of course, but he managed to get himself back to base. He might have had to sneak on base with the cops hot on his tail, but he'd manage.

My favorite guy to drive around was my Assistant Officer In Charge (AOIC). Most AOICs are new guys themselves or only have one platoon under their belt. Our AOIC was a seasoned prior enlisted guy, the best kind of officer. He had played guitar for a band growing up and could shred to anything. His favorite bar was a karaoke place that stayed open until 4 am. The place had a full suite of instruments to play along with whoever was on the mic. He would sit up there all night, drunk off his ass, and riff to any song that came on. Brittney Spears, Journey, you name it, he could make it sound better. He ended up having to get out because his brain ate one too many breaching charges. Breaching charges are the explosives used to blow open a locked door. We calculate minimum safe distance but we can't always abide by it in a cramped house. Too many shockwaves to the brain takes its toll. He seems to be doing ok, even put out a country album.

I earned my first nickname for the way I drove guys to the bar. The older guys started calling me Crazy. It paired with another new guy they called Lazy. We were Crazy and Lazy. Lazy didn't stick because the other new guy was actually a hard worker. Crazy did. My LPO from that platoon still greets me with "How's it going, Crazy." As head sled dog an LPO has to bump elbows with the boys in the trenches and go to meetings with the head shed. He's not the one who makes the big decisions, but he makes sure those decisions get implemented. An LPO is key to a platoon's success and my first was a good one. I'll simply refer to him by his nickname, The Stripper Slayer. He looked like the kind of guy a girl dates to make her dad regret missing her ballet recital.

My first experience in a strip club was with that platoon. One of the support guys we liked from the team was going to BUDS and we had a going away party. Maegan and I had already discussed the fact that strip clubs and bars would be part of being in a platoon and she had accepted it. To her credit, she always trusted me to be faithful. The club we went to was a favorite of theirs and The Stripper Slayer had already dated a girl out of that club. We called her the spider monkey. While most strippers spend their time flopping on the floor, this one could climb to the top of the pole and do some impressive gymnastics. On this particular night The Stripper Slayer had his sights set on a different girl. This girl took a liking to his gorgeous locks and came to dance at our table. She was wearing white underwear. Trust me, this becomes important. While the two of them were in their own little world I sat awkwardly wondering what to do with my hands. I noticed a drink had spilled on the table and thought someone should probably clean that up. Being the helpful guy I was, I used a few napkins to soak it up and pilled them at the edge of the table. The girl stopped dancing and looked about the table for her underwear.

She screamed, "What the fuck!" As she pulled an alcohol-drenched G-string from a pile of napkins.

I thought they were a fancy napkin. The kind you get at a nice restaurant; it was a classy joint. Luckily, she wasn't a clever girl and I got away scot free. She ended up dating my LPO for quite a while after that. She came to the gym and worked out with us as well as attending a few platoon lunches, never knowing I was the one who cleaned booze with her expensive underwear.

Most of that platoon was single, but I wasn't the only married man, or father. Matt had a wife with a boy around the same age as mine. We would take turns watching each other's kids and our wives became good friends. When Matt and I were home, we would sometimes watch the kids so the women could have a ladies night out. Matt was an excellent cook and would have us over for dinner. We only lived a few blocks from each other.

Being at my team during a landlocked war sucked. I was diving day and night while my classmates from BUDS were getting ready to go to Iraq. My older brother had joined the Army after I completed BUDS, and he was already in Iraq. He completed basic and jump school, then shipped out with the 82nd right away. I cried when he told me he enlisted and I'm not sure why. I think it's because I had always looked up to him and the thought of him being degraded in boot camp was hard to think about. Not that it's anything he couldn't handle, I just didn't want anyone treating him as less than he was. When I went to jump school in Fort Benning after BUDS I was able to see him. He was still in basic and cleared it with his drill Sergeant. Unfortunately, when I came to visit, the Sergeant on duty had not been told and was a bit of a dick. I showed up with my long hair and old school BDU's; long and old school by Army standards. They had already switched to those gray glow-in-the-dark uniforms. The Sergeant told me to get the fuck out of his high bay without letting me say a word. I didn't want to screw my brother over, so I left without a fuss. I wasn't going to stand for it, though. I went straight to the base Chaplin and explained I might not get a chance to see him again with the war going. I didn't realize at the time how close we would come to that possibility. The Chaplin threw his rank around and got me in to see my brother. I slipped him a cell phone so he could call his wife and we talked a bit. He ended up having a three day pass before I left airborne and I was able to take him out for the weekend so he could enjoy a cigarette and a beer. Before I got to deploy he was sent to Iraq. He was stuck working a guard tower for a spell, then got in with a scout platoon. He was hitting the streets of Baghdad, kicking in doors. While I was spending my nights under water breathing the same recycled breath for hours.

His deployment was cut short, however. On his way back from an op, the armored cattle car that grunts have to ride in fell off an overpass. Nine guys died. My brother was one of the worst off of the guys that lived. He broke several ribs, resulting in a collapsed lung, broke a clavicle, and shattered all his lower vertebrae. Maegan gave me the news when I got back from work one day. I held together. He had been flown to Germany and wasn't out of the woods yet, but somehow I knew it would be ok. I was certainly more composed than when he told me he enlisted. I thought about what my mother, his wife and children would be going through. I think back now and it helps to put my own problems in perspective. I had signed up before my brother and still hadn't gone to Iraq. Here I was diving night and day while my brother almost died fighting in the war. My brother pulled through. His lower back is all steel and can't be bent, but he doesn't let it stop him and I still got to go on hikes with him when I visited.

Deployment came and it was underwater and underwhelming. I wanted to be in Iraq with the other guys from my BUDS class and brother. Of course the powers that be thought it was a mission of strategic importance, but that matters little to a sled dog like me. Good news came when our Chief told the new guys we would do the Assaults block of training with a team 5 platoon and deploy with them to Iraq after we got back. This was a dream come true. Most of my classmates who stayed on the west coast went to team 5. Going through their Assaults block would allow us to establish a reputation before we deployed. It was the light at the end of the tunnel for most of the deployment.

Chapter 7

Coming home from deployment for the first time, I had a number of fantasies playing out in my head. Every movie and story about a soldier returning home served to build up my expectation. I pictured my wife crying with joy or jumping into my arms and wrapping her legs around me. All that stuff I see in YouTube videos of soldiers returning home. We trickled back from deployments in ones and twos. I flew back to Hawaii in the dead of the night and called the duty driver to pick me up from the airfield. I crept in to find my wife asleep with our son. I crawled into bed and squeezed them both. My boy was confused, but not afraid. He had forgotten me, but he knew deep down I was something to him. I had woken Maegan up in the middle of the night, so I didn't feel too bad about her just wanting to go back to sleep. It was certainly not the fantasy I pictured, but I was too happy to be home to care.

The joy at being home was short lived, however. I need to explain what a dive supervisor (dive sup) is for this next event. I won't bore you with the details, but it's important to understand. It's related to something that would color my outlook the rest of my career. A dive sup is overall in charge of a training dive. Notice I said training; we don't use them for real world operations. They probably have one listed on a piece of paper somewhere, but it's just a formality. The dive sup makes sure everyone stays safe during the dive. More importantly, he gives the military someone to blame if something goes wrong. No training dive can happen without a dive sup so it is essential for my team to maintain enough qualified personnel. The course to become a dive sup is two weeks and fairly easy; it's geared toward the minimal diving a regular team does. After the course however, one must do extensive on the job training and pass a difficult board to become qualified to supervise dives at my team.

Some officer had the bright idea to get all the new guys at the team qualified as dive sups in one course. That way the team would be set for the next five years. This officer allocated funding to pay for the dive sup instructors to fly out to Hawaii and teach the course. Unfortunately for us new guys, he scheduled the course right in the middle of team 5's deployment. This course was his pet project and it would make a great bullet point on his FITREP (Officer report card). When he found out we were going to Iraq he had us all pulled off our augments so his project would have max attendance.

Only recently have I experienced something that pissed me off so much. This was 2008 when National Guard units were still being sent to Iraq to fill demands. Meanwhile some of the most highly trained and hungry warriors were sitting around Hawaii waiting for what amounts to an administrative course. This put a bad taste in all our mouths and only a few guys who took the course stayed in the Navy. We all purposely avoided the required follow on training to become dive sups. It wasn't hard to do, either. In order to finish the qualification, one must supervise multiple dives under the instruction of another dive sup. Being under instruction means you're on the surface boats watching the dive. As a new guy, your ass is getting in the water, not sitting dry on a boat watching. Overall, the project was a complete failure and I lost out on a 2008 deployment to Iraq.

To say I was bitter for the rest of my time at that team is an understatement. I never let it affect my performance and I headed into my second platoon with a good rep. The team was trying an experiment by dropping us down from four platoons to three. Bravo Platoon 2008 was put together from members of my old Bravo and the guys from Charlie's previous cycle. We were all solid guys for the most part, but the Charlie guys had some bad blood between them from their last go around. Something that would bite us in the ass down the road.

I got another nickname in my second platoon. For some reason, whenever we finished a training evolution, I ended up coming out the dirtiest or most haggard looking. After a few days living in the jungle I came walking out looking like a Vietnam vet strung out on heroin. One of the guys called me Viet Dan and the name stuck for the rest of the platoon. Since most of those guys never reenlisted, no one calls me that anymore but I think it was my favorite nickname.

At the start of the platoon we were all excited. We had a pack of meat eaters and were going to be the best platoon at the team.

At the first meeting our new LT said, "I want us to be the golden platoon. I want us to be the platoon that can do no wrong in the eyes of the team." We were cursed to be black sheep from that moment on.

Before we started any real training, Chief busted his ankle fast roping. For those who don't know what fast roping is, its when we slide out of a helicopter on a rope like a fireman on a pole. He stayed Platoon Chief while he recovered, but wasn't able to participate in training. You can't lead a SEAL platoon from the sidelines.

That was probably the first crack in the platoon, but things really started to go off the rails on our first training trip. We flew into San Diego and stayed the night before driving up to a training site in central California. That night we hit the bars as team guys often do. Most of us hadn't been back to San Diego in a while. One of our shorter guys had a girl he'd call up when he was in the area and took her out with us. They started to dance, but they were both drunk, obnoxious and kept bumping into people at the bar. One particular patron started to get annoyed and made it known. He had two friends next to him leaning against the bar. The platoon started smelling blood and moved to be in better positions. The unsuspecting patron I will call "Sorry" didn't realize the drunk short guy in front of him was a trained killer with a platoon of trained killer friends slowly surrounding him and his buddies.

Our guy had his back to Sorry and flipped him the bird. Sorry made the mistake of grabbing the finger and trying to twist it. Sorry disappeared in a tornado of team guys all trying to get a piece of him. His two friends quickly became strangers and bailed. I was sober and had it in mind to defuse the situation, but didn't anticipate how fast drunk team guys could move. I reached the pile of bodies and started pulling them off one by one, trying to get to the center. At the bottom of the pile I found a bleeding Sorry. One of our other short guys had him in a head lock that looked like it would pop Sorry's head right off his shoulders. My guy was mumbling some kind of profanity in his ear as he squeezed the life from him. I knelt down and laid a hand on my guy's shoulder and said something to get him to release Sorry. He let Sorry go and I tried to get the platoon moving out of the bar. Most guys got out, but a few were stopped by the bouncers and they didn't want to start a full on brawl. I stayed back with the guys in cuffs and waited for the cops. When the cops arrived, I said I would make sure they all went straight home if they released them to me. Sorry was sitting on the curb bleeding from a cut on his head with a bewildered look on his face. He clearly had no clue what had happened. The cops released my guys to me, the only guy who looked like he had his shit together; one of the many times not drinking has been a good decision for me.

We hit a couple more bars, but the problem wasn't my crew, it was the guys who got away right after the fight. One of our guys cut his hand when he broke a glass on Sorry's head. He and another guy rushed to the military hospital to get stitched up. While in the waiting room, they realized if he was seen it would be reported, so they bailed. Unfortunately, they had already checked in. A guy cutting his hand in a bar fight might have been swept under the rug, but a wounded man fleeing the emergency room went right up the chain of command.

Training trumps all in the teams, so consequences were deferred until we got back. Little did we know the bar fight would be forgotten in a slew of other fuckups by the time we got back. We left San Diego the next day to road trip up north. The training site was in the boonies, so we stopped at the last Walmart for supplies. A platoon of guys aren't going to finish stocking up on dip and wet wipes at the same time, so a lot of us ended up waiting in the parking lot. The driver of our box truck was fortunate enough to have a car with a pretty girl park next to him. Her boyfriend went in to pick up beer, leaving his girl in the passenger seat to be chatted up by our guy. She told him about all the nearest places with a night life in case we got a day off. The last of our guys came out of the store and it was time to leave. The box truck driver said goodbye to the pretty girl and started to back out. He cut it too hard and proceeded to run the pretty girl's car over. He didn't hit it, he ran it over. Her entire trunk got crushed under the midsection of the box truck. She took it pretty well. It was her car, so the boyfriend wasn't too perturbed either. Getting in an accident is a pain in the ass but it's compounded when a government vehicle is involved. We had training to get to so all of that would wait. Lt still had to call the command the day after the bar fight to tell them we just ran someone's car over. Some golden platoon we were shaping up to be.

Training started out as a shit show, but we got some better cadre on loan from the east coast and the trip ended up being fun. Saint Luis Obispo was off limits to us because team guys had gotten in so many fights there in the past. Naturally it was the first place we went when we got a day off. We took a picture with Chuck Liddell by telling him we were a lacrosse team. Apparently he's gotten in a lot of fights with team guys, so we thought it was best not to tell him. After stealing a rug and a painting of Biggy Smalls for the platoon space, we headed back to the barracks. One of our supply guys, not a SEAL, came out drinking with us. He got lippy back at the barracks and one of our new guys had to lay him out on his ass. We'll call this supply guy Dumbass. He has a part to play later, so remember that name.

The training block ended and the team decided they could save money by sending us straight to our next block instead of bringing us home to rest and refit. We flew out to a little island off the coast for maritime training. If you're really interested, it's not too hard to figure out what island. This was without a doubt the worst training block I've ever been through. I won't go into too much detail, but it involved driving rubber dinghies in black squalls, being slammed by heavy surf into rocks, running through cactus fields in the dark, puking as I worked on outboard engines in heavy sea state, then paddling the rest of the way back to the barracks. The whole thing was a shit show, largely due to the crusty old timers running the training. There are only a few times I thought I was going to die, and that trip claimed two of them.

All that wouldn't have mattered except the bad blood I talked about earlier came to a boil. The short guy who nearly tore Sorry's head from his shoulders, we'll call him Pit Bull, had a beef with our Lt from their last Charlie platoon. I never found out the details. Pit Bull came back from the one bar on the island with a few other guys. Lt was out washing his gear with the hose. Pit Bull, in his inebriated state, thought it would be funny to sneak up on Lt and spray him with the hose. The others looked on giggling as Pit Bull crept up. He jumped on Lt and the others burst into laughter, then their jaws dropped in terror. Lt didn't appreciate being ambushed in the night, and before anyone knew it, Lt had Pit Bull's hair in one fist and was pummeling his head with the other.

The fight was broken up, but Pit Bull had a huge gash opened up on his head. We could have kept the incident in house, but training required us to swim in the ocean for long stretches. Having a fresh head wound in the ocean isn't a good idea, so we had to explain to the training staff why one of our guys couldn't do certain evolutions. So now Lt had to call the command and explain one of the enlisted guys was missing training because Lt, the guy who is technically in charge, opened the enlisted guy's head up with his fist.

When we got back from one of the worst trips of my career, the command fired Lt and Chief. They went to admin jobs to await another chance at leadership. To replace LT we got an officer who was probably too early on in his career to be in charge of a SEAL platoon. I felt he rose to the occasion, but he still didn't last. From now on, when I say Lt, I mean this guy. For a replacement Chief we got a legend, Eric Shellenberger, Shelly for short. Shelly was a Recon Marine before joining the teams and had kicked in doors in Iraq with a west coast team before coming out to our shit hole. Back when I first got to the team, the commodore had come to visit and blow smoke up our asses. If you're not familiar with the military, a commodore is a big deal. He went on and on about how important our team is to the national strategy and how they were working on a pay incentive to get more SEALs out to our team. Shelly stood up and told him it didn't matter how much money he threw at team guys. If they couldn't go to the sand box to shoot bad guys, no one would want to come out to our team. Shelly would have said it with the same amount of confidence if it was the president standing there. That's the kind of guy Shelly was. Always looking out for the boys and calling out bullshit.

When Shelly first met his new platoon, he made it clear it was now his platoon. He berated us for a few minutes, telling us how fucked up we were. After laying down the law, he promised he would get all of us to Iraq. He got everyone in his last platoon augments to Iraq and Afghanistan except two guys. One guy Shelly felt hadn't earned it, and the other didn't want to go for some fucking reason. If we put out for him, he would put out for us.

The sled dogs couldn't be more excited. The shit show was behind us and we had the baddest motherfucker at the team running the show now.

Our next block was the most complex and difficult type of dive training. I'm confident no one in the world can pull off the type of things we can underwater. I was in charge of the diving department for the platoon. Making sure each evolution went off without a hitch was my responsibility. At a regular team, diving department is a cake walk, but at my team it was the linchpin. I worked my ass off getting multiple dives in the water each day. Shelly took notice and I still treasure the evaluation he wrote praising my abilities. Shelly was the team guy everyone wanted to be and he was impressed with me. His opinion is one of the biggest validations of my abilities.

The entire attitude of the platoon changed for the better. Shelly had the knowledge, skill and could drink us all under the table. Our platoon of meat eaters had a lion at its head. Luckily, I wasn't a new guy anymore. One of Shelly's favorite new guy traditions was the dance of the flaming butt holes. For those not familiar with the dance, I will explain. The participants grip a length of toilet paper at one end with their butt cheeks. The other end is lit on fire and the participants dance around for as long as they can. The last one dancing wins.

Maegan was pregnant again. This time it truly was a birth control baby, or at least Maegan says so. I have learned that she is not a truthful woman, so I'm not sure anymore. Maegan always said it was her hardest pregnancy, with the implication it was because of me. She was always an insecure woman, and I didn't help by looking at porn. I've never hidden the fact that I masturbate from her, but it bothered her most when she felt ugly. I never neglected her. Anytime I've been home, we had sex on an every other day if not daily basis, and it was no different when she was pregnant. I was of course always the one in the driver's seat of our sex life, pregnant or not. Supposedly some women get more sex drive when they are pregnant or drunk. Maegan gets more mopey, insecure, and sleepy. Despite those unattractive qualities, I still couldn't keep my hands off her, but she always went to sleep early and I'm a night owl. I would have sex, then go down for a snack and TV show while she went to bed. Inevitably, I would get horny again and want a release before bed. I could go upstairs and try to grind on a grumpy unresponsive wife or just take care of it myself. Most of the time I would just take care of it myself. If sex is dinner at a nice restaurant, rubbing one out is ordering a pizza. Sometimes you want to eat and put out as little effort as possible; doesn't mean you like eating out any less.

I'm not trying to justify my behavior. I think porn is bad and I should have the willpower and consideration not to use it. I've acknowledged this to Maegan multiple times and admitted it was a weakness of mine and not at all her fault. I live with myself by saying most guys use it and I don't have a lot of vices. *I don't drink, I don't gamble, I've never lied to her, I've kept every promise, I've always provided, she can deal with that flaw,* I would say to myself. *Her sister gives her husband pocket pussies and porn. Why is she giving me such a hard time?* Because a man should have the self control and respect for his wife to not look at porn when he knows it bothers her.

Maegan and I did not fight a lot. From what I've seen of other couples, we fought very little. I'm not the kind of person to let things fester, so if there was a problem we talked about it. People say communication is key to a relationship and we certainly did plenty of it. I kept no secrets I wasn't professionally obligated to. I've also heard a happily married old geezer asked what the key is to a happy marriage. His answer was, "Lie your ass off." If two people have a disagreement, it's because they both think they are right. I have always been good at getting my point of view across because I usually think things through. Maegan is not good at getting her point across because often she doesn't know why she does something. The result is very one-sided arguments. She would complain about me and I would make a logical counter argument. Because she is a quitter, she would throw up her hands and say something like "Of course it's always my fault," or "I'm just a stupid, ugly horrible person," even if appearance and intelligence were never part of the debate. It's the same default to victimhood tactics her sister and mother used all the time. You act like someone has verbally assaulted you because they made a compelling case why they didn't want to spend a day off with the in-laws.

I tried to talk about everything with her. She didn't always open up to me because I don't lie to make someone feel better. It was easier for her to complain about me when I was not there. I'm sure she complained about me when she was with her parents, but she didn't even like spending time with her parents. When I was deployed or on training she would often spend time with my family. As I am now learning, she spent a lot of that time complaining about me. Most of the women in my family are easy to talk to, and they loved her like a sister or daughter. They would not betray her trust and knew it was not their place to get involved in any of our issues, so they made for a good neutral third party, a shoulder to cry on.

Our first daughter was going to be big. Maegan looked like she would burst. It did nothing to diminish my sex drive, however. A baby that big puts a lot of stress on a woman's pelvis. While having sex one night, she cried out in pain. We rushed to the hospital worried about the baby. It turned out our exertions had separated her pelvic bone. She was going to need to stay off her feet for a while and we still had a son to take care of. I went into work and explained the situation to Shelly. He told me to stay home for a few days. The platoon thought it was the coolest thing they'd ever heard. How many guys could say they split a woman's pelvis during sex? I explained it was mostly due to the strain of a human being growing inside her, but they didn't care. I spent the next week taking care of her and my son, missing out on what turned out to be a horrendous training evolution.

Any time you push a boat out of the back of a helicopter and into the ocean, something seems to go wrong.

Maegan went into labor before her water broke this time. We went to the hospital calm as can be, it wasn't our first rodeo after all. She got settled into a bed and her water broke. I rushed to help clean up right when she had a contraction. A fire hose of water shot out from her vagina and I had to spread my legs out like a rock star to avoid it. She struggled through a contraction while sputtering with laughter. We were feeling good. This delivery was going to go smoother than the last. The pregnancy was the hardest, but it was all going to be better now.

The doctor came in a while later to check on her dilation. He stuck his fingers up inside her and turned to the nurse and said "prolapsed umbilical." Now I had no idea at the time what that meant. For those of you as ignorant as I was; a prolapsed umbilical cord is when the cord comes out in front of the baby. This is bad because the baby will pinch off the cord when it tries to come out, killing itself in the process. The room filled with panicked nurses and doctors and we both started to realize something was wrong. No one in the room was going to take the time to tell us, either. They started wheeling my wife out with the doctors hand still up inside her to keep pressure off the cord. I have never seen her so scared. She screamed for me. In her darkest, most fearful moment, it was me she cried out for. I was the one she called for when fear gripped her. I was the one who would protect her. God willing she'll never be that afraid again, because I won't be there for her.

The doctor performed an emergency C-section. Within minutes of the doctor sticking his fingers up there, my fat little 10 lb 7 ounce daughter was out into the world. Those minutes were the most terrifying I had experienced. They brought my daughter out and she had an inch long cut across her forehead where the rushed scalpel cut too deep. She still has the scar. She was fat, happy, and sleepy. Meagan was wheeled out and the nurse had to massage her stomach, to keep the blood from clotting, I think. It caused Maegan a lot of pain. It's an indescribable feeling to watch someone you love go through so much pain. I could only stand there and cry. I tried not to with all the people around, but I couldn't stop.

My oldest daughter slept through her first night and pretty much every night after that. When she learned to talk, she would tell us she was ready to go to bed. Imagine a two year old asking to go to bed! That doesn't happen! She would still wake up sometimes and yell "Papa!" until I came and got her. Waking up and getting out of bed sucked, but it was worth it. She would be laying in her bed with her arms extended, too lazy to sit up. I would bend all the way down so she could wrap all her limbs around me before lifting her up. I treasured every step back to my room. After laying down she would always make sure to stay attached to me for a few minutes, showing how important I was to her.

I got to stay home for a while after she was born, unlike when my first was born. Maegan was not much help after her drive-through style surgery. For those first weeks, it was me taking care of both of them and my son. I can't remember if Amanda was staying with us already or if she came later, but she had her son to deal with. My daughter was so fat she made weird sounds in her sleep and I kept getting up to make sure she was breathing. Maegan always complained about how hard those first weeks were with my oldest son, but I remember taking care of Maegan and my daughter as some of the happiest times of my life.

Chapter 8

Work was only going to give me so much time off, and eventually I had to fly out to Washington where my platoon was starting cold weather diving, one of the shittiest things we do. Washington is a great place, but spending hours in the cold black of the Puget Sound takes the fun out of it. There are a few inactive aircraft carriers parked along piers that we use for training. They are all parked nose in, with their props pointed out into the channel. We drive our Mini Sub underneath them, practice some secret squirrel shit I am not going to get into, then drive back to a boat ramp to get pulled out of the water. Now I'm going to go into the most detail I'm willing to discuss, so pay attention.

The task needed four guys. We had a guy to pilot the Mini Sub, we'll call him Hollywood. Shelly was the navigator and mission commander. A guy we'll call Frat House and myself sat in the back. It was Frat House's and my job to swim out and actually complete the task once we were under the target vessel. Each guy wore a drysuit which requires at least 40 extra pounds of weight to keep you from rocketing to the surface and causing an air bubble to burst in your heart. Shelly and Hollywood used rebreathers the size of a rucksack because they weren't supposed to go far from the sub and the full face masks allowed them to talk underwater. Frat House and I used smaller, sneakier rigs designed for swimming distance. Overseeing the whole evolution would be two surface boats called RHIBs. One boat had the Dive Sup and was called the Sup Boat. The other boat was called the Chase Boat. Its job was to be an extra pair of eyes and chase off traffic that got too close. Driving the Chase Boat was our old friend Dumbass. I told you to remember him.

The Sup Boat positioned itself on the port side of the target vessel. You don't need to know which side is port just know it is opposite from the starboard side. Frat House and I were supposed to complete our task on the port side of the boat. The Chase Boat with Dumbass at the helm was told to stay out in the channel to block traffic and watch the starboard side of the target vessel. This didn't matter to us underwater. We are supposed to pretend the two boats aren't there. Hollywood parked the mini sub under the target vessel smooth as he always did. Shelly said his mask was fogging up so signaled Frat House and me to get started before getting out to clear his mask. Underneath an aircraft carrier at night is probably one of the darkest places in the world. Everything has to be done by feel. I climbed out to get our equipment ready and Frat House swam forward to check in with

Shelly. He couldn't find him in the jungle of slime and funk growing on the bottom of the in-active ship. Instead he swam to Hollywood's side and got a signal no diver wants. Four rapid squeezes, the signal for an emergency. Frat House swam back to me and squeezed my arm four times. My hands were full of shit so I crammed it back into the sub and squeezed inside with Frat House. Unlike the front seaters, Frat House and I could not talk or hear anyone else. We slid the hatches closed and signaled Hollywood we were safely in-side. Hollywood gunned the throttle, but we were stuck on something. Whatever it was broke free and we bounced along the bottom of the Aircraft Carrier until we reached the sur-face. Imagine wearing arctic gear stuffed inside an economy car size trunk with another guy, filled with ice water, while it drives over speed bumps.

On the surface, Frat House and I opened up the hatches in the back to see what had happened. Hollywood was fighting to keep Shelly's head above water. We swam up to help and I could see white foam coming out of Shelly's mouth. Frat House and I found Shelly's quick releases and dropped all his weight. We looked around and could only see one boat out in the channel. It was some distance, but I could see the vertical lights and knew the red, white, red, was the Chase Boat. We lit Shelly's emergency flare and waved it over our heads. The boat didn't move. The entire flare burned through and the boat in the channel didn't move. Hollywood tried to give CPR, but it's no easy task in ice water and full kit. We lit off each of our flares one by one and screamed at the top of our lungs. One flare was a dud, but we went through three flares and still the boat in the channel didn't move. I was starting to doubt it was the Chase Boat but any mariner should still recognize an emergency flare.

I realized the boat in the channel wasn't going to help us. We were on the starboard side of the target vessel and I figured the Sup Boat must be on the other side of the ship. There was basically a floating city between us and help. Our last flare was inside the sub so

I swam down and pulled it out. I started swimming, but saved the flare until I could get out into the channel where I could be seen. Before I cleared the back end of the carrier, the Sup Boat came motoring around. They knew something was wrong, but I lit the flare to hammer the point home.

We fought to get Shelly into the boat for what seemed like an eternity. Shelly was a good 200 lb plus man when he was dry. Even with all his weight dropped, his kit still added at least 50 pounds. Frat House, Hollywood and I finned underneath him while the crew tried to pull him on board. We ended up having to cut him out of all his gear in order to get him over the lip of the boat. Probably the only time I've actually needed a dive knife. Hollywood got in the Sup Boat with Shelly and they gunned it for shore. Frat House and I stayed with the mini sub and waited for the Chase Boat to come tow it to the boat ramp. Low and behold, the boat out in the channel was the Chase Boat. They just watched, doing nothing, while we lit off three emergency flares. The crew may have been a couple of supply clerks, but they were in the Navy and should know what a fucking emergency flare is. Dumbass came motoring up in the Chase Boat and ran over Frat House, myself and our very expensive Mini Sub. Frat House and I were too tired for anything more than profanity. Dumbass got his boat under control enough for us to rig our crippled sub for tow. We made it to the boat ramp and drove back to base in silence, waiting for news. The rest of the platoon was waiting for us back at the high bay. I went outside and started to wash my gear. Frat House came out and put a hand on my shoulder.

"He's gone man." Is all he said. I found the nearest dark corner where I could let my knees buckle and cry. Frat House stayed with me until I was ready to head inside. Later, we tried to piece together what had happened. When you wear a full face mask with a re-breather your face will warm up, even in cold water. If you've ever jumped from a hot tub into an ice bucket you'll know about the involuntary intake of breath. We think Shelly took his mask off to clear it and the cold shock made him suck in water. Hollywood said he came back into the sub and managed to get an emergency regulator in his mouth, but by that time he had probably inhaled too much water.

The next few days were the closest to what I am experiencing now. The pain and loss can only be experienced, not described. Most of the guys spent them in a constant state of intoxication. I still didn't drink, so I spent them sober, as I am now. I had to give statements to the NCIS and the investigating officer. NCIS was just a formality, but the investigating officer was another matter. All NCIS had to do was officially declare there was no foul play involved. The investigating officer had to figure out who to blame. When something goes wrong in the military, a reason has to be found and a policy put in place to prevent it from happening again. On paper this is a good thing, but in practice it becomes a witch hunt. The military always needs a scapegoat.

An officer from outside the community is always chosen to lead the investigation of a training accident. This provides an unbiased investigator, but also means the investigator doesn't know a single thing about what he's investigating. The big wig fleet officer in charge of the investigation didn't know a single thing about special warfare or diving. During my interview I spent more time explaining the various things we do and why we do them, instead of talking about the event. Eventually he finished his report and I never bothered reading it. I heard enough from the guys who did to know it would just piss me off.

Big Navy wouldn't accept a final report saying, "it's a dangerous job and shit happens." The problem is the investigating officer had no fucking clue why it happened. His solution was to point out every little flaw he could find in us and say it was a culmination of all these little breaks in good order and discipline. When I heard he cited our platoon's out of regs grooming standards as a contributing factor, I decided the report was full of shit and not worth the read.

Shelly was from Pennsylvania and his family wanted him buried there. I was chosen to escort his body back. It is an experience I will never forget. We started by transporting him from the morgue to the airport. We pulled up to an access gate leading strait onto the airport tarmac. Every firetruck and police car in Bremerton must have been there with their lights going. Red, white and blue lights combined with saluting firemen and cops to create a corridor of patriotism leading straight to the plane's luggage ramp. It is a humbling sight. We carried him slowly in our dress blues and loaded him directly onto the plane. Hollywood, Frat House, myself and three others were escorted through ticketing and security so we could board.

At the layover we got off the plane first and were escorted to the luggage compartment so we could carry our brother onto the next plane. As his coffin came down the conveyor, the windows of the terminal filled up with crusty old vets giving their salute to the fallen. Grey beards with assorted pins in their ball caps from world war two, Korea and Vietnam. The best of America. Old timers who saw what was happening and came to pay their respects.

In Pennsylvania, we delayed the offloading of the plane so his family could come down to the tarmac and greet him coming off the plane. The luggage crew heard he was coming and apparently they had a color guard. I would have never thought those men and women you see scurrying about the bottom of the plane before takeoff would have a color guard, but they do, and a sharp one at that. They paraded the stars and stripes and saluted Shelly as he came down the conveyor with all the snap of the best active duty color guards.

Shelly was a rare man. Team guys and marines flew out from all over the country to attend his funeral. The AOIC from my first platoon said something at the wake I'll never forget. He said Shelly died fighting the enemy. Everything we do is fighting the enemy. If we are not engaging him directly then we are preparing for the next engagement. Shelly died preparing for the next engagement. Combat operations have gone relatively smooth for me, training has claimed most of my friends. I don't think Maegan ever realized what we all risked every time we went to work. For her I was just going to have fun jumping out of airplanes and diving. She never considered I might die every time I went under the water or took that leap. Honestly, I don't think she would have been all that broken up about it.

Shelly's parents had a home in the country with his favorite bar not far away. For the next few days, over a hundred of the roughest men on the planet drank nonstop at both locations. The owner of the bar was a good friend of Shelly's and he didn't spend any of those nights serving drinks. Team guys served the drinks while the owner spent the night plastered with a team guy's arm around his shoulder, along with Shelly's fiancée, father, brothers, mother, and even grandmother. Two families who had never met, discovering they had a brother and son in common. When I die, that's what I want. My two families celebrating together. If anyone is still unsure when that happens, Maegan is not invited.

Chapter 9

After a few days, the platoon started flying back to Washington to finish the training block. I only stayed for a little while because Shelly had given me one last gift. I was finishing my first enlistment in the Navy and was going to reenlist, which came with a handsome bonus. Shelly had set me up with a training trip to Thailand so I could fly through a tax free zone and get my bonus tax free. I stopped in Hawaii for a day to kiss my wife, son and new daughter, then hit the road again.

When I came back from Thailand, our command got the platoon together to talk about the future and health of our platoon. They carried on about how Shelly would want us to carry on with the mission. You don't need to tell a team guy this, it's ingrained in his psyche. Problem was we were done with our training cycle and our mission was an indefinite amount of time off. I stood up and told our big wigs the worst thing they could do is have us sit around and do cookie cutter dives for a mission we didn't have the details for yet. They needed to find meaningful work for us. There was a war still raging in Iraq and they needed to send us to it. That's what Shelly would have wanted. Of course they thanked me for my input and said they understood. Months went by with the command finding busy work for us and our platoon continued to fall apart.

Pit Bull and I were doing a proof of concept/busy work dive. The sea state was rough and the nature of the dive kept us near the surface and at its mercy. Pit Bull fought the Mini Sub for hours trying to keep it steady. All the strain probably caused him to hold his breath at some point, and he ended up with an Arterial Gas Embolism (AGE). Google it if you want the details but in layman's terms he had a hole punched through his heart by an air bubble. He survived, but he can never dive open circuit again, so his time at our team was over.

The next blow was a personal one. I need to go back a bit and tell you about my uncle T first. Uncle T did a stint in the Navy when I was a boy. He got to meet the cast of Top Gun when they filmed on the USS Ranger to give you a time frame. At the time he was the only family member I spent time with who had served. Naturally, I looked up to him quite a bit. When the war broke out, Uncle T joined back up with the Navy reserve as a Seabee. Seabees are naval construction teams, if you didn't know. His unit got activated and he did a tour in Iraq. When he got back, he decided to go back to active duty, but the Navy wanted to drop his rank in order to enlist. The Army was hurting for guys, so he became an Army engineer instead, and got to keep his rank. While I was diving in Washington, Uncle T was doing route clearance in Afghanistan. His truck hit a roadside bomb and uncle T caught a good chunk of it.

Once again, I came home to find my wife in tears and news of another family member fighting for his life. Once again, I fell into my role as man of the house and decided every-

thing would be ok. Uncle T was in the woods for longer than my brother and never recovered as well, but he's a hard motherfucker. By this time, tragedy was becoming a common
part of life and I was getting good at coping. Uncle T can still walk, but he'll certainly never
be the same. Plenty of organizations stepped up to take care of him and it's good to see
the country take care of its vets. The degree of that care can vary widely depending on the
conditions. Uncle T was wounded in combat, while my brother was wounded in an accident
driving back from combat. No purple heart for my brother, no foundations lining up to make
sure he and his family were taken care of. Uncle T and my brother are both getting by and
aren't the kind men who need handouts. I just want people to understand how easy it is to
fall through the cracks.

By this point, my second platoon proudly wore the mantle of black sheep and we didn't
give a fuck. What were they going to do us, continue to not let us go to war? The one
bright side was getting a solid chief to replace Shelly. He was much more mild mannered,
but every bit as competent. He was the kind of guy who could explain to you why you're an
idiot, then you would realize you are an idiot and thank him. He had some kind of psychology degree, I think. The man had six daughters while trying to get a son, so patience was
definitely one of his virtues. From now until my next platoon, this guy will be called Chief.

Our team was responsible for making sure the large Navy submarines equipped to
launch SEALs had crews trained to do so. One submarine on the east coast needed certification while another out in Guam needed to be loaded for a future certification. Our platoon
was sitting around waiting for a yet undefined mission, so naturally we were picked for both
tasks. The platoon was split in half and all the officers and enlisted leadership went to the
east coast while the sled dogs went to Guam. Guam is notorious for being a place where
Navy guys get in trouble. They have a *Days since last DUI* counter at the front gate and it
never needs the second digit long. The guy in charge of the Guam crew was the short guy

who started the bar fight at the beginning of the platoon. He was an excellent team guy and leader, but even he joked about how the team obviously didn't think its decision through. We thought for sure we were being tested. The team sent all the sled dogs from its trouble maker platoon hoping we'd burn the island down so they could shit-can us all.

A more well-behaved group of Navy personnel never went to Guam before or since that trip. We showed up, did our job, and enjoyed a few mellow nights out on the town. When we flew back, we found out our head shed was fired.....again.

Ok, it wasn't our whole head shed, just our LT and LPO. If you've forgotten, that's the guy who is overall in charge of the platoon and the head sled dog, respectively. Apparently the film crew from *Act of Valor*, the awful movie that never should have been made, needed to get some cool Navy SEAL diving shots. The Navy, not our platoon, decided the film crew could get their shots while the leadership half of my platoon certified the sub. Certifying the sub doesn't involve anything super secret, so the film crew was allowed to swim around and film as long as they didn't get in the way.

Our Mini Sub has waterproofed computers inside, complete with monitors. My LT and LPO thought it would be funny to load porn onto those computers so they could watch something while the film crew tried to get their shots. Everyone thought it was funny until someone important didn't think it was very funny. You see, those waterproofed computers had classified material on them, and our LPO and LT loaded porn onto them. Loading unsecured software onto a secret government computer is a big no no. Kind of like storing official government emails on your private server. Soldiers have been prosecuted for charging their phones with government computers, but if you're the Secretary of State you get a pass.

The axe fell and the platoon lost two solid dudes. I haven't even mentioned some of the other guys we lost. Some just made rank and needed to move on, while others got injured or got in trouble. That guy who cut his hand in the bar fight got chopped, for instance. Every guy in the platoon had a magnetic name tag to go on the tracker in our platoon space. When we lost a guy, we would put his name tag on an ever growing stack attached to our safe. We called it the bone yard. At this point the bone yard had more names than the roster on our tracker. The team was running out of people to feed our platoon, so they gave us back the original LT they fired at the beginning of the platoon.

The platoon was in a rut, so we decided to do what every pissed off platoon does. We had a bitch session or kangaroo court, as some call it. Basically, we closed the doors to the platoon space, disregarded rank, and spoke our minds without consequences. Frat House and I ganged up on LT. I pointed out how I predicted all this after Shelly died. I won't go into detail about what was said, it was a private platoon conversation after all, but the next day Frat House and I were told we were going to Iraq.

Chapter 10

The American public does not realize the amount of bullshit holding our military back from defeating the enemy. For those who don't know, there're two forms of Islam: Shia and Sunni. The two separated very early in Islam's history and have been killing each other ever since. I won't go into the details, but you should probably look it up. I would encourage everyone to learn as much about Islam as they can, especially its early history. The area of Iraq I went to was predominately Shia. This meant we had to go through an extra approval process to go after Shia targets. Because Sunnis were a minority in the area, the majority of the population couldn't give a fuck if we went after Sunnis. Because America wants to respect their culture of discrimination, we often couldn't get approval for targets we otherwise would have gone after. Every middle east deployment I've been on, we've known where the bad guys are. IED makers, Iranian agents, recruiting mosques, smugglers, ships carrying lethal aid, you name it. We can watch bad guys on one screen while watching a Schwarzenegger marathon on the other. Somewhere up the chain of command is some big wig who is more politician than soldier and won't approve the mission. We listen to bad guys brag to their friends about how the Americans will never find him; all the while we are staring right at him. Little does he know there's some political speed bump keeping him from swallowing a Hellfire.

We were forced to work with the Iraqis on all of our ops. We kept them in the dark as much as possible, because our supposed allies would tip off our target. Make no mistake, the wars in Iraq and Afghanistan have dragged on not because the enemy is competent but because Americans lack the resolve of our forefathers. The Apaches, Comanches and Sioux were far more competent adversaries.

Our main focus was countering the smuggling networks that brought Iranian manufactured IEDs and rockets across the border. These weren't old leftover munitions some terrorist snuck over, either. One of the rockets they shot at us was a dud. Its date of manufacture wasn't even a year old. This stuff is coming right off Iranian assembly lines and finding its way into Iraq to be shot at Americans. The day after I left, one of those rockets landed in some Army cat's bed while he was sleeping. Remember that the next time you hear about our leaders making deals with Iran.

I'm editing this portion not long after Trump shwacked Soleimani. Almost every deployment I was on, the Iranians were a major factor. On this Iraq deployment, one of our Army brethren was cut in half by an Iranian EFP (Explosively Formed Projectile); little roadside coffee cans of death that can be clustered in an array. Iranians aren't that clever. We usually know right where they are and what they are doing. We are forced to tip toe around them to avoid an international incident. The Iranians know this and are blatant with their ef-

forts against us. They know we won't attack them outright so they flagrantly kill our troops

with only the flimsiest of facades to give them deniability. Shoving a Hellfire (I assume) up

Soleimani's ass was long overdue.

We had to road trip three hours to stage for an operation against the leadership of a

smuggling ring up north. A large generator needed to be brought along to power the TOC

(Tactical Operations Center): that place in all the movies with the computer screens and tech

nerds monitoring the mission. Some old guy with a cigar is in there saying *Hang in there*

son, we are coming to get you. The generator was supposed to be hooked up to an RG-33

(big armored truck), but it had the wrong tow hitch. Instead, it got hooked to my underpow-

ered HMMWV (hummer/humvee), already weighed down with an armor package. I drove

three hours blacked out on night vision across war torn roads. Every rut and pot hole tried

to send the generator one way or the other. We made it to the staging point and executed

the operation. We found the guy we were after, but it turned out he was also chief of police.

After a frustrating night of arguing with the commander of our Iraqi partner force, we ended

up leaving the guy and packing up to head back south.

I was told I could switch out and make someone else drive the generator, but I said I

would drive it back. The thing was a bitch to control, but I had practice driving it up and

didn't want to make someone else learn it all over again. I had to keep the gas pedal buried

to keep up with the convoy. The HMMWV topped out at 55mph. That's how fast we were

going when the generator caught a rut I couldn't pull it out of. We pitched sideways and

went into a barrel roll. I had enough time before the first roll to realize the shit we were in.

Being inside a high speed rollover is like being a bean in a maraca. There is a butthole

puckering moment as the inertia takes control, then its complete chaos. I gripped the wheel

as hard as I could and pressed my feet against the floorboards thinking I could pin myself in place. I tried to keep my limbs close, not wanting them to get pinched off in twisting metal. Later I found out that's not what you're supposed to do. I remember my grip on the wheel giving way, but the thing that stands out the most was the sudden stop. I don't remember leaving the vehicle. I was a bean in the maraca, then suddenly I was face down in the Iraqi dust; looking at the guy who was sitting behind me a moment ago. He was screaming because his pelvic bone had been shattered. He was one of our tech guys and I had just met him before the trip. Before moving, I told my fingers and toes to wiggle. They listened and I let out a breath. My buddies came running from another vehicle to render aid. I told them I was fine, so they focused on our tech support guy. Fuel was pouring all over us so we needed to move. The tech guy was dragged away as carefully as possible, but it still made him scream in a way I'll never forget.

Our skinny little interpreter helped me up and I walked as far away from the wreck as I could. A bout of nausea hit me like a freight train and threw me back to the ground. I rolled to my back and took stock of the situation. First off, I had shit myself. Later I found out that's a defense mechanism. When your body encounters extreme stress, it ditches all unnecessary weight, at least it's what I was told and I'm sticking with it. My right arm was missing a good percentage of the skin that was supposed to be covering it, but all in all I wasn't in bad shape. My hips hurt like a motherfucker, but they weren't as bad as the guy screaming next to me. They found our turret gunner a ways back. He was an EOD (Explosive Ordinance Disposal) officer and had no fucking clue where he was. EOD guys are bomb techs, you know the guys from the Hurt Locker, only the Navy version is way more badass. He was sitting up and completely bewildered at what was going on. Someone was trying to explain to him he was in Iraq. He had a cracked vertebrae in his neck and had a concussion. Being in the turret, he fell out early and didn't go for the full ride. Our navigator, the guy sitting shotgun and the only other team guy in the vehicle, was the only one who managed to stay in the vehicle. All he had was a cut between his eyes from his night vision goggles. I asked him later how he managed to stay in the truck.

"I spread out like a starfish to make myself bigger, like we are taught." Being from a team where we drove vehicles with propellers instead of wheels I had never been taught that.

"Didn't work for me." I laughed, feeling stupid for trying to keep my limbs close. *Try your fancy starfish maneuver when a RHIB flips and you'll be the one feeling stupid.*

Laying on the highway was killing my hips and I felt like I could walk it off. Very slowly, I rolled to my hands and knees. When I tried to stand, the nausea hit again. I settled for crawling. I probably made it a few feet before the GFC (Ground Force Commander) noticed me. With his arms crossed and not so much as a change in tone he calmly requested.

"Someone please stop Swift from crawling away." By now they had sedated the tech and called for a Medevac. One of my buddies ran over and told me to stop moving. I protested.

"I just need to walk around so my hips loosen up," I reasoned.

"Dude! You just flew out of a HMMWV. You're not going to fucking walk it off."

As I write this now, I think back on when I fell off the sea cliff in 8th grade. It's comforting to know that when shit happens, my first instinct is to get up and keep walking. The Medevac bird came and they loaded us onto the helo. The crew knew their business, putting me on the stretcher laying on my side. They braced my hips in a way that took away all the pain. The feeling of relief made me feel like I could fall asleep, even if I was still laying in my own shit. That relaxation came to an end when we reached the hospital tent. The surgeon was a yoked chick with a shaved head and more tattoos than me; a real life Rosie the Riveter. She figured out real quick I would probably be fine and focused on saving the life of our tech with the shattered pelvis. I, however, was a good training opportunity so the JV team stepped up to take care of me. The medical tent was staffed by mostly women. I found one of the few dudes and told him as discreetly as possible that I had shit myself and wanted to clean up. He assured me I could as soon as they were done with all the initial probing around you get when you go to the doctor's office.

They cut my shit-covered pants off and he brought a blanket, trash can and wet wipes. In a tent full of women, I cleaned the shit off me with nothing but a blanket to hide my shame. Once I was clean, the real fun began. I had been moved from my comfortable stretcher to a rigid spine board and my hips were killing me again. I just wanted to get up and walk around so they would loosen up. They still needed to take X-rays, so that was out of the question. Until they knew nothing was broken, I couldn't move.

The head nursed asked, "Who hasn't put on a pelvic brace before?" Two junior nurses piped up and they set to trying to put one on me. I didn't get a good look at this thing, but for something supposed to help, it sure caused a lot of pain. The first two chicks tried getting it on using their body weight to try and squeeze the two ends together. I gritted my teeth as best I could, hoping and doubting the pain would end when they finally closed the clasp. After much effort on their part and internal profanity on mine, they acknowledged they were the weaker sex and called two dudes over. Once they went to work I wanted to beg for the girls back. The dudes failed as well, and the head surgeon returned from saving our tech's life. She said to forego the brace for now and consigned me to a new hell. Apparently, there was blood mixed with the shit in my pants, so they needed to put a catheter in me to see if there was blood in the tank. For those who don't know, that's when they shove a tube up your dick.

And so, my blanket was removed, exposing my shriveled dick for all the pretty nurses. In my defense, I had just been thrown out of an armored vehicle, so it was hiding pretty far in. Again, a nurse with no experience in the matter was selected to shove a tube down my urethra. I gripped the edges of the spine board and steadied my resolve. She failed once again, though not without giving it her all. It certainly made it in, but then she had to twist and wiggle the tube around trying to get it all the way to my bladder, or however deep it was supposed to go. My dick was not having it. It was scarred out of its mind and retreated as far into my stomach as it could go. The head surgeon finally called it off and the nurse withdrew the tube.

I jovially exclaimed, "Put me back on the highway!" Laughing as hard as I could, trying not tear up in front of all those women.

The head surgeon put a hand on my shoulder. "I think we've tortured you enough. Do you think you can just pee in a cup for us?" *Why the fuck didn't we try that first?!* I thought but didn't say. I managed to pee and the X-rays came back. I was good to go. A nurse picked the gravel from the raw meat of my arm and wrapped it up. I could walk around, but I no longer had any clothes. The medical tent in the middle of the desert didn't have any of those open ass hospital gowns, either. It seemed it was also laundry day and everyone's clothes were drying outside. All the dudes had left by this point, but there was a bigger girl who had a pair of purple briefs I could wear. So, wearing nothing but purple women's underwear, I strolled around the hospital tent. I found the section where our tech and the EOD officer were waiting to be flown out to Germany. The EOD guy was a Brad Pitt looking fucker and was hitting on the nurses while wearing a neck brace. Our tech, however, was still sedated and had tubes running in and out of him. I lost it then. I had been driving, I had caused this. I cried, in front of everyone, I cried.

The nurses took it in shifts to keep an eye on me through the night. Every 30 minutes or so I had to get up and walk around in my purple underwear. In the morning, a girl brought in a pair of cammo pants and a T shirt for me. Two of my guys had stayed back with me, but the rest kept driving back south. The local Army Special Forces guys came and picked us up so we could wait in their camp for a helo ride back to our neck to the woods. The first meal in the SF camp, a flag pole blew over and landed on the bench next to me. Everybody else was able jump out of the way, but I wasn't going anywhere quickly. The metal pole was heavy enough to crush me and only missed by a foot or two. Everyone just stared in silence at the good or bad juju of it. Being me was a safe enough place to be, but you were gambling by sitting next to me. I've sat in the vehicle next to men while they've gotten holes punched through their heart, drowned, cracked vertebra, shattered a pelvis, and choked on their own mucus for 30 minutes from pressure induced pneumonia. We'll get to that last one later. I generally end up relatively unharmed.

We got our flight back in a few days, and I hobbled out to the airfield. Riding on a helicopter in 120 degree weather was more than my stomach could handle, and I puked into a bag. I don't think anyone saw. When we got down south, I called Maegan to tell her I was ok. She didn't seem too shook up about it. By now I was used to her emotional reactions being less than expected. She only ever got emotional when she had to tell me something had happened to someone else. I can't think of a time she shed a tear for me. I found out later she got quite emotional when I called to say I would be getting out of the Navy. Her financial future was uncertain and that shook her up quite a bit. Despite having always taken care of her, she still doubted my ability. That's still a ways off, though. The rest of the deployment was much of the same. There were still plenty of bad guys when I left. We knew right where they were, but couldn't go after them.

Frat House had been with a platoon up north, and we hitched a ride back to the states with an entire battalion of regular Army. They packed the plane. The two of us were the only guys in civilian clothes with hair longer than an inch. One of the big wig Army guys knew us for what we were and bumped us up to first class. We flew into Baltimore to be greeted by a crowd of proud Americans with gift bags of candy and such. Cheers and thanks greeted us when we walked off the plane. It's quite an event flying back with a conventional force, like the celebration at the end of some war film. This is what it felt like to have someone happy to see you home, and these were complete strangers. The two of us had tickets waiting to get us back to Hawaii. For some reason I thought maybe coming back from a combat zone where I almost died might have earned me that soldier's greeting, but once again I set my hopes too high. My son was old enough to remember me now, and he was extremely excited until he got distracted. He was still at the phase were he got excited when I came back from a day at work. Treasure those moments. My daughter had forgotten me and I was ready for it this time. I sat on the floor and smiled at her. She gave me a confused look then scooted over and sat in my lap while she played. Few things have ever made me so happy.

Chapter 11

Playing cool guy was over for now, and it was time to start diving again. My platoon was in full swing and I needed to learn the new profile they were using, or so I thought. Shortly after I got back, Charlie Platoon lost their older guys to transfers and they were short on experience. The rest of Bravo still hadn't gotten to deploy yet, so Frat House and I were offered. Our name tags were moved to the bone yard and I started my 3rd platoon.

Charlie platoon's first LT was one of the best officers I've worked for. As soon as Frat House and I got in the platoon, he set us up with augments to Afghanistan. We would be part of the second round of guys from the platoon going. The platoon's LPO was on the first round, so I took over as LPO while he was gone. Charlie had already been together for a while and things ran smoothly. Every morning, I would check out 1000 rounds and shoot through them all with only LT to help. You would think that's how every Navy SEAL starts his day, but we had to do a lot of shady paperwork to let that happen. Charlie's LT was all about doing what's necessary to get his boys the best jobs and the best gear. He wasn't worried about his own career, just being the best team guy he could be. Contrary to what you might think, SEALs are not given the best gear on the market. We are part of the military and the military is part of the government. The government will find the lowest bidder to make the "best" equipment. All the equipment is good, but when you're going to war, every guy wants the best. Most guys end up buying a few key pieces of gear themselves.

One area the military is always a step behind in is plate carriers. This is the harness that allows us to wear body armor. At the time, London Bridge Trading was making the best carriers. Of course we were getting decent knockoffs issued to us. Each platoon is given money every year to buy gear outside of what is issued, however, you can't use the money for a piece of gear with an equivalent already in the standard issue. To get around this, LT called the company and had them change the notation on the invoice from plate parrier to life vest. A little fudging the system, and LT was able to send his guys to Afghanistan with top of the line plate carriers.

Charlie platoon was the command's golden child, the platoon who could do no wrong. I returned with them to the same island that got my Bravo platoon LT fired. This time around we had a good time. The good time was shattered when we got news of a helo full of our dudes going down in Afghanistan. One of my BUDS classmates was on the helo. Adam Smith or Smitty rolled into my class in second phase and graduated with me. I remember him saying, "Optimism in BUDS is just foolishness." He was a top performer. The thing making me feel the worst was not feeling bad enough. Losing Shelly and almost losing my brother and uncle made me callous to loss. I hadn't seen Smitty in years, and I wish I had. It would be my turn soon enough to go to Afghanistan.

Afghanistan was, and still is, my best deployment and that's all I'll say about it. This biography is basically just a bitch session and I have nothing bad to say about my time in Afghanistan. I enjoyed it so much I would have stayed longer, but my team needed guinea pigs to test new dive profiles. A few months after I left Afghanistan, one of the helicopters I had been riding in got shot down. Another BUDS classmate was on board. Jesse Pitman was born to carry a belt fed gun. Again, the worst feeling was not feeling enough.

My platoon had a mission on the books and we needed to test new dive profiles. If you're not familiar with dive physics, I'll try and break it down in layman's terms. Pressure on the body increases as you go deeper in the water. If you've ever swam to the bottom of a deep pool you've felt the effect of that pressure on your ears; similarly, if you drive to a high mountain or fly in a plane you feel the effect of lower pressure on your ears. To give you some perspective, someone at a depth of 33 feet is under twice the pressure as someone standing at sea level. When the body is under increased pressure, it absorbs gasses differently. Pure oxygen becomes toxic below 20 feet, the nitrogen in the air we breathe can make you loopy. All this increased absorption means the body needs to release these gasses as you ascend or you will get some nasty side effects. Remember my buddy who got a hole in his heart? There are published dive tables one can use to plan a dive and make the necessary stops to give the body time to release the built up gas. The kind of diving we did at my first team is an entirely different beast. Oftentimes the missions we were tasked with had never had anything similar done before. Therefore, we had to invent new ways of doing things. This can be one of the most rewarding aspects of being at that team. This time however, it wasn't.

My platoon had to test new profiles that had never been tried before. They shut us in a flooded chamber and pressed us down to a certain depth for a certain period of time. Think triple digit depths for hours, not minutes. They were able to pipe in some Metallica, Slayer and Pantera. A weighted chess board helped pass the time. Periodically, we would have to get up and walk on a self powered treadmill with kettle bells. Yes, you can use a treadmill underwater. The entire time I was wishing I was back home with my wife and children or back in Afghanistan going after high-value targets. At the end, we'd be poked prodded and observed. We were all given pink pages on the tops of our medical records exclaiming in bold print DO NOT REMOVE FROM THE TOP OF RECORD. INDIVIDUAL HAS PARTICI-PATED IN EXPERIMENTAL DIVING! Years later, despite such plain and obvious text, some dipshit in the Eugene Naval Reserve Stations medical department took one look at it, some-how didn't understand what is was, and threw it away.

Once we proved our dive profile wouldn't kill us, it was time to start training in the open ocean. We found us a deep spot off the coast of Hawaii and anchored a boat over it. After the first day of throwing up, I got my sea legs and my experience was at least equally shitty to everyone else living on a boat. For a Navy man I really hate living at sea. Hawaiian wa-ters are generally considered warm, but if you go deep enough or long enough you will start to jackhammer. Guys started wearing arctic dry suits to keep warm. One sorry officer from the vanilla teams forgot to hook up the air bottle used to counter the pressure on a dry suit. When he came up, he had angry welts from neck to ankle caused by the seems of the Lul-ulemon like thermals worn under the dry suit. If only that was the worst of it.

My dive buddy had been down hard with a bug, but finally got medically cleared to dive. He was feeling healthy and nothing grates on our kind of men more than being side-lined. The dive started fine. We hit bottom, did what we needed to do, and started to de-compress. At first he was able to say he was having a hard time breathing. Very quickly he started to sputter and choke. We didn't know it, but the pressure had induced a kind of pneumonia. His lungs were filling with fluid. We still had over an hour of decompression to burn off. If we ascended now, we could kill the rest of us and him. There are few experiences like sitting next to your buddy while he drowns in his own lungs. The choking, the effort not to panic, it's hard to give it justice in text. He was still choking when we got to the surface, which was a good sign. I completed my second and first successful real world buddy rescue. My buddy lived, but never dove again.

I returned home and just like my homecoming from my first deployment, Iraq, and Afghanistan, I imagined a Hollywood-worthy reunion with my wife that I knew would not happen. The kiddos of course made up for it. Maegan always seemed to think my life was just an adventure whenever I left. To be fair, it was, but she never appreciated that going to train for war was just as dangerous as when I left for actual war.

We spent a lot of time training for that op. Once we had a plan it didn't take long for us to become proficient at it. What takes the longest is waiting for the big wigs to get their shit together. By big wigs I mean a lot of old white guys, one old white hag, and a black dude. We spent a lot of time proving it could be safely done. Not because anyone worried about our safety, but because it would be an international shitstorm if something went wrong. We went back to being guinea pigs a few times and practiced with our supporting assets until they were also proficient. A lot of it felt like busy work and I felt the same frustration as after Shelly died.

Maegan and I had our second son. I would say that of all my children, my relationship with him is the least complicated. The main reason is he is the most like me. Our relationship is like the relationship I have with my father. We don't need to say a whole lot to each other, we understand. He is the most stubborn, headstrong, angry, and independent of all my children. I feel, and my mother echoes, that my two boys are a repeat of my brother and me. My older brother always kept his toys organized and knives sharp. When he eventually handed them down to me, they would be destroyed. There are boys who are good at building things and boys who are good at destroying things. The world needs both.

Boy 2 had to be a planned C section after girl 1. I got to watch this time, and it is a far less delicate process than you might imagine. It looks more like gutting an animal than it should. At one point, a nurse used a spatula-like hook to grip the slashed edge of my wife's stomach, then leaned with her body weight to keep the skin out of the way so the doc could dig deeper. Boy 2 two came out the smallest: 8 pounds 5 ounces. Maegan might have been able to push him out, but we weren't going to risk it after all 10 pounds 7 ounces of girl 1. Like girl 1, boy 2 was all mine for the first few weeks while Maegan recovered from being treated like a trophy kill.

While boy 1 came out with blue eyes wide open, boy 2 wasn't opening them for no one. I would sit with him in my lap forever, just trying to catch a glimpse of his blue eyes. So much of that time is forgotten. The thing that stands out about him was our nightly routine. All the kids would wake up in the middle of the night calling for Papa. I would carry them into our room and they would cuddle up to their mom. When boy 2 was done nursing, he would lay on top of me to fall asleep. I kind of feel bad for him. When I go through pictures it seems like we skipped right from girl 1 to girl 2. He seemed to get lost in the shuffle. I don't think I need to feel bad for him. He doesn't need validation from anyone or anything. My oldest was an only child for a while and always needed attention. Being the youngest of five I could never understand why he couldn't just play by himself. Boy 2, on the other hand, can entertain himself for hours. Boy 2 certainly holds the record for most spankings. Yes, I spank my children. I also can't count how many times people have told me how well behaved they are.

I'm going to go off on a tangent and Boy 2's story is the best place for it. Spanking is good for your children and the younger you start the better. When your kid starts to crawl is when they first start getting into trouble, when their actions can have dangerous consequences. Problem is, they can't understand shit. You can't ground them, you can't put them in time out, you can't give them a gold star for good behavior or any other new age bullshit. You can speak to them in a stern voice and they'll react a bit. You'll see a bit of confusion on their face and they might not like it. If that's all you ever do they will see there is no consequence and become desensitized to it. Pain is the most basic teacher and everything understands it. Say your kid crawls across the floor and reaches for the power socket. You can tell him in a kind, positive tone, "Don't do that little Timmy." All he's going to understand is your positive demeanor and continue with what he's doing. After experiencing the pain of zapping himself in the socket, he will probably have learned to stay away from the socket, but he won't have learned to listen to you. You can pick him up and put him in the time out corner, in which case he'll crawl back over to the socket. You can bait him away with a treat, but he'll crawl back when he's done. You can reward him with "positive reinforcement" when he's not going for the socket, but his young brain isn't going to make the connection. What you need to do is tell him in a stern voice "No!" as he goes for the socket and stop his hand. Most likely you'll get confusion and maybe some tears. He'll go for it again. That's when you whack his hand. It doesn't need to be hard, just hard enough for him to not want you to do it again. He'll cry, but you have to let him go for it again. Again, you sternly say "No!" and whack his hand if needed. Once he's given up on the socket, you pick him up, carry him away, and console him so he knows you still love him. He's not going to understand what "No" means yet, but he will understand your tone, more importantly, he will understand what comes after that tone if he doesn't stop whatever he's doing. Boy 1 learned very quickly and eventually all I had to use was my tone, the dad tone. Girls learn even quicker.

Amanda, my wife's sister, did not spank her kids. Every time she stayed with us her two boys would bite my children. I would hear my child cry in pain and we'd all come rushing to find that one of her boys had been eating one of my kids again. She would try one of her new age techniques and of course the biting would continue. Because she could not control her children, she became overwhelmed and resorted to abusive language which led to the darkest day in my household.

Amanda would come to live with us when her husband was deployed. It would never take long before Maegan and Amanda would start their passive aggressive bickering and I would have to listen to my wife talk shit about her sister before bed. In an effort to keep the peace, I can say with honesty I defended Amanda against my wife's judgmental nature more than I talked my own shit about her. Amanda always had a hard time controlling her boys and refused to use any real discipline. After one of the boys, which one, I can't remember, did something I also can't remember, Amanda grabbed him and yelled, "Why are you such and awful boy?!" There was genuine anger in it and if words can be abuse, these certainly qualified.

This was not the first time she had done something like this, and my wife had been complaining about it to me. Maegan had enough and grabbed Amanda. She shook her like Amanda had just shaken her son, and yelled that she couldn't treat him like that, something along those lines. By this point I was starting to look up from my computer. Most of the time I tried not to get involved directly in their arguments, because Amanda would accuse me of some kind of verbal abuse afterward. This was escalating quickly, and I should have acted sooner.

Amanda said some tried and true Cooper family victim statement and sent my wife over the edge. Maegan was shoving Amanda as they yelled at each other and I lost sight of them around the corner. I scrambled out of my chair. I'm pretty sure Maegan punched

Amanda in the face while they were standing, but I can't be certain. By the time I made it around the corner, Maegan had thrown Amanda to the couch and was dropping fists on her face like a cage fighter's ground and pound. Amanda was kicking from her back, but my wife was pure rage. Amanda had always been the dominant one, a big reason why she didn't like when I came around. Maegan had released a cruelty and rage I had not thought she was capable of, and I should have been more worried by it. Maegan was not going to stop beating her sister so I dove in between the two, shielding Amanda from my wife. Fists tried to get around me and Amanda kept kicking in panic. I held Amanda protectively and gently pushed my wife away. Maegan stopped and Amanda stumbled for the front door. All the kids were standing there screaming as scared as they had ever been. The noise was deafening as my wife began crying as well.

Now that the violence was stopped, I started to worry about the cops being called. Amanda was bleeding from the nose and headed out the door. I grabbed her with as little threat, but as much control, as I could manage. I did not want to get physical, but I couldn't have her stumbling into the street bleeding from the beating my wife had just given her. Maegan had realized what she'd done and was no longer a threat. I pleaded with Amanda and got her to come back in the house. I sent Maegan to our room with our traumatized children. I did not treat her like the wrathful monster she had just acted like. Despite showing she was capable of extreme violence against her family and loved ones, I knew the children were safe with her and she needed them. I know now *she* is not capable of such consideration. Everyone but myself was crying uncontrollably and Maegan wanted to apologize to Amanda, but I told her not to go near her. I went to Amanda's room where she cradled her two boys who were scared out of their minds. I cleaned up Amanda's nose and held her, trying to show that they were safe. I made them spend the night apart and luckily the cops never came. In the morning, I checked on Amanda's nose and made sure it was ok for Maegan to come down and apologize.

Amanda stayed with us the rest of the time she had planned, but it was awkward. It wasn't hostile, because everyone was allowed to see each other, talk and heal. We told Amanda's husband, of course. My son would confide the traumatic incident to my mother much later, but we kept it contained and everyone healed. If I wasn't there to control the situation, the cops would have come and arrested Maegan. I don't know if Maegan would have stopped beating her sister, she certainly didn't look like she planned on stopping when I dove in between them. As soon as Amanda got the chance, she headed out the door. She made no effort to gather up her two children. She would have stumbled bleeding right into the middle of the neighborhood and the cops would have been called. Amanda is definitely the kind of person who would have wanted charges pressed had I not calmed her down.

The ducks started to fall in line for what was considered to be one of the biggest missions our team had undertaken. I don't know what's been done since, but at the time it was a pretty big deal. I signed non-disclosure agreements that would send me to prison if broken. Now I can't be certain if this is true, but this is what I was told. When my head shed went to DC to brief some big wigs on our mission, supposedly, they saw a list of strategic priorities for the United States. At the time we still hadn't found Bin Laden, but the search for Bin Laden was somewhere in the teens on the list. Our mission was high single digits on the list. When we found Bin Laden, I'm guessing killing him jumped to number one, but at the time our shit was more important, or so I was told. Just to give perspective and toot our horn a bit.

The mission went off without a hitch for the most part. One guy got minor decompression sickness or "The Bends." Considering how high risk the diving was, that's not bad.

The President wasn't able to roll it out for his re-election campaign like the Bin Laden raid, but we all got Legions of Merit, so somebody was happy.

That mission was my longest stretch living under water. Sub life sucks. I don't know how some people do it as a permanent occupation. Subs usually have talented cooks and the food always starts out good. Eventually ingredients start to run out and its fried frozen fish day after day. You can't drown out the taste in ketchup either, because it runs out a few weeks in. Working out is a pain in the ass when every motion has to be adjusted to get around a valve or pipe. The worst are the fucking thieves. For that trip, I built an entertainment system in a pelican case. Velcro tape held a Playstation in the box and a small TV in the lid. Everything plugged into a power strip secured in the pelican case. I just had to find an outlet to plug into and a place to sit, the latter being the hardest to find. We loaded the sub in the states and flew to meet it at a friendly foreign port. I had buried the case under our comms (communication) gear. When we got on the sub for the mission, the case had been gutted. Everything gone. For the first week of the underway I would corner members of the crew and interrogate them. I made printouts offering a lenient beating in exchange for the stolen goods and posted them all over the sub. Eventually I was told to stop threatening the crew and I never found out what happened to my Playstation. If the thief ever reads this, you're a real dick.

We got off the sub and finally saw daylight. It takes a while for your eyes to adjust to natural light. Even a cloudy day will make your eyes hurt. Everyone always wonders why you're not tan, being stationed in Hawaii. It's hard to get some color when you're under water. Our pasty white asses and our token black guys had to wait a few weeks while our flight home kept getting canceled. Eventually we hitched a ride home on the sub crews' flight. They, of course, were not going the same place as us. That flight home was the longest and most roundabout flight I have ever taken. We crossed the equator and most of the lines of longitude.

Chapter 12

I arrived home once again to a wife who wished I was still gone. It was clear she had been managing. My being home wasn't going to make a difference. No matter, I had three children who were happy Papa was home. It would be nice to come home to a woman who wanted to tear your clothes off, but three little goblins as excited as Christmas morning makes up for it.

Bliss never lasts long, however. I was sitting at home enjoying a short work day when Maegan came in the room with the same look on her face as when she told me my brother and Uncle were hurt.

"Matt's missing," she said. Matt Leathers, my sea daddy from my first platoon and family friend, had been free diving off the west coast of Oahu. His platoon was looking for a suitable place to train for their upcoming mission. Matt had the longest breath hold I had ever seen and liked to push it. They had been diving down and lost track of Matt. I immediately drove down to the command to join a search party. I grabbed fins, mask and a dive knife from my locker and loaded our dive boat. We spent days on that boat with guys on the bridge looking across the ocean with binoculars. The coast guard and marines mobilized aircraft and one of the largest searches in history was underway. Matt was one of the best waterman there ever was, and that kept hope alive for a while. *If anyone could survive this long, it's Matt.* Days went by and we all came to terms with looking for a body.

After several days they put us ashore on Kauai. The currents consistently wash from the Big Island in the southeast along the island chain and dump all the debris on Kauai in the northwest. We divided the shoreline and assigned teams to search each stretch of beach. A close friend of mine, let's call him Boozer, was assigned to search a rocky section with me. Boozer and I had done everything together from BUDS, including our first platoon with Matt. We got up in the morning and walked our section of beach all day. Walking a Hawaii beach all day with one of your best friends doesn't sound bad. When you're looking for the body of your other friend it puts a black cloud over it. At night we slept in a house being sold by one of the Coasties stationed on the island. Everybody picked a place on the floor and crashed. I can't remember why the team couldn't find us lodging. We never found Matt. I remember how sad Maegan was when she told me Matt was missing. He was her friend, too. Imagining her finding out I was missing always terrified me. I pictured one of my friends knocking on the door to tell her what happened. When I was being dashed against rocks by some of the nastiest surf, wearing 1,000 rounds of 5.56 at night, the thought of my family finding out I didn't make it to shore is what kept me kicking.

The dive boat came to pick us up and bring us back to Oahu. On the way back, we got hit by the biggest sea storm I have ever experienced. Our bunks were small cubby holes in line with the direction of the swell. I would go from standing on the wall next to my feet, to doing a hand stand on the wall above my head.

Back at the command, it was time to go through the all too familiar mourning process. I hate funerals. We have ways of bonding and coping with the loss of a teammate. When you see what it has done to his parents, wife and children, there is no preparing. This was the first time the loss really affected Maegan and my children. Maegan and Matt's wife did cross fit together, Matt watched our kids and we watched his son quite a bit. The boy didn't understand at the time. I finally got to meet his daughter from a previous woman. A long time later, I would run into his wife and son in San Diego. The boy recognized me as someone who knew his father and asked me where his dad was. I have never been at such a loss for words. His mother saw me struggling and hurried off with him.

The rest of the time at my first team was spent trying to leave my first team. Maegan was pregnant with our fourth child. I thought maybe God was trying to tell me to settle down and be a family man. I called Maegan and told her I was getting out of the Navy. She was staying in Oregon with my mother at the time, something she did often while I was gone, especially after it became awkward to stay with the sister she beat bloody. When I called her, she acted like she was ok with the decision. I now know that she cried her eyes out to my mother after I got off the phone. Money was of course the reason. She didn't care what I was going through at the time, she was worried she wouldn't be taken care of. Despite me proving I could always put a good roof over her head and food on the table, she doubted me. My mom assured her I, her son, would always find a way. During Maegan's fourth pregnancy she told my sisters and mother she wished she would miscarry. This has only recently been revealed to me. I am not perfect, but I have never been so horrible a husband that my wife should wish her child dead. That fabrication of hardship is her creation.

She didn't have any reason to worry, of course. I still had a while before my enlistment was up and I was already coming up with ideas for a job. One of my uncles was a California Highway Patrolman. We barely ever saw each other, but when we did, we were old friends who could swap stories for hours. He had been a Marine and spent an entire career in the CHP. He always seemed to love his job and had good stories. I had a squeaky clean record and an impressive resume, so I figured a police department would hire me. Federal agencies were my first choice. FBI required a college degree I didn't have. My assumption about them, which would be confirmed when I learned more about them, was that they were like the CIA: a bunch of stuck up Ivy League pricks who think they are cooler than they are.

In reality, they are mostly pencil pushers. I'm being unfair, of course. I've liked most of the spooks I've worked with. The stereotype of both organizations as a whole is not unfounded, however. DEA and Marshals would both waive degree requirements for military experience. The problem however, was federal agencies are not always hiring. I needed to put food on the table for six as soon as I got out.

I kept my eyes on federal jobs, but started looking at state agencies. Being from Oregon, I started there. Getting hired by a police agency is a very long process. It requires multiple physical, academic and psychological tests spread out over as long as a year. Washington State Patrol, however, had a special process for out-of-state applicants. They conducted their entire screening process over two weeks. While Oregon was my first choice, Washington moved faster. The physical tests were easy, even in the worst shape I had probably ever been in. Women's standards were even easier. The thing is, there were probably women who could pass the male standards, but they still lowered the standards for them. Academic tests were not too difficult. I only went in front of one board with three or four senior troopers. The interview was not long and I know now I got a few questions wrong. They mostly want to see your thought process, or make sure you at least have one. The most arduous screening was the psych portion and polygraph. Police agencies hang their hat on psych testing way too much. Some academic and a fill in the bubbles test are not going to tell you who will thrive under pressure and who will know when, and when not, to squeeze the trigger. The process weeds out a lot of the alpha protectors you want defending the herd and lets through a lot of betas on a power trip.

First, you have to take a 600 question test where they ask you a hundred times six different ways if you want to, or ever wanted to, kill yourself. At the time I could honestly answer no to all of them. Now, I could still just answer no to all of them and no one would know the difference. They do the same for substance abuse, torturing animals and doing kinky stuff with animals. Supposedly, that last one drops a lot of candidates. Lastly, you sit down with a PhD who's only ever had harsh language aimed at him. He asks you the same questions, but with the intent of trying to piss you off. As long as you're consistent with your answers and don't let him get under your skin, you're good. I think most of the team guys I worked with would make good cops, but most of them wouldn't make it through the screening process. A lot of people that shouldn't, do: see current events.

Girl 2 was another scheduled C section. This time we decided to use a civilian doctor. Government sponsored health care is great until they slice your kid's head open. We went to the doctor's office for one of the last checkups and boy 2 needed his diaper changed. I changed it like I had a million times before, not thinking of it. The doctor, who was pregnant with her first, said "I hope I get that good at changing diapers." She was genuinely impressed at how quickly I changed my kid's diaper. I realized I had three times more experience with children than the woman who was going to deliver my baby. For some reason I had assumed she was an old hat with babies, but she probably had nothing to do with them after delivery. Not many people have four children these days. Being a new father and a new team guy had passed me by a long time ago and I never noticed.

Girl 2 is my most outgoing, not that I would call Girl 1 shy. Boy 1 is certainly shy and Boy 2 can be at times. Both my girls are Daddy's girls and I wouldn't have it any other way. Again, the first few weeks after Girl 2's birth she was all mine. I changed her, held her and put her to sleep. I also took care of Maegan while she recovered. She was grateful at the time, but as always, she would forget it and think I never did anything for her. She would tell my mom as much. Mom always kept her trust, but one of the times Maegan was degrading me to my mother, my oldest boy said, "We don't like Papa, do we Mama?" My mother told me about it because it scared her. I wasn't as worried as I should have been but I tried to make things better. I figured Meagan was venting too often and didn't realize my son could understand. He was just commenting on what he heard. It hurt to hear but, I knew my son loved me. I should have been more worried. Even then, she was trying to manipulate the children into thinking their father was a bad guy.

The end of my enlistment came and I still hadn't heard back from the Washington State Patrol (WSP). My plan was for my family to stay in Oregon with my parents until I got a job. I was confident in getting the job at WSP, I just didn't know when I would start. As I dropped my car off to be shipped stateside, the WSP called and said they wanted me to start the academy Monday. It was the Friday before. I rushed home to tell Maegan I had the job and we would be in a bit of a hurry. I would still technically be in the Navy for another few weeks on terminal leave, but I was processed out for the most part. I still needed to swing by the command to pick up some paperwork. I tried to sneak in and out, but I was spotted by Master Chief. He told me my Legion of Merit had finally come in, and they needed to present it to me. I told him I was catching a plane in a few hours and he'd have to hand it to me or mail it out. As it happened, the command was already mustered in the classroom for some mandatory General Military Training or GMT/waste of time. Master Chief dragged me into the classroom and I had a Legion of Merit pinned on me wearing a tank top, board shorts and flip flops.

Running behind now, I rushed my family to the airport. While getting through security with four kids, one of them a newborn, my oldest puked all over the floor. We cleaned it up and boarded for the five hour flight to San Fran. I feel entirely confident in saying San Fran sucks. I have had flights delayed and cancelled in San Fran more than any other city. It's also one of those airports where you have to leave security when changing certain terminals. I'm sorry, if your city isn't squared away enough to have all their terminals connected, your city sucks. Our flight was cancelled and we would have to wait until morning to catch a flight to Oregon. Rather than take the kids to a hotel, then go through the same shit show in the morning, we hopped a plane to Seattle that night. I wanted to get out of San Fran that much.

We grabbed a rental in Seattle and drove to Shelton, WA where the WSP academy was located. I hate Maegan now, but there was a reason I loved her for 15 years. She stayed in a shitty Super 8 motel for a week with 4 kids and found a house to rent with no help from me. I was in the academy marching, doing pushups, getting yelled at, and having my room destroyed…. again.

Chapter 13

The academy was easier than Navy boot camp in some ways, but harder in others. It was certainly more fun. Physically, it was probably a touch easier then boot camp, much easier than Marine and Army boot, I'm guessing. We would get yelled at and have to run out of the classroom to get beat. Beat or goon squad is what we called it in BUDS, but the academy used the Army term, smoked. A smoke session is basically an unscheduled workout for messing something up. The instructors yell at you and make you do pushups and such. The worst part was having to do it in a button up shirt and bowtie. The WSP brags about being the only police agency sporting bowties, not something to brag about in my opinion. The sessions never lasted too long, but I would find out later the WSP academy is one of the last old school academies. We went home on the weekends, but it is also longer than any boot camp. Academically, it's probably harder than any bootcamp, but still not too bad. Learning law is probably the most study-intensive. I took more written tests than I ever have before. Everything you learn has a practical test and a written test. Even the ASP has a written test. An ASP is that telescoping stick cops use when they need to do a little Rodney Kinging. They literally have a written test on a piece of metal similar to a radio antenna. One of the questions asked what ASP stood for. It's an acronym for the company name that makes them. I can't remember what it stands for because it doesn't fucking matter! It's all to cover the agencies ass, so when they get sued for an officer pulling a Rodney King they can produce paperwork saying he was properly trained.

I'm going to talk a lot of shit about the police as an organization and some of the individuals, but I must preface with saying there are a lot of good cops and they do a tough job. I have newfound respect and disrespect for cops after being one.

The big problem with police agencies are their standards and hiring process. They put all their faith in the hiring process and it's next to impossible to fire someone in the academy for non-performance issues. Once you start the academy, you're hired, and it's as difficult to fire you as any other job. People turn around and sue the agency. An instructor can't decide someone is not the type of person we want to give power and shit-can them. In BUDS, the students are put in as high stress an environment as reasonable safety allows. All that time, they are watched and evaluated by experienced operators, guys who know what it takes to do the job. If they see someone they have doubts about, they zero in on him. He'll get one on one attention until he proves himself or quits. If someone isn't a team player or doesn't put out, the class will push him out. Doesn't matter if he can pass what's on paper. You can't distill a job like that down to a curriculum. Once they decided women could go to BUDS, civilians were hired to audit the BUDS program. Anything that wasn't in the curriculum was a target for them. On paper, BUDS is hard, but it's the creativity of the gatekeepers that make it so effective. The toughest evolutions in BUDS don't have a passing time or quantity. They are designed to expose weakness to watchful eyes that have experience in hardship. The auditors tried to get rid of the unscheduled one on one attention and extracurricular activities. All this was so they could make BUDS easier while being able to claim they hadn't lowered the standards for women. I have to point out that I heard all this from an instructor and did not witness it myself. Some Navy big wig who is more politician than soldier will probably say this isn't true, but I've learned to view the word of anyone above O3 with skepticism, especially if it's about a program they were in charge of. I'm confident the gatekeepers will do their job. A BUDS instructor will always find a way to make your life hell.

The academy isn't nearly as stressful, but it gives experienced police officers a chance to observe candidates in stressful situations similar to the job. It allows them to decide if a candidate has the necessary psychology far better than some nerd with a PhD and a 20 minute interview. Problem is, they aren't given the authority to shit-can a candidate if they think they'll make a bad officer. Our head combatives instructor managed to come up with a way to really test a student and shit-can them if they didn't have the mentality for the job. The final test he designed was a practical one, a traffic stop that goes horribly wrong. You were pretty much guaranteed a fight. He had a grading sheet that would allow instructors to grade based on their opinion of how the student performed. After a large portion of students failed, most of them female, the academy required he restructure the test. The instructor resigned after my class rather than compromise his standards. I was fortunate in my academy instructors. The previously mentioned instructor would spar with me after hours and we became good friends. The two lead instructors were prior Marines with all of the Corps good qualities and only their hair cuts to represent the bad qualities. I count them both as friends and good cops.

Guest instructors were common, and I began to see some of the bad mentalities and power trips cops develop. Too often, the attitude was not to serve and protect, but punish and regulate. Agencies encourage this by evaluating officer performance based on arrests and citations. We as a society are also partly to blame. Most cops do their job with the constant fear they might get fired. If the agency fires an academy kid, he can turn around and sue them. Once a cop is on the street, an agency will throw him under the bus if it saves them a lawsuit. Shit-canning an academy kid exposes you to a possible lawsuit while shit-canning a beat cop might save you from one. We punish and pick at every little mistake these human beings make and they have become robots. We've taken away most of their discretion. Sure, now they can't skim a little off the top of a drug bust or put in one extra kick to an asshole who deserves it. They also can't or won't cut you a break when you need it.

Many road cops make personal policies that reflect this. Some cops stopped everyone going at least 15 mph over the speed limit and always ticketed them no matter what. Why waste his time by stopping someone he is not going to ticket? So why not just put up a RADAR, camera and send the ticket in the mail? Cops are out there because we want human beings protecting and serving. Law enforcement agencies are full of blanket policies designed to avoid liability, and it removes the human factor.

The head instructors would often teach compassion. I believe those two also practiced it when they were out on the road, but the guest instructors reflected the agency's attitude more. The agency wanted robots who racked up the numbers and didn't get them sued. I started a long list of people I was not going to be like.

Shooting, as always, was fun, but police don't do it nearly enough. One of the instructors stated with pride how many rounds we would shoot throughout the academy. The candidates were of course impressed, but I was thinking I would go through that same amount in a day or two as a team guy. As a SEAL, I was not allowed to carry a concealed weapon in communist California. When I finished shooting in the military, my gun was locked in an armory. By SEAL standards, law enforcement officers are given an intro to firearms, then sent out amongst the public with guns on their hip every day. At the end of the shift, each cop takes his gun home. On top of that, every law enforcement officer is allowed to carry concealed anywhere in the United States. How much fucking sense does that make? Your gun is a last resort as a cop, but you're carrying it around the general public all day. You and your agency have a responsibility to make sure you master that weapon. After graduating, you're given 50 rounds a month to practice on your own. I would go through that in five minutes. WSP probably has one of the better firearms programs in law enforcement to boot. Just to be clear, this is my assessment of the amount of training cops receive, not an opinion on gun control. I think we should all be like Arizona where every law abiding citizen can carry a gun however they like.

Combatives in the academy was pretty good, thanks to the efforts of the lead instructor. Several times a week, we would get in full uniform, throw on a hockey helmet and head out to the gravel pit to brawl. These were good fights with few rules. Problem was, the instructor couldn't get rid of you for getting your ass kicked every day. I learned another key insight during these brawls. If someone can't fight, then they are more likely to shoot you. Being one of the best fighters in the class, I played the bad guy a lot. I would always be shot by the end of the scenario. You have to understand a cop cannot lose a fight. To lose a fight means you've been incapacitated in some way. An incapacitated cop is at the mercy of the criminal. That could be a death sentence; you have no way of knowing and you're not going to take that chance. The amount of police officers that have been shot with their own gun is staggering and embarrassing. Therefore, if a cop is losing a fight, they are justified in shooting their assailant. What does that mean for the agency who armed and sent a cop out on the streets who couldn't handle themselves? Many of the aggressive alpha males who make good fighters are weeded out in the screening process. Those are the kind of men who get the agency sued. They are also the kind of men who make good protectors and can restrain someone without hurting them. You're less likely to shoot a man if you can handle him with your hands. What you end up with is too many guys with little man syndrome who will drop a knee on a man in handcuffs because they are too afraid of what he might do if he sits up, or they are finally getting to punish all those people who picked on them. God forbid an agency discriminate against hiring someone who can't fight. I was always confident I could fight the people I was dealing with and, if needs be, kill. Confidence in my ability allowed me to be courteous and polite with everyone. I never had to show up and pull my dick out to let everyone know who was in charge. I could ramp it up and dial it back as needed. Most guys who can't handle themselves ramp up too quickly and can never dial it back.

You can always use the Taser as a crutch, but I didn't trust that thing. It hurts like a bitch, and when it works, it will immobilize the target. With all the research done, it's also pretty sue proof, which is a plus for the agency. A lot can go wrong, though. Both prongs need a good stick, and thick clothing can stop it. OC (pepper spray) is the worst. The pain isn't as intense as a Taser, but it doesn't go away for a good hour. It doesn't hit you right away and it just made me want to kick someone's ass even more, just to keep my mind off the pain.

Driving was the most fun. I'm lucky enough to be a natural at a few things: fighting, shooting, skydiving, but driving isn't one of them. I'm not bad by any means. I've done other courses since. I usually start out about middle of the pack. I can learn anything but grammar, so I steadily progressed. I'm a pretty damn good driver now, but there were certainly guys far better than me in the class. Emergency Vehicle Operators Course (EVOC) training is one of the things police agencies do well. The reason for it is police-related accidents cost agencies a fortune every year. The only way to make a dent in that price tag is to make your officers better drivers, so they do it right.

Collision investigation is a huge part of being a state trooper. They call it a collision, not an accident, because an accident implies no one is at fault. The WSP believes every car crash is preventable. Bald tires; you should have taken better care of your car. Bad weather; you should have slowed down. I can see the truth in this philosophy. What I don't like is that the WSP and most agencies think a citation should be issued at every collision. Next time you get in a fender bender or see a fender bender, think twice before calling the cops. The cop is showing up with the goal of giving someone a ticket. A big reason why I didn't agree with this was my experience in high school when I wrecked my truck. Yes, it was my fault. Plowing into a ditch taught me never to do it again. If that didn't do it, then having to get a ride to school from my mom did. If that didn't do it, then hundreds of dollars in repair, storage and tow fees did. The ticket the dickhead cop gave me just made me hate cops. I call the cop a dickhead, but you can get in trouble for not writing tickets at collisions. You also get evaluated on how many tickets you write. Yea, we'll get to police quotas later.

The academy chilled out on the boot camp stuff and started to be fun. I had some genuine good times, made good friends, and gained a lot of good knowledge. The academy proper ended, but we all still had to pass our field training trip (Coaching Trip). It's three months of being a road cop with a real trooper riding shotgun to teach and evaluate you. A good program overall, and a chance to let someone who knows the job shit-can someone who isn't fit for it. Problem is, there are already too many shitty cops, ergo, too many shitty training officers, ergo, a lot of shitty candidates make it through. Being a training officer is a prestigious position, so guess who gets those positions? That's right, cops who write a lot of tickets. Again, I'm not being fair; both my training officers were good dudes. I did my coaching trip in the Shelton county detachment. The detachment was a tight group who was more interested in catching bad guys than writing speeding tickets. It wasn't a highly trafficked area, so the agency didn't expect big numbers from them. Meth was big in the area, so they racked up felony cases. This kept the higher ups off their back, but didn't earn them any kudos.

There were three agencies in the county: State Patrol, Shelton County Sheriff's Department and Shelton City Police Department. If I was on a stop, it was normal for a Sheriff's Deputy to back me up even if I didn't need it. The main reason was to shoot the shit after. If the city cops had a warrant they were serving, they would drop by our office to see if we wanted to tag along. Guys from different departments would fish and hunt together. This is where I learned how to be a cop, and it was a good place to learn.

It wasn't all peaches and cream. A middle aged/old lady took too many meds and blazed past me on the road. I arrested her for DUI, but since it wasn't alcohol-related we needed blood. Washington State doesn't use piss. I wrote up the warrant and informed the lady we would be taking her blood. She refused, and I told her it was going to happen. I gently took her by the arm and led her to the chair. The old hag bit me! It wasn't bad, and she eventually calmed down. We got the blood and I started to process her. I charged her with the DUI and my coach said, "What about the assault?" I found the most minor assault charge and added it. He wanted me to add assaulting a police officer which is no minor charge and made her a felon if it stuck. I was unwilling to charge a mostly harmless old lady with a felony for a bite that didn't even break the skin. It was my decision, and he let me go with it, but he had a lesson when we got back in the car.

If a cop is going to arrest someone, you use the most severe charge and add every charge you can justify. For one, it gives the prosecutor more to work with when intimidating a defendant into a plea deal. Second, it looks good on your end of the month numbers. Regardless of whether or not the charges stick, you get credit for the arrest. Cops do not determine guilt or innocence. Reasonable doubt is not a consideration for them. Probable cause and reasonable suspicion are how they operate. Put simply, *I'm 51% sure he did it* and *he might have done it*, very low burdens of proof. The main thing is, there is no punishment for getting it wrong. If you arrest a guy for a felony and they are found innocent, nothing comes back on you as long as you don't violate policy. You and the agency still get credit for a felony arrest. There is a good reason for this. You can't have cops scared to make arrests because it might come back on them, there is already too much of that. It doesn't help the guy who was arrested, though. He is going to spend some time in jail, which sucks if you haven't tried it. His bail is based on the laundry list of charges the cop racked up to pad his stat sheet, all of which he only needed to be 51% sure of. He has to call into work to let them know he was arrested, something that won't be forgotten even if the charges are dropped. If he wants to stand a chance against the government salary prosecution team, then he won't want to rely on the bottom of the barrel, over-worked public defender. All in all, even an innocent man is going to be looking at a lot of heartache, embarrassment, time, and money if he is arrested. All this will be before he ever gets a chance to defend himself in trial. If he is found innocent, he won't be compensated. I'm not saying cops should be punished if someone they arrested is found innocent. A little compassion and not treating a man as guilty before he ever stands trial would be nice. I definitely think people like prosecutors, who don't have to make their decisions out on the street, should be held accountable for the turmoil they put people through.

Several facts about a beat cop became evident. Police work is more paperwork than excitement. When you do get something exciting, the accompanying paperwork increases substantially. 90% of the time you're making somebody's bad day worse. 90% of the time the event is over by the time you get there and you help no one. Skill matters little, seniority and doing what you're told is what matters. I would never come to terms with these facts. There is the other 10%, and it kept me going as long as I lasted. I got to feel like I helped someone once during my coaching trip. A call came in for a collision way up in the mountains. My coach had no idea where it was, but I had taken the family up there often for campfires and marshmallows. I got to drive all out for a good hour with lights and siren going. We hit dirt roads I was very familiar with and my coach's butt puckered as I found my groove. An ambulance had launched from much closer and arrived on scene a good 20 minutes before us. We started getting a picture of the situation from the radio chatter. A truck packed with an entire family had gone off a mountain road and lodged in a cluster of trees above a lake. I knew the spot. The slope was short of being called a cliff but not by much. The driver was pinned between a tree and the A post of the truck. The A post is the frame of the windshield just to the left of the steering wheel. It sounded like he wasn't going to make it.

When I arrived, the family was clustered on the road looking down the slope. They looked distressed, but not panicked. I walked up slowly, thinking I was about to console a grieving family after the bad shit was already over. Before I said anything, I heard a woman's cry come from the truck. I realized with a shock there was someone still alive and stuck in the truck. I leapt down the slope grabbing a tree with one hand, and used the other to frisbee my stupid Smokey the bear hat to the road. I approached the truck carefully and realized an EMT was already down there. As I had made my way down the hill, the driver fell free of the truck and scrambled up the hill, fit as a fiddle, leaving his sister in the truck. I was careful not to put weight on the truck as I peered in to see a terrified young woman with her foot jammed on the brake. She had been jamming her foot on the brake for an hour thinking it was the only thing keeping her from plummeting to the lake while her brother was cut in half. The EMT came to my side and we came up with a plan. He would stand above me on the slope and I would reach into the truck to rip her out, passing her to him as quickly as possible and getting my weight off the truck. I told her the plan, trying to make my confidence rub off on her. I gripped her belt line with both hands and counted to three. On three, I did the most explosive barbell snatch I have ever done. The EMT snatched her out of my hands and they climbed up to the road. The truck didn't move an inch. She could have crawled up with the rest of her family and everyone would have been fine. Save for some scrapes, no one was hurt. It didn't make me feel any less badass, though.

Everyone was crying, but I felt good. I finally got to help someone. It didn't take long for the other 90% to shit all over my good day.

My coach leaned in and whispered, "You should probably run field tests on the driver." As it turned out, the family had been camping and drinking when they decided to drive down to the lake. The driver loaded his two children into their car seats in the back with their mother. His sister and some guy, I'm guessing her boyfriend, rode up front. I ended up arresting the guy for DUI after his brush with death. I didn't feel too bad after he almost killed his family. Unlike me, he would still get to see his children. The coaching trip ended without topping that story. We all returned to the academy for graduation. I got top marksman and top combatives or Control Tactics, as WSP calls it. Defensive Tactics is what most agencies call it. Defense implies to a jury that such tactics are to be used defensively. Control means you used a tactic to control the situation. It explains why a cop might act offensively to prevent a potentially deadly situation, rather than wait until he has to defend himself. That mentality fits in nicely with the philosophy I had already developed with the teams. It becomes important later to understand why I do certain things.

After the graduation, I got to take my family one by one out on the drive course. We were told not to go over 35mph, but of course we all ignored that rule. Rarely do I get to show my family all the cool things I get to do. Boy 2 was especially excited by the ride and tried to describe it in what words he could manage. Few things feel better than when your son thinks your awesome.

Chapter 14

I ended up getting Grays Harbor County for my beat. It was another rural county right next to Shelton County where I did my coaching trip. Grays Harbor's biggest city was Aberdeen, where Kurt Cobain grew up. I would even end up volunteer coaching the wrestling team Kurt's stepfather made him join. It was similar to Shelton with a lot of country. The kind of place I wanted to raise a family. I thought the rural small town nature of the area would mean the various agencies would have a similar culture to Shelton. I was to be very disappointed.

First we had to buy our first home. More accurately, I needed to buy Maegan her first home. One of the perks of being a Stater is you can work any county a reasonable distance from your residence, I forget the exact mileage. We started looking for places close to the county line in case I wanted to transfer later on down the road. I had spent most of my adult life sleeping somewhere other than my home, so I wasn't picky. I wanted land. There were tons of large land plots with manufactured homes well under our budget, but Maegan didn't want a manufactured home. I can understand the reasons, but would have been happy in any number of places. After an extensive house hunt, we finally looked at a place deep inside Grays Harbor, nowhere near a county line. Maegan fell in love with it. I liked it a lot, too. The 11 acres of forest didn't hurt. If we bought the house, I was throwing my lot in with Grays Harbor for good, and I had just started to learn about the place. I saw how much Maegan loved the place, and there were so few things I did that could make her happy. When we moved to Hawaii, she complained about how much she hated it and missed San Diego. When we moved to Shelton she complained about how much she missed Hawaii. It was always better where we just came from. This time I would make her happy. One of the thoughts to help me let go of the teams was the idea of finally put my family first, so what if I ended up not liking my beat?

I didn't like my beat. All the agencies stayed in their lane and there was none of the camaraderie Shelton had. There was the Grays Harbor County Sheriff and several small towns with their own departments. The first time I backed up one of the deputies, he looked at me like I had a dick growing out of my forehead. When we finished the call, I introduced myself as one of the new Staters and said I looked forward to working with him more. He was friendly enough and liked the idea, but I could tell it wasn't the normal practice in Grays Harbor. I had similar experiences with other deputies and a lot of the city cops. They all got used to the idea of a Stater showing up to help out from time to time. The one who didn't like the idea was my Sergeant. My Sergeant was your stereotype of an overweight cop close to retirement who didn't want to do any more than he had to. His favorite trooper was equally overweight and fished the same water hole in an unmarked car day after day, writing an ungodly amount of tickets. Sergeant wanted me doing the same. He didn't want some new guy running around helping people and bringing down the detachment average. What is the detachment average, you say? Well, now it's time to talk about quotas.

Officially, there are no quotas. Police departments do not see the revenue from tickets. Most of it goes to those don't drive drunk ads you see. What they do have is an "expecta- tion," as it was explained to me. In the WSP's official policy manual it states an officer is to use the least enforcement necessary to cause a change in behavior. When I checked in to my detachment I was given a printed out packet with "expectations," decided on by the leadership. If I worked a 10 hour shift, I was expected to stop 12 cars in that shift. Fair enough, you need to prove you're out there working and interacting with the public. The thing I took issue with was the expectation that I would take enforcement on 55% of those stops. The math isn't exact, but that basically means out of the 12 cars stopped, I needed to write seven of them tickets. To anyone who can taste the difference between bullshit and ice cream, that's a quota. To add to it, I was expected to ticket every seatbelt violation and take enforcement action on every collision. Revenue isn't the driving factor, but the budget plays a role.

Police work today is driven by numbers. If an agency can show on a spread sheet or graph that by doing A they have decreased B, then they have justified next year's budget increase. In the case of WSP, and no doubt other agencies, they have spreadsheets showing when speeding tickets go up, vehicle collisions go down. Every trooper is evaluated against his peers by how many enforcement actions he takes. In the case of WSP, traffic citations are chief amongst them. How many people he helps doesn't matter a damn. Changing some old ladies tire doesn't fill up an impressive spreadsheet. How do you quantify gratitude?

The first sign of trouble was my first evaluation. Sarge sat me down with a spreadsheet showing the whole detachment and our numbers. He pointed to the amount of cars I had stopped and I was second in the detachment, well in front of everyone else, but well behind his favorite trooper. I spent my shifts driving from one end of the county to the other, listening for calls and stopping targets of opportunity. Such a tactic meant I was able to be the first guy to show up on a lot of calls where people needed help, but made it difficult to stop a lot of cars. Still, I managed to outperform everyone else except the guy who sat in the best spots with a RADAR gun, stopping every speeder and ticketing them. After praising my work ethic, he shifted his finger over to the citation column where the amount of tickets I wrote was well below everyone else, with zero seatbelt tickets.

"You're bringing down the detachment average," he said. There were other stats I led the detachment in, but it didn't matter to him. Things like helping stranded motorists didn't matter. Most cops hate showing up to stranded motorist calls. I loved them; it's the only time you get to show up and be the good guy. If cops like Sarge's favorite trooper couldn't avoid a stranded motorist call, they would show up and just offer to call a tow truck, which the stranded motorist would have to pay for and could have done themselves. I know for a fact I changed more tires than anyone in the detachment, maybe even the WSP, and none of that was reflected in my evaluation. Another area I led in was what I think was classified as an assist or some other term meaning *not important*. An assist is when you back up your fellow officer. I learned the bad areas of my county quickly and always made sure I was near one. When the call went out to the deputies, I would usually be closer and able to respond quicker. I thought it a good thing to be close by when people needed the police. Whether I was first or second to the call, deputies would take jurisdiction. Therefore, a two hour call in a dangerous situation would be classified on my spreadsheet as an assist. Sarge couldn't give a damn about assists. All that mattered were traffic tickets.

I left my first evaluation with a new strategy. Sarge wanted more tickets, but he didn't specify how expensive they had to be. If I had to write more tickets, then I would write tickets for the least amount possible. The dollar amount for a speeding citation increases every 5 mph over the limit. Going 62 mph in a 60 mph zone is the same amount as 65 mph in the same zone. I would only ticket cars going at least 20 mph over the speed limit. When I wrote the ticket, I would write it for 1 mph over the limit, just to make it sound like I was going as easy on them as possible. You would be surprised how many people thank you after giving them a ticket. Of course the ticket would still show the actual speed they were going. A ticket might show 80 mph in a 60 mph zone, but the dollar amount would be for 1 mph over the speed limit. At the time, 5 mph over was just under $100.00. Half way into my first year it increased to $105.00, if I remember correctly. Sarge's favorite would stop 12 to 15 cars a shift and ticket every one. At a minimum, he was taking $1,200 dollars a day from the citizens. 4 shifts a week brings him to $4,800. 4 weeks a month to $19,200. For the year, he's fining the public $230,400 a year. This is an extremely low estimate for Sarge's favorite trooper and probably a low estimate for what every trooper takes from the motoring public. Every road trooper brings in enough money to buy a large house every year.

It didn't take long before my new strategy caused problems. Somebody who was speeding at least 20mph over the limit went down to the courthouse to complain over a speeding ticket for 1mph over the limit. Way to fuck it up for everyone else, dickhead. This asshole couldn't be happy with having his fine reduced well below what his speed warranted, so he went and complained about me. This is why most cops turn into machines. When you try and be empathetic, some ungrateful douche shits on you. Sarge took a deeper look at my stats and saw I was only fining people for 1 mph over the limit. It didn't matter that the ticket showed these people were going at least 20 mph over. Sarge was upset, to say the least. Speeding tickets weren't the only problem. I still refused to write seatbelt tickets. To add to Sarge's dislike of me, I was letting single car collisions off the hook as well. WSP wanted 100% enforcement on collisions. I would write a ticket to the party at fault in a multiple car collision. If only one car was involved, I figured the driver had learned their lesson. If not, a ticket wasn't going to change that. If they were drunk or reckless, then of course I would take enforcement action.

One month I had a more than average amount of collisions and wrote one ticket. Most were deer collisions, which most troopers avoided. I, of course, didn't. A large chunk of the non-deer collisions happened on one night. Rain rolled in with a strange intermittent temperature drop, Washington weather at its best. While helping one guy who slid off the road, I got a call for another collision up north. Five minutes later, a third collision came out at the same location as the second. I decided I wasn't going to ticket the guy I was dealing with, so I could check on the people up north. En route, a third collision at the same spot came out over the radio. The rain was bad, but the temperature was not that cold. As I approached the area of the three single-car collisions, I slowed to a crawl. In my headlights were three cars spread out in a ditch and a teenage kid sliding along the road like it was an ice skating rink. I slowed as much as possible and took every precaution on my approach. As I applied the final bit of pressure to the brakes, my patrol car kept sliding. Luckily, it stopped before I made a fool of myself. I was as careful as humanly possible, and I still almost went into the ditch. None of these people were getting tickets. The section of road was in a dip that had created a cold patch. Everywhere else, the rain hit the road and washed off, but in this one spot it had layered up a thick sheet of ice.

While I was checking on everyone, a fourth car came sliding into the ditch, just missing my patrol car. We were out in the boonies and a tow truck was going to take forever. Luckily, a country boy in a tricked out 4x4 showed up and started pulling everyone out. I took the country boy's info to pass on to Sarge and maybe get him some kind of recognition. Sarge was upset I had four collisions in one night and no tickets. I told him about the guy who helped me pull everyone out and asked if WSP had some way of recognizing citizens who go above and beyond. According to Sarge, they don't.

My monthly reviews became re-runs of Sarge telling me I'm doing great in some areas, mostly the areas falling under serve and protect, then trying to chew me out for not writing enough citations. I say *try* because he was always nervous when he had to reprimand me. He would call me into his office where he sat behind a desk with my stat sheets. Rather than sit on the other side of the desk where a chair was waiting for me, I would pick up the chair, carry it behind his desk and sit right next to him where we could better go over my stats together. He would try to point to an offending column on my sheet but his hands would shake so bad he couldn't get his finger to rest on one number. The problem was I never violated policy. In fact, my practices were more in line with published WSP policy.

Lack of tickets was only one of my flaws. Another thing that got Sarge's goat was my habit of going to calls of people in need. One fine Washington day, I was driving back to the detachment office when two Hoquiam PD cops flew by me with lights and siren blaring, running code as we call it. I didn't know what was happening, but if two officers were risking the inherent danger of running code through the city, then something serious must be going down. I flipped on my lights and jumped in behind them. I called my dispatch, told them I was following Hoquiam PD running code, and asked them to call over to find out what was going on. The HPD guys must have been monitoring my frequency, because they immediately came over and said they were going to a robbery in progress. They must have initially put it out over some internal frequency I didn't know about. We showed up on scene and went to the back of the house. At the back, I found a rather rotund senior HPD officer looking at a tall chain link fence, exasperation on his face. Inside the backyard, a junior, more spry HPD officer was already stacked on the back door waiting for a partner to help him make entry. Being isolated by yourself in a backyard is not a good situation, so I vaulted the fence, stacked up behind the HPD guy and gave him a squeeze. The squeeze startled him and I remembered I wasn't working with team guys.

I leaned in and whispered, "I got your back. Go ahead and make entry." We cleared the house and found nothing. I wish I could make it a cooler story, but it was the thought that counted. I found out later a neighbor had seen someone in the house and knew the owners were on vacation. That someone ended up being the person the owners asked to feed the cat. Regardless of the fact that we got all worked up for nothing, the rotund HPD guy thanked me for showing up and admitted he was never getting over that fence. We shot the shit a bit and I finished my shift.

A day or two later, Sarge called me into his office. Apparently, backing up your fellow officers was a big no no. He was genuinely pissed off. I wasn't going to get too worked up about it until he said Hoquiam PD didn't want me to help out on their calls. Now I distinctly remembered one of the officers saying, "Thank god you came along, because I wasn't getting my fat ass over that fence." Sarge was outright lying to me. I don't remember what I said, but I'm pretty good at being both hostile and respectful at the same time. I knew I had the high ground. Telling an officer not to back up his fellow officers sounds like shit no matter how you spin it; didn't stop him from trying. He wasn't altogether lying about HPD not wanting me on their calls. The HPD commissioner, that's the boss, had called Sarge about me showing up to the call. Hoquiam was a small town and many of its citizens questioned whether or not they needed their own police department. The HPD commissioner didn't want the citizens getting the idea that deputies and Staters were enough to keep them safe. He would rather one of his junior officers clear a building alone than compromise his budget for the next year. The guys on the road doing the job wanted my help, but the boss behind a desk wanted his salary. Sadly, this disconnect between sled dogs and leadership is a common theme. This is because the way to get into leadership is to play it safe and kiss ass.

My confrontation with Sarge reached up to the LT sitting at HQ in Bremerton. Now LT's in the police force are not like LT's in the teams. LT's in the teams are in the trenches with the boys and go out drinking with them. LT's in the police force are more like that boss you rarely see. He comes around every once in a while to give some hollow motivational speech or when someone is in trouble. It was the latter for me. LT, Sarge and I sat down in the Sarge's office and LT attempted to reasonably mediate the situation with a positive atmosphere. He was one of those really nice guys who embodies political correctness, like that blackface dude who runs Canada now. I listened politely to his explanation of why I needed to write more tickets, then I respectfully said no. He was of course taken aback, but to his credit, tried again. I quoted WSP policy and told him I was not going to fill a quota.

With the slightest hint of annoyance, he said, "It's not a quota. It's an expectation." My simplified reply was that he could keep on expecting. We went back and forth a bit and his veneer started to crack a bit. Have you ever seen someone get angry who has no experience wielding aggression? It's like a cheerleader throwing a football.

Eventually he gave up on trying to get my consent and brought out instructions he had already typed. They outlined what was expected of me over the next few months. The instructions were careful not to put a number on speeding tickets, but stated I must write close to the same amount of tickets as other officers in my detachment. I can't remember the exact wording. I never intended to comply with it. It did put a number on seatbelt tickets, at least six a month. The final stipulation was that I not respond to any non-WSP dispatches without asking for permission from my Sargent. I didn't imply that I was going to comply with any of the instructions, but LT wanted to get out of there as soon as possible. As a parting gift, he said I had been signed up for a seminar titled Dealing with Difficult People. It wasn't a punishment, he stressed, I could take my patrol car and attend during my shift. It was obvious I didn't have a choice.

The seminar was taught by one of the noodleiest guys I'd ever seen. He would have gotten along with LT. The Dealing with Difficult People seminar seemed to be attended by all the difficult people and not the people who had to deal with them, myself included, I guess. You know the fat lady behind the counter at the DMV doing her nails? imagine a room full of them. The class was a couple hours of how not to be a wimp, taught by a wimp. I still have my graduation certificate.

The next month, I scanned the city and county frequencies waiting for a call to come out. I would ask sarge for permission, then go to the call whether he gave it or not. All radio traffic is recorded, so he would have to tell me not to respond to someone in need over the radio. The month ended up being a slow one, however, and the opportunity never came. Before the deadline for my compliance arrived, Sarge retired.

The new Sergeant was from another detachment, but had worked Hoquiam before. He had been waiting for the old Sergeant to retire so he could take his spot. I was worried the new Sergeant was old chums with the outgoing Sergeant. We all got appointments for sit-downs with the new Sarge, and I was not looking forward to mine. Sarge asked me how I got along with the old Sarge and I probably gave some kind of tactful answer.

Sarge's reply was, "Yeah I hated that fucking guy."

Relief washed over me and I got to know my new Sarge. He was the kind of hard charger you want to be a police officer, which meant he probably wasn't going to make it past Sergeant. He was confident, capable, and humble. After spending most of his career on the SWAT team, he had to give it up in order to get a Sergeant's spot. Sarge was the kind of guy who would have fit in nicely with a platoon. We went over LT's list of expecta-tions together, which still stood. First thing Sarge did was give me preemptive permission to go on any calls I wanted to. As far as tickets went, he said I just needed to show some im-provement so he would have ammo to fight for me. He said I should take one day a week to go out and work nothing but speed. I didn't need to ticket people I didn't feel deserved it, but I would have to work extra hard to find those people on the road being jackasses. After a solid shift of racking up some tickets, I could spend the rest of the week doing real police work. For seatbelts, he said to find people doing something else worthy of a ticket and just hit them for the seatbelt. If I could do that for him, then he could go to bat for me with the head shed. I took his advice onboard and never heard from LT. No doubt LT was more than happy to avoid coming down to deal with me again. If Sarge was happy with me, he was happy with me.

Quality of life significantly improved with the new Sergeant. After a few weeks, he told me he had gone over all the old Sergeant's write-ups on me and they were absolute bullshit. Not just me, but the other new guy as well. The whole situation had been mishandled by

the old Sergeant, and he had told the head shed up in Bremerton as much. More than happy to shift blame onto someone who was retired, the head shed agreed with the new Sergeant's assessment.

Despite work atmosphere improving, police work had already put a bad taste in my
mouth. One night in particular really pissed me off. A call came out for an attempted suicide. A brother and sister had been driving down the highway when the brother slit his
wrists. I never found out the details, but the car stopped and the brother took off into the
woods bleeding. A fellow Trooper and myself were first on scene. We found a blood trail
leading into the woods and started to follow it. The Deputies started to show up and follow
as well. We reached a shallow stream and I could see where the guy had broken brush on
the other side. I started to move across the river and a deputy told me to stop. He was a
portly fellow and he felt like the brush was getting too thick. He wanted to pull back and
wait for the dog. This is a pretty common mentality for cops. Pulling back and waiting it out
is usually the best option for most police situations. There is usually no reason to rush in.
The longer you wait, the more back up arrives, the more time your perp has to rethink his
choices. This mentality is so pervasive, most active shooter courses spend half the time on
changing the mental state of officers. In an active shooter situation, you have to charge in
and get things done.

In this particular situation, we had a fresh blood trail and our victim/perp was bleeding
out. The K9 unit wasn't on duty, so it would be a while until he arrived. The biggest reason
not to wait was that the K9 unit sucked. There was one K9 in Grays Harbor and I had already participated on a few man hunts with it before. Each time we Troopers were put on
perimeter and the dog turned up Jack and shit. One of those "Man Hunts" was for a fat girl
and she still got away. Needless to say, I wasn't confident the dog was going to find our
bleeding suicidal man when it showed up in an hour. There was some risk to ourselves, but

I saw being in the woods late at night as an advantage. I stressed to the deputy that we had a clear trail to follow and we didn't need the dog. He was not too keen on heading into the bush and I could tell he was ready to pull his jurisdictional dick out.

Sheriffs are elected officials and the ultimate law enforcement authority in any county. They are the oldest form of American law enforcement we inherited from the Brits. Every other police entity operates within a given county with the permission of the Sheriff. I was about to get into an argument with the deputy, but my buddy said we were leaving if the deputies wanted to handle it on their own. We drove up a road that potentially crossed our perp/victims path. While we were looking, the deputies requested over the radio that we get back in our cars because we were contaminating the trail. That pissed us both off and we left the scene altogether. Of course the deputies never found the guy and tried to blame it on us. They didn't think the dog showing up an hour late with a near 0% success rate was a factor. Fortunately, the guy didn't bleed out. He turned up at a family member's house the next morning.

Home life was good for the most part. On my days off we would explore a new logging road. Whether we found a good spot or not, I would build a fire to cook everyone hot dogs and marshmallows. We would shoot guns, throw knives and walk trails. I was finally able to raise the kids the way I wanted to. My boys would have adventures like I experienced as a boy.

One particular adventure was not one I wanted to experience. We did an egg hunt for Easter in one of our favorite spots. Once we found all the eggs, we started to walk back. It was a minute walk, max. When we got back to our camp, boy one was missing. He had been right behind us with his basket of eggs a moment before. He was old enough to do his own thing, so I yelled for him. No one answered. I yelled again and walked back on the trail. There were no steep drop-offs and the lake was farther away than the camp. I yelled louder and louder but got no response. Panic is both an action and a feeling. I have not panicked since I was in kindergarten and couldn't breathe. The panic I felt at that moment is a kind of terror I wouldn't wish on anyone. I ran down the trail yelling his name and trying to listen. The area he could be in was smaller than a football field. I knew some animal carrying him off was one of the most unlikely things possible, but it has happened. I have never felt so afraid. I yelled and looked for what seemed like an eternity and finally I spotted him running up a hill towards me. The relief was immeasurable. To this day I'm not totally sure what happened. He must have stopped for a second and lost sight of us. He had grown up in suburbs and lost his bearing in the woods. If he had taken a few steps in the right direction he would have seen the campsite. After walking the wrong direction for a few steps he must have panicked and ran. That's the only way I can explain how he got so far away so quickly. Rather than yell back when he heard me, he tried to follow the sound of my voice. He was shaken and all his candy filled eggs were lost when he tripped and fell. I felt so bad for him I tracked back through the woods to find his candy. The feeling of not knowing where your child is, is one of the worst in the world. Maegan experienced the same feeling that day, yet would later willingly inflict that feeling on me again.

Job life improved and home life was good from where I was sitting. Maegan, of course, had plenty to complain about. Like always, wherever we were before was better than where we are now. Shelton had a grocery store ten minutes away and now we had to plan an all day Costco run once a month. When I was in the military, we could go eat out whenever we wanted. Now Maegan had to cook more and it was a good 20 minute drive to any restaurant when we did want to eat out. WSP pays its troopers poorly compared to other departments in the state, but we were not poor. I was able to support four children, two cats and a wife. We owned our own home and had two cars. We couldn't afford swim lessons for the kids like before, but now I could teach them things in the woods. Meagan was still unhappy.

Working four ten-hour shifts meant I had three days off, so we went home to Oregon often. Maegan's conversations with my mother were more frequent. My mom tried to warn me thatMaegan was unhappy. Mom couldn't really be specific. She didn't want to betray the trust of someone she loved like a daughter, and she didn't want to see her son keep making mistakes.

I am very much like my father. I understood that my mother was trying to explain Maegan was having some of the same feelings she had about my father. I still didn't know exactly why my mother left my father, but I didn't think we were anywhere near that point. Maybe I needed to help out around the house more. I was the sole provider for 8 mouths and Maegan's job was to take care of the kids and house, so I felt I was doing enough. I took out the trash, maybe not right when Maegan asked me to, but it would get done. I kept our two acre yard mowed and tried to kill as many moles as possible. I chopped wood so we could have a fire in the evenings and ran the grill. I fixed what was broken. I handled discipline and kept the peace. I held the kids when they skinned a knee and cleaned it up. Maybe I'm wrong, but I didn't think I needed to do a whole lot more.

I didn't help out with bed time much, because when I did, Maegan wasn't happy with it. Maegan would always fight with them for twenty minutes, trying to get them into pajamas. She'd yell for help and I would tell the kids with authority it was bedtime and in a matter of minutes they would be in bed, pajamas or no pajamas. It worked like a charm the nights I had the kids to myself. Eventually, it came down to me brushing the younger kids' teeth then watching TV while Maegan took twenty minutes to do whatever it was she thought was absolutely necessary, then I would come kiss them goodnight. Mom would often point out how I helped out with the kids more than my father ever did with us, and my father helped out with us more than my grandfather did with him. I figured I wasn't perfect, but I was doing pretty good. I would like to point out my grandma had nine children and a husband who didn't change a single diaper. She stayed married to him her entire adult life and loved him until the day he died. I've tried to ask my 96 year old grandma about my grandfather who I never knew well. She struggles to remember, but it's obvious she loved him. Happiness and contentment can be a decision. Some people make lemonade, others complain they wanted apples.

I had realized a long time before that Maegan was a negative person. I didn't expect her to be perfect, and I loved her anyway. I thought she was doing the same for me. I was unhappy at work, she was unhappy at home. Something needed to change. It became very clear when I went to an awards ceremony up in Bremerton. There, I watched as the WSP awarded fat officer after fat officer for writing ungodly amounts of traffic citations. We are talking hundreds of seatbelt tickets, thousands of speeding tickets. Not a single award was given out for most citizens helped or bad guys caught. At the ceremony, I met the head of the SWAT team, an old team guy. We shot the shit about the good old days and guys we knew in common. My first year was almost up and I would be available for the SWAT team. I expressed how much I missed the teams and he said the SWAT team was not going to scratch that itch. SWAT was a fun distraction, but it wasn't going to feel like being back in the fight. He had the only full time SWAT position, for everyone else it was part time. I needed something or I was going to lose my mind.

Chapter 15

First thing I did was sign up for the Naval Reserve. The reserve program is one of the slowest in existence, so it never really became a factor. I looked into federal agencies again, but they still were not hiring. A spot opened up in Medford PD, the town I went to high school in. It just qualifies as a city and has a pretty serious meth problem. We could move back to our home town and I might get a little more action. The pay was only a little bit higher than WSP, but it was back in Oregon and city agencies are less focused on traffic. I went down for the interview and everything went well. I told them about the issues I was having with WSP and they were sympathetic. They said they would never ask me to write more speeding tickets. It didn't take long for them to hire me. A couple we befriended agreed to rent our home and we got ready to move down to Oregon.

Since the day we were married, I trusted Maegan with all our finances. She had complete control of our money. She made sure the bills were paid on time and told me if the account was getting low. She would bring any major purchases to me, and I would give them the final ok, but otherwise she had free reign with our money. I don't have expensive tastes and guns were the most expensive purchases I made for myself. Before I bought any gun I would ask her if we could afford it first. The system had worked for 10 years. Neither of us were the kind of person to go out and buy a bunch of ridiculous shit.

We were going over our finances for the move, and I discovered we had accrued quite a bit of debt on one of our credit cards. She had been paying the bills with the credit card and making minimum payments on it. I grew up in a family that struggled financially and saw how much stress it caused. Getting into debt was something I had avoided like the plague. We didn't buy our first car until I had enough in the bank to pay it off if I needed to. The house was the first thing I bought without having the money already in savings. The fact that our credit card debt was slowly climbing meant we were spending more money than I was bringing in. Having more credit card debt than I made in a single paycheck was not acceptable to me. I was furious with her, probably even a bit of an asshole. The fact she had let that much debt build up without telling me really damaged my financial trust in her. The worst was finding out that I wasn't actually making enough to provide for my family. Luckily, I had a higher paying job lined up in Oregon.

Before we made the move down to Oregon, the straw to break the camel's back landed. Maegan came to me with that dreadful look on her face and told me Brett Marihugh had died. Brett and another guy had been training breath holds in a pool and drowned. I never did a platoon with Brett, but his personality was so big everyone at the team was his friend. He was a good friend of Matt Leathers. At Matt's memorial, Brett walked to the podium in his uniform carrying a beer, and knocked it back before delivering Matts eulogy.

I had gotten to know Brett more during the last few months of my enlistment. Brett had worked for a sheriff's department in the Detroit area before joining the teams, so I picked his brain quite a bit. I still never got as close with him as I was with Matt or Shelly, but his death hit me hard. When Matt, Smitty, Jesse, and Shelly died I was a team guy. I was in the teams, surrounded by my brothers, taking every hardship together as we always did. When Brett died, I had none of my teammates with me. I wasn't in the fight. I was at home on the couch without another team guy in sight. Once I gathered myself, I told Maegan I wanted to go back to the teams. I would be around less and make more money, so she was onboard. I called up my old master chief and told him through my sobs that I wanted back in. As I tried to get a hold of myself, he told me he was sitting in a chair next to Brett's father, smoking a cigar. I knew I was making the right choice.

The ball started rolling on me getting back into active duty, but it wasn't a sure thing. I continued on with the move to Oregon to start with Medford PD. Every move to that point had taken three to four professional movers three to four days to load my household goods. I rented a U-haul and Maegan put all the small items into boxes. I loaded all the belongings for a family of six by myself in a single day then drove 8 hours down to Medford, Oregon.

I'm quite proud of that. Meagan of course wasn't impressed, despite her always complaining about how long professional movers took.

We would be staying with my mother until we found a place in Oregon. I made us tighten our belt until our debt was paid off. That would have meant Maegan had to cook more, but since we were living with my mom for the time being, she didn't. My mother made my wife, kids and I breakfast, lunch, and dinner. Not since my older siblings moved out when I was in high school had I had a regular breakfast cooked for me. I didn't even have to ask for it. Meagan was a very good cook and cooked more than your average modern career woman, but she never got the concept of planning meals for the week. It wasn't rare for me to come home after being under water for most of the day and ask what was for dinner only for her to reply "I don't know." Most of the time I would just decide we were going out to eat. I would inform her that the family would be needing dinner tomorrow too, and about 50% of the time she would plan something. We got a lot of compliments on how well our children behaved in restaurants because we ate out quite a bit.

Medford is the biggest city in southern Oregon and Medford PD is the biggest department. The agency probably had the same turd to stud ratio, but I worked with more officers than in WSP, so I found more guys to get along with. Medford had quite a few old timers who I tended to gravitate to, guys who got hired before police agencies got neutered. I couldn't start policing until I did the transition course up in Salem, so for the first few weeks I did ride alongs with the various departments in the agency.

Riding with detectives was fun. They actually worked in pairs like you see in the movies. Most patrolmen fly solo. I suppose some big cities can double up in a patrol car. Detectives in Medford OR aren't working homicides all the time. The guys I tagged along with were working a department store robbery and a drive-by shooting. They seemed to like their job and the occasional homicide came their way. For the drive-by I got to walk around the yard and help them try and find all the bullets. Tracing the bullet path had a fun CSI vibe, but it wasn't my cup of tea.

Narcotics detectives had the most fun. Medford has been called Methford in the past. Supposedly, back in the day, our neck of the woods was the number two producer of meth. I've never fact-checked that, and don't feel like doing it now, but suffice it to say we had a meth problem. Southern Oregon's rural nature made it ideal for meth labs. Logging roads crisscross government land, allowing trailers to reach secluded places. Home cooked meth has died off for the most part, so I was told. Mexican cartels can get it across the border in such high quantity and quality it's just not economical for locals to cook it. U.S. anti-drug laws have made acquiring the ingredients for meth very difficult.

Narco detectives carried concealed and wore jeans and sport jerseys to work. Their hair was long and they didn't have to cover their tattoos. Needless to say, it appealed to me. Sitting in on their meetings, it sounded like each guy had something good he was tracking. One officer was ready to move on one of his projects. An illegal alien was running a distribution center out of his house in the hills. Shipments of meth would come up the I-5 highway from Mexico, and he would drive it to individual dealers across the valley. The detectives met with a source out in town, just like a scene out of *The Wire*. Some junkie climbed into the back of the detectives' car and told him his dealer said to come back in a day or two for a large purchase. With that short of a timeline, it was good odds the supplier in the hills was stocked up.

The detectives met for a briefing and it reminded me of being back in the teams planning for an op. Instead of Afghanistan, the area was a place I had driven through a thousand times to go shooting and four wheeling with my brother or cousin. The detectives posted up on every road leading to the supplier's house. Once the supplier was spotted driving to his house, we all converged. The raid went off without a hitch and I was only there to observe. The dog hit the property and turned up four pounds of meth in the biggest crystals I have ever seen. The supplier got his meth from someone. Now the detectives needed to decide if they were going to offer a deal and keep following the trail, or take the bird in hand. The supplier was an illegal and they knew he would disappear to California the second they let him loose, so they decided to take what they had. I looked around the property and realized this guy was living on a piece of land I had always dreamed of, while I was looking for the cheapest rental in town.

Oregon has one police academy that certifies all peace officers for the state. No agency has its own academy like the Washington State Patrol. The Oregon Police Academy runs a two week transition course for officers from other states. Along with another WSP trooper, my class had quite a few Alaska State Troopers, some Nor Cal deputies, and one San Diego Officer with a British accent. It was all classroom work for us, but the regular academy was going on around us. The whole thing felt more like a college campus than a police academy. I definitely did not get the feeling I was in a place that produced the protectors of the populace.

Being in Salem for the course put me closer to the SEAL recruiter for the state of Oregon. Despite having already been a SEAL, I still had to pass the screening test again. I scheduled a test after class one day and put up the worst scores I have ever gotten on the test. I had gotten out of shape. There is a reason so many cops are fat. You spend ten to twelve hours in a car, and at the end of the day you are exhausted, but haven't really gotten any exercise. Police agencies make a big deal out of professional image, nice uniforms, crisp haircuts, and I had to wear long sleeves to cover my tattoos for Medford PD. For some reason, police agencies don't think being a fat ass looks unprofessional. In the military, working out is part of the work day, but most police agencies only give their SWAT teams paid workout hours. The rest have to do it on their own time. As any American citizen can attest, most don't. If agencies really cared about professional appearance, they would give all officers paid workout hours. Unfortunately, officer wellbeing is usually last on an agency's list of priorities.

I had to go through a probation period after the transition course, where a senior officer rode along with me. Medford PD had its disadvantages and advantages over WSP. The main selling point was them not caring whether I enforced traffic law or not. Another plus was always having a call to go to. In WSP I had to find work, but in Medford I had a stack of calls waiting when I got in the car. If you ever call the cops and it takes them a long time to show up, it's probably because your problem isn't that important. If it is important, it's still going to take a while. Everyone should understand that the cops are not going to get there in time. I would advise being able to save yourself.

A big downside to Medford PD was they did paperwork for everything. If someone showed up at the hospital intoxicated, they had to go to the drunk tank to sleep it off. I would have to write a full report for transporting a dude from the hospital to the drunk tank, and this happened several times a shift. Making an arrest on an outstanding warrant for the WSP required a short generic blurb. Medford PD wanted a full write up, even with every-thing recorded on video. All of this was of course to cover the agency's ass. They would rather their officers do hours of paperwork for menial tasks than have more time to respond to calls. Medford PD also had a no vehicle pursuit policy, which was the biggest downer. Enough pursuits ended in accidents, injuries, deaths, and lawsuits that the department gave up on catching the bad guy. The excuse was "we'll catch him later." The unspoken part of that philosophy is "while he's committing another crime you could have prevented if you had caught him the first time."

One thing I missed about WSP was running code on a daily basis. Every accident that came out, you got to flip on the lights and hammer the gas until "no injuries" came out over the radio. The way I worked in the WSP was to stop cars in the oncoming lane. If I'm going 60 mph one way and a car passes me going 90 mph in the other direction, then I get to flip a U and get my car well over 100 mph to catch him. As a city cop I did very little high speed driving. In my short time at WSP, I probably did more real-world high-speed driving than some career city cops. One of my favorite things to do in Washington was practice my driving. At 2:00 am in Grays Harbor, Washington, there is no one on the road. I would scream down every back road in that county, learning every curve. This is a big no no, but I felt entirely justified in my shenanigans. I was learning every curve and dip in my beat, so I could drive every road as quickly and safely as possible. They only gave me 50 rounds a month to practice my shooting skills, but I had hours of night shifts to practice my driving.

Medford was certainly not the place for practicing your driving skills. Its a small city, but you'll find someone on the road at all hours. I liked working nights in Medford. Foot chases were not uncommon, and I still hadn't gotten in one. In certain neighborhoods, all you had to do was stop someone on a bike after dark and you were guaranteed to find meth, heroin, or an outstanding warrant, often all three. No one ever ran from me. I worked one case where a guy stole some chainsaws from a hardware store. Any high-dollar item can be pawned or traded directly to a dealer for drugs. I spent all day with my training officer tracking the guy down to a men's shelter downtown. The guy who ran the shelter said our perp would be back that evening. Our shift was almost over, but I wanted to work overtime to wait for the guy. My training officer wanted to go home so we handed it off to the oncoming shift. Of course when they went to wrap him up, he bolted. Some other guy got to chase him down and tackle him after I did all the leg work. I had to listen to the awesome story the next day.

Medford PD was a little more exciting, but a lot more paperwork. I also had the disadvantage of working where I grew up. I played football in high school with one of the guys in the department, but I also had to arrest a guy I played ball and wrestled with. I was still working on getting back into the Navy on my off time. We cleared our credit card debt and moved into a nice rental home. Of course Maegan preferred when we were in Washington. The kids started going to the same elementary school I had and I coached my old high school wrestling team as a volunteer assistant. Things were tolerable, but I could still feel Maegan's unhappiness with me.

It was a Thursday around 3:00 pm when I got the call. One of the most helpful people in all naval administration told me I was getting back in the Navy. She said I would be getting a call from the Military Enlisted Processing Station (MEPS) in Portland with the details. She warned me that I might be leaving sooner than I expected or wanted. I thanked her and said I couldn't be leaving soon enough. I figured after I got the final word on my reenlistment, it would be a month or two before I shipped out; plenty of time to put in my two weeks' notice. I hung up the phone and it rang a minute later. Portland MEPS called to tell me I was shipping out Friday, the next day, at noon. Portland was 5 hours away and it was 3:00 pm on Thursday.

I hadn't told anyone at Medford PD that I was working on getting back into the military. Despite the upcoming logistical challenge, I couldn't be more excited. I called my mother to tell her we would be dumping the kids off for the night. Maegan would have to drive me up to Portland. I drove to the station while Maegan got the kids ready. The duty Sergeant was shocked to find out I was leaving for the Navy that very moment. At the time, I didn't know why they needed me to ship out so fast, but I did nothing to stop the Sergeant's assumption that it was a matter of national security. By that time they all knew I had been a SEAL and I just let their imaginations run wild. My best guess was there was some shit billet in Bahrain needing to be filled.

I grabbed everything I owned out of the locker and said goodbye to the guys at the station. I rushed over to the high school to say goodbye to the wrestling team and met Maegan at my mom's house. We hit the road to Portland no later than 5:00pm. A hotel room was waiting for me in Portland. Maegan and I got to spend a rare night together without the children. I think we probably had not even had ten since the first was born. Like every other night, she worried about the children instead of enjoying her husband. It wasn't like he was leaving in the morning for an unknown amount time to an unknown place or anything. Now I know that she was relieved to have me leave. By her own admission, to which several others can attest, I never abused her or even raised my voice to her; she just simply preferred me gone.

For those unacquainted with MEPS, it is a slow and painful process. MEPS is military and government bureaucracy at its worst, the DMV on steroids, the embodiment of the hurry up and wait philosophy. The first time I was there at 17 years old, it took all day for them to generate a tome of paperwork on me. When I came back at 18, it took another day to add another volume to the tome and I shipped/flew out the next day. I had no idea how they would get me on a plane by noon. I showed up before the butt crack of dawn with all the wide eyed kiddos leaving home for the first time. Like so many years ago, I stood outside the building in the cold, waiting for it to open. It would take an hour for everyone to get through security, then we would all sit or stand in waiting room after waiting room. The doors opened and someone yelled my name. I went to the front of the line and they rushed me inside like I was the only doctor at a delivery ward. Everyone inside was standing by, ready to check my boxes, cross my T's, and dot my I's. I have never seen pencil pushers panic before. The whole place was a flurry trying to generate a mountain of paperwork on a guy who didn't have a sheet with his name on it yet. At this point, I was really starting to wonder what was going on. I knew I wasn't that important.

To their credit, Portland MEPS had me on a plane with a new tome of paperwork by noon. About a hundred new recruits had to wait while the facility focused on one guy, but they got it done. My first destination was Chicago, the home of Navy boot camp. I didn't have to go through boot camp again, but Chicago is where the Navy in-processes all enlisted personnel. Why the Navy chose Chicago, I'll never know. Why anyone ever stopped in Chicago, I'll never know. I understand the first settlers giving the place a try, thinking they might have shown up at a bad time of year. After the first year they should have realized, there is no good time of year, and moved on. I showed up just before Christmas and found out why there was such a rush to get me shipped out.

The Navy has recruitment quotas for each year. As one might expect, Special Warfare recruitment is a hard quota to fill. Despite already being a SEAL, my reenlistment counted toward the Special Warfare quota. If the Admiral in charge of recruitment could get me to Chicago before everyone left for Christmas vacation, then he would meet his yearly quota for Naval Special Warfare. The Admiral made it clear: get this guy to Chicago before Christmas or else.

Now that I was in Chicago, the pressure was off. Everyone could relax and take their vacation, everyone except me. I showed up right when everyone who needed to process my paperwork was leaving for the holidays. I was stuck in a barracks room until the new year. There is a special wing for former service guys getting back in. The Obama downsizing was in full effect, and it seemed to hit the Marines the hardest. Most of the guys with me were prior Marines who weren't allowed to re enlist in the Corps. With snow and ice on the ground, the heater broke in our wing. The Navy was in no hurry to fix it so some prior service guys could stay warm. We all raided the unused barracks rooms for extra blankets to survive. It took someone pointing out the temperature had dropped below safe levels as per Navy regulations before someone came and fixed it.

It was the first Christmas my job caused me to spend away from my children. My wife would be responsible for the second. *(It's now three as I edit this.)* The teams tried their best to take care of your family. If there wasn't a good reason to miss Christmas, they would do their best to make sure everyone could spend it with their family. Big Navy doesn't give a fuck, however. There was no reason for me to be in Chicago. In this modern era of email, all my paperwork could have been done electronically while I was training in San Diego. At the very least, I should have been able to fly home for Christmas. I still wasn't fully processed into the Navy, so I was not allowed to take leave. Even if I was, my budget was tight and my family would have to survive a month or two without pay. Though I wasn't allowed leave, I could take weekend liberty. My oldest sister lived within driving distance, so I was able to spend Christmas with her family. It had been ages since I'd seen her, so there was a silver lining.

Once the Christmas leave period was over, everyone came back and my paperwork started to move at the pace of a government employee, this time without the Admiral's fire under their asses. I would go down to the office every day to check on the progress only to be told, "I'm waiting to hear back on my email." Eventually, I would just sit across the desk from a portly government employee and look at her expectantly all day. From my spot, I could see another equally bovine woman shop for drapes on the internet. The lady responsible for my paperwork eventually got fed up and with clear displeasure, picked up her phone. "Yes this is Shaniqua with NAV VET processing. What's the status on Swift's package...............Oh! You replied yesterday. I'll check my inbox.......Ok I see it, thank you."

I was furious, but I kept composed. This was on a Friday afternoon. If it was up to her she would have ridden the clock out until the weekend. I would have been stuck for another weekend with no progress being made. Of course she didn't acknowledge what a piece of shit she was, but now I had ammo. I stayed with her the rest of the day and made sure she processed as much of my paperwork as possible with the time remaining. I showed up bright and early on Monday and didn't leave until I had a plane ticket out of that shithole.

Chapter 16

I had been out of the teams for 2 years, which meant I needed to do the core blocks of SQT again. If you don't remember, there are two schools you have to go through to become a SEAL. The first is BUDS and the second is SQT. BUDS is the kick in the nuts and SQT is where you actually learn shit. I only had to redo part of SQT as a kind of refresher course. Rather than do some research on my history and evaluate my capability, the big wigs just hit the easy button and made me redo part of the pipe line. The right thing to do would have been to look at my specific circumstances and evaluate my skill level. I had only been out for two years and I wasn't sitting in my mom's basement smoking weed. I had been a police officer the entire time. Some guys never leave the teams, but spend three years at a cushy desk job and then cycle back into a platoon without any refresher training. Most of the time those guys end up fired. It wouldn't have been hard to call up my 4 surviving platoon chiefs who would have confirmed I didn't need any refresher training. But, it was simply easier to make me do part of SQT again, so I kept my mouth shut. The first time I went through SQT, I had a team guy in the same situation in my class. He, however, needed more than a refresher. I was determined to be a better example to the students.

I was excited about the first block, because it was winter warfare in Alaska. My first trip to Alaska was one of my favorite trips, as it is for most team guys. The team I came from gave me more experience humping a ruck through the bush while avoiding detection than the average team guy gets. I tried to impart as much knowledge as possible, but I wasn't always a positive influence. The final exercise was a three-day land navigation course. Early the second day, we had to cross a stream. The class learned techniques for crossing a stream and staying dry, but the spot the instructors made us cross didn't allow for any of the techniques. The instructors wanted the students to get wet and be miserable. I didn't feel like spending the rest of my crisp March day in Alaska with wet feet. I took off my boots, socks and pants. I never wear underwear, commandos go commando. With a ruck, rifle, and dick hanging out, I crossed the river as ninja as any ninja ever was. Everyone had a good laugh, but a few important people were none too pleased. I'd do it again, even in a war zone. History is full of warriors fighting in their birthday suits.

The next block was Close Quarters Combat (CQC), fighting inside a house, basically. CQC made it very apparent that I didn't need to be doing a refresher course. The instructors started lobbying to get me out of the course and on to a team where I could be training on my level. The head shed wasn't having it. They wanted to set a standard. If an E6 with my experience had to redo the course after being out for two years, then they could just make everyone who wanted to get back in do the course. I have no problem with setting a standard, but in this case it was to make things easy for guys behind desks and it diminished the potential quality of the teams. I could have been spending those months getting new skills and qualifications to benefit my future platoon. In the time it took to get through SQT, I could have gotten my Dive Sup qual, Range Safety Officer qual, gone to Jump Master school or Joint Terminal Attack Controller school; all qualifications the teams are constantly starving for. Don't worry, I'll explain those later if they are important to the story.

Land warfare was the next block, and the only block I felt diminished in quality since the days I originally went through. Maritime operations (diving and boat shit) was the next block. If there is one kind of training I didn't need a refresher in, it was maritime operations. In all the other blocks the instructors were at least close to my level or better in the skill they were teaching. For diving, I was light years ahead of any instructor. It is hard to overstate how much more diving experience a guy from my team has over a vanilla team guy. In SQT,

I spent more time waiting for other divers to finish than I did diving. Luckily, it was the last block I was required to complete, and the instructors let me play hooky the last week.

Now it was time to decide which coast I wanted to go to. I had spent a lot of time in Virginia Beach and augmented the east coast teams in the past. I liked what I had seen of those teams, and preferred to live in a state that allowed its citizens to defend themselves. In communist California, all the criminals have guns and carry them, and the law abiding citizens are only allowed certain guns, good luck trying to carry one legally. I knew Maegan wanted to go back to San Diego. Her twin sister Amanda lived just north of the area, and she would be spending more time wherever I got stationed than I would. I pulled the trigger on the west coast teams, and we moved the family down from Oregon. Again it took 4 men several days to move exactly what I had moved in a day just a few months earlier. I was more than happy to let them do it, since it was on the government's dime.

The school system in SoCal sucks, so Maegan wanted to homeschool the kids. I knew the kids would get a better education with her, but I was doubtful of Maegan's ability to handle the stress. She already acted like she was completely overwhelmed, and now she wanted to take on schooling the kids. I expressed my concerns and made it clear she would not be able to count on me for help, not with my job. I said I'd rather just put them in school. If they struggled with reading, writing or arithmetic, we could get them help. Academic education is probably the least valuable thing you get from public school.

I agreed to try it out for a year and see how she handled it. I had already come to terms with my wife's tight round ass and toned legs never coming back. We would be eating out regularly, and I would be coming home to sweat pants and hair in a bun, the floppy white trash kind, not sexy librarian. It had been a l while since she cared about impressing me anyway, if she ever did. After girl 1 was the last time she'd put any real effort into working out, and that was only after an argument where I spoke my mind. I made sure to stay in shape for her and wished I got the same in return. Our youngest was nearly three. Mae-gan's genetics were good and she had a good figure even when she didn't try, minus the devastation the kids did to her mid-section. She would complain about it incessantly. Her stomach never bothered me. She had earned those stretch marks. She should have worn them as a badge of pride like I wear my scars, but as I've said, she was never one to make lemonade.

I checked in to my team and was assigned a platoon. Walking into a platoon space full of pipe hitters was a homecoming all its own. There wasn't a single guy I had met before, but they were all brothers by the end of the day. I was back and it felt good. Getting out and getting back in allowed me to do an extra platoon as a sled dog. Only the platoon chief had more experience than me, and I was now part of an older generation. My fourth platoon was solid. We had the best new guys hands down, six in total. Three were short and the genetic product of Spanish colonization. We affectionately dubbed them our little brown ducklings. Our older guys were all aggressive, smart and humble. Our LPO knew his shit, both tactically and administratively. Our officers knew how to lead and when to listen to their enlisted.

I showed up at the team right as they entered the block used to send guys to individual schools. At this point I was a Lead Breacher and Comms guy, but neither of those skills got you augments with other teams anymore. Sniper was a sexier school, but it wasn't in high demand either. The two jobs you need to fill on every above-water operation are Medic and JTAC (Joint Terminal Attack Controller). In layman terms, the JTAC is the guy on the ground who makes sure the bombs land where they are supposed to. Medic appealed to me more, but it was six months long, where JTAC school was five weeks. Talking pilots onto targets didn't appeal to me, but being a JTAC increased my opportunities to go down range. There isn't much to say about JTAC school, but Trump got elected when I was there, so that should give a good time reference for you. We were gearing up to start taking the fight to ISIS and I wanted my piece of the pie.

My team had to wait its turn. I lobbied to augment one of the other teams already up to bat, but I still had responsibilities to my own platoon. We were busy getting ready for our own deployment when they took Mosul. A platoon work-up is always a kick in the nuts, but it makes good memories. It's hard to put platoon life into words, but I can remember one scene to illustrate the experience. We were a couple weeks into one of the tougher blocks waiting for a training evolution to start. Everyone was kitted out, waiting for the helos to show up. A huge desert storm was crossing the horizon. If it came our way, the helos would cancel and we might get the night off. One of the guys found some Native American chant on his phone and started playing it. All the guys broke out into their best rendition of a rain dance. Something about a Filipino American doing a Native American rain dance on top of a Hummer in full kit makes for a fond memory. The storm passed at a safe distance and we ended up working our asses off all night. Once the platoon finished its core training phase, I was free to whore myself out. My LPO was a medic and had the same idea. He drank frequently with an old BUDS instructor of mine. Said instructor was now a big wig at the team getting ready to make the western push to the Syrian border. After a few beers at the favorite bar, my LPO and I were headed to Iraq.

Iraq had changed a lot since the last time I was there. If you're unfamiliar with the situation, I'll give you the cliff notes version of the Iraq war. First, we started off with the invasion. That type of war is America's bread and butter, see D-day and the island hopping campaign in the Pacific. Needless to say, that phase was over fairly quickly. After a successful invasion, America decided against tried and true business models like puppet dictators; where things go to shit long after you've left. Instead, we went for the friendly neighborhood occupier like in Vietnam; because it's worked so well in the past. This began the insurgency phase of the war, which was my first experience in Iraq.

The war is officially broken down into rebuilding phases, surges and other PC crap like that, but for the boots on the ground, we've been fighting insurgents. America had bases spread all over Iraq where we could launch operations to snatch up insurgents. Deployment consisted of hanging out on base all day while the intel guys tracked a target, then going out to get him at night. The powers that be wanted it to look like the Iraqis were fighting the insurgency, so we always had to take a partner force out with us. We called the shots, though. We decided when and where. Eventually, the insurgency died down, and Obama thought it was time to pull out. America handed over all the bases, giving the Iraqis armored Vics, night vision and TOW missiles, hoping they could defend their own country. Then came ISIS.

The new kids on the block came rolling in from Syria, driving pickup trucks. Rather than repeat the success of Desert Storm and let our fly boys have their way with them, we let the ever competent Iraqi Army handle it. True to form, the Iraqi Army tucked tail and ran, leaving behind all that night vision, TOW missiles, and armor. ISIS took over northern Iraq and we settled into a standoff reminiscent of WW1. We actually had a front line for the first time in decades. Giant defensive networks contained ISIS in between Iraqi forces in the south and Kurds in the north. There was still an insurgency in the south, but our guys weren't allowed to go after them. We mostly fought a defensive campaign, which is not how we are supposed to be used. This was all going on while I was a cop, but some of the guys got lucky when ISIS rushed their position, only to find out it's hard to win a straight up gun fight against Americans. Traps and roadside bombs are what you use against Americans. The Vietnamese learned more of them would die if they tried to trade bullets with us. Medieval English archers grew up shooting arrows, our boys grow up shooting guns.

Once the administration changed, we were allowed to take the fight to the enemy. The big show was Mosul, which I missed, but we still had to push them out of the west. Now you're up to speed.

I'll talk more about the push west, since you can Google most of it, and it won't reveal our tactics. We started in Al Assad, one of the few secure bases Americans could operate from. When I was last in Iraq, we dictated the timelines and movements. Now we had to wait around until the Iraqis decided it was time to go. When they finally got their shit together, we were told to pack for five days out in the field. My element was a four vehicle package mixed in with the Iraqi Army. Two roads traversed the west of Iraq to reach Al Qaim on the Syrian border. The northern paved road ran along the Euphrates and was the primary route for normal traffic. My element would be taking the southern unpaved service road with several industrial targets along the way.

The first day was an uneventful trip to a staging area in the middle of the desert. We circled the wagons and laid out the cots. Little did we know, our bed down location was right next to the High Mobility Artillery Rocket System (HIMARS). I awoke to the sound of a space shuttle taking off. The Marines were softening up the town we would be taking the next day. If it was an American Army we would be assaulting at night but the Iraqis had a hard enough time not shooting each other in the daylight. At least we started moving before sunrise. The Iraqi Army was only able to clear a single route of roadside bombs. The road was choked with tanks, dozers and all manner of armored vehicles as far as the eye could see. No one dared risk driving off the cleared path. I imagine the Republican guard looked the same way when they were getting the shit kicked out of them by coalition aircraft back in '91. I tried to picture an A-10 turning in the air to strafe me with 30mm and got a chill. I didn't have to imagine the Apache Gunships circling overhead. If you want to know who cleared ISIS out of western Iraq, it was Apache pilots. If anyone is thinking about being a pilot, forget being a fighter jock, fly Apaches.

The main threat was from three sources. The first was mortars. Periodically, a mortar would land off to our side, but it wouldn't take long for the Apaches to fix that problem. The other threat came from Vehicle Born Improvised Explosives (VBIDs). ISIS's bread and butter was the VBID. When the Iraqi Army abandoned all the armored Vics we gave them, ISIS found themselves in possession of tools they couldn't use for their intended purpose. Armored Vics are for those straight up fights Americans like. Instead, ISIS packed them with explosives and told some poor sap he would get laid by 72 virgins if he drove it at the Great Satan. We started calling them kill dozers.

Kill dozers are a single use item. Once they got low on U.S. supplied armor, they started to weld steel plates onto regular vehicles. Imagine a Mad Max suicide car. Up in Mosul, ISIS would hide them in garages and dugout pits until we got close. We expected to run into a lot during the western push, but there weren't many. I saw a few half-way built kill dozers in the towns we took, but they were not as prepared as they were in Mosul. The third threat was fairly new for us, and we'll get to it later.

Assaults would frequently bog down, and we would just sit like we were in LA traffic. My LPO even hung his ass off the side of the truck to take a shit as we crawled along. The Iraqis would always be done fighting by noon, regardless of progress. If they couldn't take a target by lunch, it wasn't happening. They would settle in for the day, and we would meet them for tea. First you have to make small talk. It's rude if you get right down to business. Next, you can talk about what you're going to talk about, then you can talk about it. After spending more time listening to tomorrow's plan than we spent fighting that day, we would find a spot in the desert to circle our trucks for the night. One night I was on watch with my LPO and we walked up the rise we were using as cover. The Iraqis hadn't managed to take the nearby town during the day, so settled into a siege for the night. With our night vision we could see ISIS and the Iraqis trading pot shots. It was like a time machine to an older form of warfare, when Germans and French camped on either side of no man's land. The entire campaign was very conventional, nothing special forces about it. Bullets and armor against bullets and armor, with the Apaches and C-130 gunship acting as the hand of God rigging the outcome.

The Iraqis took the town the next day, and we had to have another meeting. I stayed outside on security for most of those meetings. The Iraqis are quick to call a town cleared, but there is Iraqi clear and there is actually clear. A dog tripped an IED a stone's throw from us, right in the area the Iraqis decided was clear enough for a meeting. There was also the threat from the Shia militia groups. Iraq has large Shia and Sunni populations. Iran has been meddling in Iraq since day one. Being a Shia country, Iran has given loads of tanks and money to the Shia militias. We were supposedly on the same side, but two Americans had already been killed by these militia groups up north. Some of our guys had been approached and told we were next once ISIS was gone. We were driving a couple of trucks designed to protect against small arms and roadside bombs. The Shia Militias were driving old soviet tanks that could punch a round right through us if they wanted to.

If you're wondering, these are the same Shia militia groups that attacked our embassy in 2019.

As we took targets, it was always foreign fighters left behind for the last stand. Often it was young boys from Indonesia who would surrender as soon as they could. They were recruited by ISIS networks and had their passports taken on arrival. I remember one kid, early twenties at the oldest, zip tied on the side of the road. You could tell he wanted to surrender to the Americans, but we weren't authorized to take prisoners. This was the Iraqi's show. That kid was doomed to a rape dungeon followed by an execution and he knew it.

A train station was the last target on our route before turning north for Al Qaim. The station had traded hands several times since the start of the war. It was a landscape of twisted metal and crumbled buildings like a flash forward scene from The Terminator. Our EOD guys cleared a route to a small area for us to set up camp. The place had been bombed, strafed and raided by some kind of U.S. Special Forces in the past. We shit in plastic bags and flung them out into the rubble, not wanting to walk on un-cleared ground and not thinking we would be returning to sleep there for the next two weeks.

The next day we headed north. We were supposed to capture a phosphate factory along with the residential area built for the workers. A dust storm rolled in and the Iraqis got their ass handed to them. It may have been an Iraqi operation, but they weren't doing shit without American air power. The invasion was put on hold for bad weather and we headed back to the train station to add to the accumulating bags of shit. That night we were caught in a sand storm I cannot embellish enough. I'm talking biblical plagues of Egypt shit. We set up camp and it started to get dark. There were still hours of daylight left but it felt like dusk. I took a quick video with my phone because the bombed out train station had an eerie look about it. There was still plenty of light for a video. I put my phone away and sat on a cot to eat my MRE. The world went black in a matter of seconds. A cot was picked up and slammed me in the back of the head, almost knocking me unconscious. I couldn't hear or see a thing. Sand peeled at my skin. My truck was only a few yards away and I started walking in that direction. Mud started to fill my mouth and nose when I reached the door. I climbed inside and we did a head count over the radio. Everyone made it inside a truck. The huge armored vehicle swayed back and forth in the wind. We stayed in the trucks for a few hours joking over the radio and coughing on the sand seeping into the cab. We found out the next morning one of our European allies got caught out in the storm for thirty min-utes. He crawled his way into a mortar pit with some Marines and had to be evacuated when the weather cleared, due to his eyes being shredded by sand. One of the Iraqi old timers with us said it was the worst storm in sixty years.

Sunny skies greeted us the next day and it was time for round two at the phosphate factory. We knew ISIS would be all pumped up from turning the Iraqis back the day before. The Iraqis had also lost their momentum, so we decided we would start the day with a good old American show of force. I got to witness the HIMARS at work again, where they landed this time instead of where they launched from. They were more terrifying when they took off then when they landed. To be fair, I was much closer when I witnessed them take off. We finished the opening assault with barrages from our .50 cals, and the Iraqis had the target by lunch. Of course they weren't going to push to Al Qaim before tea time, so we went back to the train station for the night. More shit bags decorated the rubble and we relaxed a bit with more terrain between us and the enemy. The snipers broke out their rifles and we had target practice knocking down power lines.

The next day we finally reached Al Qaim. It was quite the little battle, but it was nothing compared to Mosul, so I won't pretend it was. I think the Iraqis had more casualties from shooting each other than from enemy fire. ISIS did get four of them with a grenade dropped from a commercial drone. Trying to take a shit while you know a grenade dropping drone is out there is like swimming after a shark has been spotted. I've experienced both. We used a five gallon bucket with a toilet seat zip tied to it. Large trash bags ensured the contraption never touched ass or its product. It stayed bungeed to the outside of the truck. When you had to go you just did your business right next to the truck. I tried to hold it but eventually gave in. Picture a soldier in full kit, pants around his ankles, sitting on a bucket, frantically scanning the sky for killer robots. No one want's their epithet to be "died while taking a shit."

Most of the combat I had experienced before that deployment had been at night. See-ing a city at war in broad daylight is quite a sight. Black clouds from burning petroleum rose up from the city and smeared the sky. Al Qaim was only the last stand for the foreign fighters. The OG ISIS fighters bailed over the Syrian border to wait for the Russians and Assad to come from the other direction.

We spent the rest of the day helping our European buddies. Several European countries had Special Forces in Iraq to search the dead and identify their citizens who went to fight for ISIS. The first night we Americans withdrew to an Iraqi artillery base just outside the city. I say base, but it was a sand berm the Iraqis had thrown up that morning. On our way out, we could see the city across the Syrian border. Several smoke trails streaked across the border toward our trucks. The rockets impacted short of our trucks. Intel had warned us ISIS had TOW missile launchers, that third threat I mentioned earlier. TOW missiles are American made, portable, guided, anti-tank missiles. For some reason, we keep giving Muslims weapons and they always end up used on us. It's almost like their religion says it's ok to turn on your allies if they are infidels. The launchers were too valuable to ISIS to lose them when we captured a town, so they had saved them, choosing to throw Indonesian boys at us instead. The Syrian border was the perfect opportunity to employ them. Despite American forces operating in both Syria and Iraq, this operation was an Iraqi effort and we could not cross the border; especially with the Russians coming from that direction. ISIS set up the launchers just across the border and waited to try and hit the Americans as we left the city. Some of the snipers who had pestered us during the day had also been trying to ID our vehicles. That night we ate our first meal in almost two weeks that wasn't an MRE. The Iraqis cooked us an impressive spread. Some of the guys passed due to the sanitary conditions the meal was cooked in. I loved it. Halal is some good shit. Even if the guy who cooked it probably still had shit on his hands.

The next day another platoon headed into the city to have tea with the Iraqis. My platoon stayed behind as an Immediate Reaction Force (IRF). I made sure my kit was staged to be thrown on quickly and found myself a cot. The platoon hadn't been gone for long when I heard an explosion. An explosion was an everyday occurrence by this point, so I didn't pay it much attention. Then I saw a black mushroom cloud rising over the city. I figured a fuel depot had been hit. It made for an apocalyptic picture, so I snapped one with my phone. A minute later the call went out to head into the city. Apparently, that mushroom cloud was from one of our trucks. We mounted up and headed for the city. Before reaching the city, we came across the platoon limping back. One truck had been left and a second had an enormous hole in the engine. Despite the damage, the truck had driven safely out of the city. I have to give props to Caterpillar engines. It didn't take long for the word to come out that our K9 died in the blast. Our guys had their bell rung and one or two had bits of shrapnel in their backs, neck and head. We called a helo in to pick up the wounded and towed the damage truck back to camp. I got the full story that night.

The Iraqis had chosen a building close to the Syrian border as their headquarters. I'm guessing it was the most comfortable. When our guys went to meet them, the trucks set a protective perimeter. ISIS TOW crews had set up on the other side of the border and gotten angles on two of our trucks. They fired simultaneously and scored two hits. One missile hit the back of our truck where the spare fuel was kept. That caused the mushroom cloud I saw. The dog in the back was vaporized and the two back seaters got fragged, but the cab armor did its job and saved our guys. The truck caught fire and they bailed out into another truck. The second truck was hit square in the teeth, it was the one that managed to limp out of the city. The extremely beefy tow assembly took the brunt of the hit, causing the armor piercing shape charge to detonate too early.

Once Al Qiam was cleared, we set up shop at the train station. Our Marines moved in and handled security, so we didn't have to stand watch anymore. Marines always come packaged with a bunch of extra rules. Before, we could have target practice where and when we wanted. Now, we had to radio the command tent and get approval. The Marines had their own headquarters and brought women, so shitting wherever we wanted had to stop. On the upside, getting women meant we got proper toilets shipped out. We of course had to clean up all the literal shit bags we had tossed all over the train yard. They all stayed sealed, but days in the Iraqi sun turned them into methane balloons. We found a pit and conducted a burn. Each bag of methane ignited with a sharp squeak, making the poop bomb fire sound like a sci-fi battle with pew pew lasers.

Within a couple days. Our private slice of mad max turned into a bustling outpost with seven nations represented. Artillery units moved in to assist mop up operations on the far side of the Euphrates River. The distant thunder of a C-130 Gunship had been a nightly serenade since the whole thing started. Now we had the pleasure of waking up at all hours to the sound of a cannon going off right next to us, along with the random Marine accidentally cracking a round off.

I woke up one morning before everyone else. My phone was almost dead and I wanted to charge it so I could have music for a jog through the rubble. Our own diesel trucks were shut off. I wasn't going to start them and wake everyone up. I could see the Marine security truck parked nearby was idling. I walked over to see if I could charge my phone. I opened the driver's side door to see two bewildered Marines. I asked the driver if I could use the charger.

His answer was, "I don't think we are allowed to."

"Just blame me if anyone asks," I said, and climbed inside to find the outlet, only to find there was none. Apparently, we had a different variant of the same truck. No doubt money was saved by not giving Marines a way to charge hand held GPS's. Even more money was probably saved by not giving individual Marines hand held GPS's. While I was digging around I noticed one of the Marines had an H&K 416. You can look into it if you're interested, but suffice it to say it was a very expensive gun the Marines were just starting to add to their inventory. I was surprised to see a Marine carrying it and wanted to finger fuck it. The Marine handed it over so I could play with it. The turret gunner asked if he could see my gun and I said, "Sure, it's hot," handing it over.

The Marine looked at me surprised and said, "You're allowed to have one in the chamber!?"

I couldn't resist the Dumb and Dumber reference and said, "Yeah!.... We're in Iraq."

I had just gotten my hands on the 416 and checked the breach. It was empty. These guys were the first line of defense and none of them had a round in the chamber. All these Marines walking around in full kit all day didn't even have a gun that was ready to fire. Even when we were our own security we would leave our kits in the truck and keep a hot weapon within arm's reach of us. At this particular point I was only wearing pants, but at least I could shoot a bad guy if I saw one. The little bastards only pop their heads up for a second and if you have to chamber a round you're going to miss your opportunity. Apparently, after the negligent discharges some big wig decided it was safer if his Marines walked around Iraq with unloaded rifles. We shot the shit with a few of the Marine officers and they said their biggest challenge wasn't ISIS or the negligent discharges, it was trying to keep 18 year old Marines from fucking like rabbits. Apparently the one or two females I had seen on my run were very popular. I went to sleep every night with a raging hard on as I thought about my wife. I can only imagine being a single Marine with a warm female bedded down on the concrete right next to me.

We helped out with some of the clean-up operations, like disposing of IEDs rigged with those chemical weapons Saddam didn't have. After a few days of relative inactivity, the boss-man decided we could drive back to base, the base we started at not the train station. We took the paved road back along the Euphrates. If you're not a history nerd like me, you might not know the significance of that river. The land between the Tigris and Euphrates rivers is some of the most important in history. Mesopotamia, as it is called, is were civilization got its start. Since the first tribes came together to make cities, men have been killing each other over that land. Just about every people named in the Bible have spilt their blood across that sand. Modern westerners think of Iraq as an Arab land but they took it from Persian Sassanids who took it from someone else, who took it from someone else and so on. Roman legions had marched along the same route I was driving.

Chapter 17

We caught a flight back to the states with a larger conventional unit, just like my first trip back from Iraq. Again, there was a crowd waiting at the gate on our first stateside stop. It's embarrassing as you walk past the cheering crowd, but you feel pretty good afterward. We won't ask for appreciation, but it's nice to see proud Americans give it on their own.

Getting home was a different story, as always. I got home the day before Thanksgiving. Meagan and the kids picked me up at the airport. Getting bear-hugged by four children after coming home from war is one of the greatest things on earth. I hugged and kissed my wife with as much affection as public etiquette allowed. Meagan had left her sister Amanda at our house to keep working on the food for the next day. We got home and I pulled Maegan into the shower as soon as I could. I started doing what husbands do to wives in the shower, and she started to rush me, making it clear the event would be a one-sided effort. I was furious, but I let it go. As always, I took a back seat to her sister. I had just fought across a country, driving back the evilest fuckers since the Nazis, and she wanted me to hurry up so her sister wasn't in the kitchen alone. I had played out all the things I was going to do to her in my head every night while I was gone. All that went out the window, because she didn't even have the courtesy to set aside the day I came home for just the family. To top it all off, we had to drive an hour up north in the morning to celebrate Thanksgiving at her sister's house. If you're married to a soldier and he just got home from war, it's a safe bet he'd rather spend Thanksgiving in his own home. It wasn't really a big deal. As a father, you learn very quickly the holidays are not about you, not even Father's Day. Being so far down the priority list after coming home from war still kind of stings, if you'll indulge me some selfishness.

December, January and February rolled by, and it was time to deploy with my team. For once, I would be deploying with the platoon I began with. Or so I thought. A week before deploying, Chief told me I would be going to Yemen with a different platoon. Whether or not we would be sending guys to Yemen had been up in the air for a while. An Army Special Forces Colonel had been trying to get operations underway in Yemen and he needed a strike element. Trust me, strike element makes it sound a lot sexier than it actually was. The Colonel pulled the right strings and got 8 SEALs sent out to his corner of the desert. We were sending guys to work very independently for an Army command, so seasoned guys from each platoon were picked to form an impromptu platoon. We dubbed it Pickle Platoon. It was one of the best groups of guys you could throw together. The LT was a smart, hardworking guy, so he was allowed to cherry pick his guys.

I should probably give you a rundown of the Yemen conflict. There are basically three areas of Yemen: the mountains, the major ports, and the rest of the country which includes the minor ports. Historically, whoever controls the mountains controls the major ports. The Ottoman and British empires both tried to control the major ports without controlling the mountains and eventually gave up. Back in 2015, the Houthi tribe who controlled the mountains ousted the Yemen government and took over the major ports. There is a lot more to it, involving Saudi Arabia and Iran as well as Sunni and Shia respectively, and I suggest everyone educate themselves about it. I'm not going to get into more detail about it, because, contrary to what our senators and representatives believe, the military isn't interested in the civil war. We were interested in how Al Qaeda was capitalizing on the chaos. The rest of the country usually doesn't care what's going on in the mountains or major ports. The rest of the country would have been fine except Al Qaeda used the lack of government to take over all the minor ports. You remember Al Qaeda, don't you? While most people associate them with Afghanistan, they got their start in Yemen and never left. ISIS tried to take advantage of the civil war as well, but never gained any real traction because Al Qaeda has always been the home team. While Saudi Arabia dealt with Iran-supplied Houthis in the mountains, the United Arab Emirates kicked Al Qaeda out of the minor ports.

Yemen was possibly a new frontier for operations, so we were cautiously optimistic. Right before we left, some politician started calling for a cease to American involvement in the Yemen civil war. We weren't going to fight in any civil war, but try and explain a finer point like that to a politician or the media. The spike in political relevance meant we were going to have more eyes on us, and leadership who didn't want to get fired. Neither of those are good ingredients for getting meaningful work done.

We showed up to a camp that was the embodiment of putting the cart in front of the horse. The camp was not ready to support the increase in bodies and the proper asses hadn't been kissed to get approval for operations. Like Iraq, we didn't want it to be America's show. This time we had to get approval from the Emiratis. Not only did we have to get approval through our own bureaucracy we call a chain of command, we had to get approval through the king of all bureaucracy, a stable Middle Eastern country. You see, that Mohamed fella was running the city of Medina while he was still getting his "visions." While Jesus only ever had twelve hobos to call on, Mohamed had a city and eventually an entire peninsula to rule. Combine that with a culture brought up controlling the middle of the Silk Road, a large portion of the world's oil, and you have a recipe for an administrative monster. Every idea, law, plan, deal, or epiphany has to pass through 100 people so they can take their cut and decide whether it will hurt or profit them. If they are unsure, it's always easiest to just say no. Middle Eastern bureaucracies are such a pain in the ass Columbus sailed into the unknown sea just to bypass one.

We hit the ground running and had viable targets in a short time, but there were too many restrictions to allow us to prosecute them. We occupied ourselves with basic recon-naissance, but the Emirates made approval for that difficult. Arab armies are very top-down. The lower ranks don't do shit without being told to. We waited months for a phan-tom letter of approval to be mailed to our base's commander. That's right, in this age of the internet and email, we waited on a paper letter to be mailed from a country that builds is-lands and the tallest building in the world.

The UAE kicked Al Qaeda out of the minor ports, but they didn't care about the rest of the country. They are colonizing Yemen. No one will call it what it is because it's not white people, but brown people colonizing brown people. What Al Qaeda does outside the finan-cially viable ports doesn't matter, as long as they don't raise a ruckus in UAE's little slice of Yemen. Our slice of Yemen was used by Al Qaeda for smuggling and recruitment. They didn't fuck with the Emiratis and the Emirates slow-rolled the Americans. Toward the end of the seven-month deployment, even the master bullshitters started running out of shit to shovel. They gave us approval for a more expansive reconnaissance. Just before we stepped off, the Emirates said an IED went off in the town we were going to recon. It was too risky for us to go out, so they cancelled the mission.

We had a drone feeding us live footage of the area they said had been bombed. The busy port had crowds of people going about their business like nothing happened, because nothing did. This is the kind of shit we dealt with all deployment. On top of the operational constraints, we had a shitty support staff that got better over time as they rotated out. Most of the initial crew had never supported Special Operations. One of the biggest challenges for special ops is to find and keep good support staff. We ran out of food and water on multiple occasions. The airfield was supposed to be run by an Air Force guy, but he bailed to go drop bombs in Syria. I was the only guy experienced in handling aircraft, so I had to learn how to run an airfield.

We got a shitty internet connection a few months in. Don't think internet equals luxury living standards. Internet is one of the easiest things to get in the middle of nowhere. With so much time on our hands, I spent a lot more time texting Maegan than I usually did on trips. Guys make the mistake of checking in regularly with their girls. When something inevitably comes up, it puts them in a panic; if your girl actually gives a fuck about you. I never made promises to Maegan I couldn't keep, and I never let her rely on something that might disappear or change. She always complained about how other wives got regular messages. This deployment I texted her every night. There was no reason not to. Here I thought she would appreciate it, but it would take her days to reply. She was always busy at Amanda's watching her kids. I had chosen San Diego so Maegan could be close to Amanda. Amanda was bogged down with work, so she hardly ever visited, not that it stopped her from dumping her kids on us all the time. They were good boys and our children had fun with them, so I tolerated it. When I left Maegan became free daycare and spent more time up at Amanda's house than ours.

Why did Amanda work so hard? I'll tell you. Her husband had been a Marine, but wasn't allowed to re-enlist because of a DUI. Rather than get a job, he decided to use his GI bill to go to college. Not a terrible idea, as you get a housing allowance with the GI bill. But instead of using the housing allowance for the house his children stayed in, he used it to shack up with a college girl. He convinced Amanda to agree to an open marriage where he spent the week living 45 minutes away with a college girl. But don't worry, he brought his laundry home on the weekends so his wife could do it between working two jobs. What about the two grade school boys? They certainly couldn't afford daycare, so when my wife couldn't take care of them, they just stayed home alone. This sounds like gossip, and it is. My wife would vent to me about how horrible Amanda's husband was. With the Cooper tendency to embellish and victimize themselves, I'm not sure how much to take as fact. Regardless, Amanda was miserable, and it was going to have a big impact on my life. Misery loves company, and there are few families that embody the saying more than Maegan's family. Maegan's mother was the worst, but her sister definitely clinched second place.

Meagan would reply after a day or two with a "Sorry, I'm at Amanda's. She's fighting with #&$*#& again and I want to leave, but the kids are having fun together." I figured it was only a matter of time before Amanda left him, and I told Maegan she could stay with us. I had loaned Amanda money and let her stay with us without hesitation in the past. Amanda was fighting with her husband, so Maegan was responding to my texts. We started talking about Amanda's prospects, and Maegan talked about how hard it would be for a single mother to find another man. I was ignorant of dating at the time and thought I would have no problem dating a single mother. I thought it was another one of her ridiculous assumptions, like men caring about what kind of car a woman drove.

I dug into the internet to find something to prove my point. What I found was countless life coaches outlining why it is a terrible idea to date a single mother. Maybe I was wrong about men not wanting single mothers. I told Maegan as much and sent her one of the videos. The content really offended her and she shot back a bunch of reasons why the guy in the video was wrong. I wasn't necessarily sold on some dude from the internet, but her arguments didn't hold water; plus, it was one of the rare occasions she responded to my texts immediately and I wanted to keep it going. Talking through hypotheticals and friendly argument had always been a healthy staple of our relationship. As we went back and forth, she started talking more about herself than Amanda. She argued no man would want a woman with her stomach and four kids. I pointed out that every time she went out without me she got hit on, even with the kids. She always came home from grocery shopping and told me about the creepy guy who hit on her. Eventually, I pointed out that it was supposed to be Amanda we were talking about. She LOL'ed it away and I didn't give it much more thought. I really should have.

I was getting in good shape on deployment and my physique was looking as good as it ever had. I decided I was going to make Maegan desire me when I got home. She never really had. Growing up, my sisters would swoon over all the characters from The Outsiders movie. Maegan was also a fan of the movie, and the actor who played Daryl sparked her fantasies, along with Val Kilmer and Vin Diesel's voice. Of course I had my own list of actresses, and we would playfully talk about our celebrity crushes like most married couples. The difference is, I showered Maegan with lust; the same cannot be said of her. Meagan never gushed over men she found attractive like I've seen some women do, so I told myself it was just her shy personality; what I fell in love with in the first place. It was still something I always wanted, for my wife to see me and get hot and bothered. This was the most common reason I started an argument. I would get frustrated at always being the one to initiate sex. Her complete lack of affection toward me was the thing I struggled with the most. She wanted me to hold her at night, but she never held me back.

Watching those videos on single mothers made similar dating videos start to pop up on my feed. I had never really dated my entire life. Meagan was my first real girlfriend and we were practically married from the get go. Romance was never a skill of mine, and I figured if I could learn something about it, maybe I could get her to desire me. I looked into all kinds of female psychology and dating advice, looking for ways I could improve myself in Mae-gan's eyes. I can't say I learned much, but I did come to the conclusion that modern dating was a mess. I thanked God I didn't have to deal with trying to find a woman in modern America.

I tried to engage Maegan as much as possible. I'd send her a video and try and get her opinion, only for her to not watch it. I finished a novel I had written and sent it to her to read and give feedback on. I think she made three or four comments on an over 100,000 word manuscript. She burned through romance novels at an incredible pace, but would go days without reading any of mine. Maybe my book just sucked. Those romance novels are female porn. Porn is often cited as giving men unrealistic expectations, but it is the other way around. There isn't a whole lot in porn every woman can't do other than some feats of flexibility. For the most part, you just have to pretend you're having more fun than you really are. The women in porn actually exist and are doing what you see on screen. It's all in the realm of possibility. I can't become a millionaire vampire doctor. I can't arrange for you to be abused in some way so I can rescue you. I can't have a werewolf pirate sail in so we can have a love triangle. A lot of research has been done on the effects porn has on the mind, but nobody's looked into what the dopamine rushes from the best-selling literature genre does to women.

Maegan was constantly at Amanda's or watching Amanda's kids. I was trying to en-gage her more than I had on any other deployment and was ignored for my efforts. She had always complained I should talk to her more on deployment and I was trying to fix that. Not getting to do meaningful work, being ignored by my wife, and being away from my children really started to take its toll. If there is one thing I wish Maegan could understand it's the feeling and mental trial of being apart from your wife and children. It was always the hardest part of the job for me, and Meagan acted like I didn't care about them. She's never had to go to sleep at night pretending her daughter was in her arms. I always coped, and Maegan interpreted that as not caring.

One of my coping mechanisms on that deployment was the stray cats around the compound. Rats had infested our tent and I started trapping them. Despite catching one on a regular basis, the more clever bastards were able to make off with the bait. One of the camp cats had a litter of kittens and I coaxed them over. The mother ditched the kittens as soon as she could, and I had three little rat deterrents. The kittens weren't going to catch rats bigger than them, but their scent kept them away. All my traps stayed empty with bait intact. I fed the cats from the bulk tuna packets and they stuck around. Just like a cat lady copes with choosing career over kids, the kittens helped me cope with not seeing my kids. The rest of the guys hated them. Their mother never taught them not to shit were they sleep before she bailed on them. We no longer had rats, but our little corner of the camp smelled like cat shit. I tried laying gravel all over the sand but the little bastards just rolled a few rocks around and shit anyway. Eventually I got out-voted and the kittens had to leave. I didn't show it, but I was pretty crushed. The guys rounded them up in a box and dumped them outside the camp. That very night I caught another rat in the tent.

Deployment rolled on without kittens or meaningful work. We all got frustrated, but I lost my shit and chewed into my LT. I had fucked up an airfield procedure, making myself look like a jackass. I was pissed off that I had to run the airfield instead of going after bad guys. The point was at least half valid, which is why my LT tolerated it. He listened to me bitch about our bullshit situation and I apologized when I was done. I was so worked up, I had to find a dark place to cry where no one would see me. One of the hardest things for soldiers of my ilk is not getting to do what you were born to do. My Yemen deployment was the shittiest and least effective deployment I've ever had. I did earn a new nickname though, Camp Nudist.

On the way back from Yemen, I finally got to spend a day out in Germany. I had flown through German airports a dozen times before, but never got to leave the terminal. This time I got to make the decompression stop you're supposed to get every time you leave a combat zone. All my other Middle East deployments had a lot more action, but because I was an augment I got lost in the shuffle. This time I was leaving with the guys I had served with. We were approved for a 24 hour vacation in Germany so we wouldn't snap and kill our wives when we got home. In the morning, we would have a quick sit down with the psychiatrist, then have the rest of the day to explore Germany on foot.

I sat down with the psych in the morning, and she asked some of the usual questions. Meagan and I were old hats at this, so I was just checking the box. I knew I couldn't help but imagine a storybook reunion that wasn't going to happen. The psych suggested I call Maegan and come up with a detailed plan of events for my first day home. It was a good idea, not that it would have changed anything. My plan would have been Maegan lighting up with joy at first sight of me, then jumping into my arms and wrapping her legs around me. When we reached the house, she would drag me into the bedroom, bend over, and say take me I'm yours. You can't plan emotions or enthusiasm. I let the psych do her thing, then explored Heidelberg during Oktoberfest. My short time with the Germans was very pleasant.

Chapter 18

The team had made arrangements for families to meet us at the boarding gate and to Maegan's credit she jumped through the hoops to be waiting with the kids when I got off the plane. The kiddos lit up with joy and gave me a group hug. Daughter number one started crying, and I held her tight trying to bury my face in her hair so no one would see me crying. She was getting older and she was starting to notice not having a father around. I know it sounds like I cry all the time, but I think I've documented every time I've cried as an adult in this story. Maegan stood there watching, seeing how not having a father around affected her daughter.

As expected, Maegan had not set aside any time or affection for her returning husband. She had plenty of things planned with her sister. I was used to it and just glad to be home, so I let it roll off my shoulder. We drove the 45 minutes north to see a movie with Amanda's family. I always liked seeing movies with the kids, and we were getting pizza beforehand. The place we went was an order at the counter kind of joint and very busy. We picked a table and sat down with the kids. Amanda and her husband got up to order our pizzas and I assumed Maegan and I would sit and watch the kids. Apparently, only I was going to sit and watch the kids. Maegan got up and waited in line with Amanda and her husband. It irked me a bit. The line was very long, and I started to stew. I sat there watching my kids and Amanda's, while my wife preferred to stand in line with her sister rather than sit with her husband who had been gone for seven months. My anger sounds childish or even feminine, but put yourself in that situation. I had been home for maybe a day or two. She had spent most of those seven months with Amanda and her husband. The three of them were standing in a very long line, chatting away, while her husband who had been gone for seven months sat by himself at the kiddie table.

Maegan had stopped even pretending she cared about me. I feel like a woman saying "you should have known I wanted flowers," but I was pretty pissed that her natural inclination wasn't to wait with her husband instead of her sister. I texted her *Are you really going to make me sit here by myself?* She walked over with that *what!?* Look on her face. I gave her some angry words and she got defensive and fell into her usual victim mode. It was a petty event and we enjoyed the rest of the evening. I didn't think any more of it at the time. She was just being inconsiderate. I'm an inconsiderate man and have been guilty of far worse, I'm sure. I usually don't expect or want any kind of consideration from people, but something felt wrong at the time.

The week continued and she was as cold as ever. Then it began. We were laying in bed and she asked, "Do you love me?" This was not an uncommon conversation for us. Maegan was always an insecure person and reassuring her had been a constant duty of mine as her husband. I told her I loved her all the time and she would still ask on a regular basis. Writing this down now makes me realize how absolutely stupid I am. Being asked *do you love me* for 15 years is a big fucking red flag. Most couples say I love you and I love you, too. Our conversation was, *do you love me?* and *of course I love you.* That's it. She rarely ever said *I love you, too in return.* I'm trying to picture her saying it in my head, and it seems out of place. I'm sure she gave an obligatory I love you when we finished phone conversations, but I can't picture her looking me in the eye and saying I love you. As we lay in bed, she said she felt like I only liked the idea of her and the kids. Like usual, she couldn't just be straightforward. I could read between the lines that night. She was telling me she liked the idea of being married to me. A Navy SEAL who would always protect and provide for her. She liked the idea, but was tired of the work it took to be my wife.

She said, "I feel like we are only together because of the kids." It hit me like a freight train: she didn't love me. I knew the moment she said it what she meant. She argues that she said, *I feel,* as if it makes any difference. Love is a feeling. Later, I asked if she did love me at the time, and she said no. She told me she hadn't loved me since before the deployment. I know now that she never loved me.

I left in the middle of the night and just started driving. When I finally stopped crying, I came home and crawled into bed with my little girls. A few days went by with us ignoring each other. I slept with my daughters every night, until one night I went to bed only to find my wife in bed with the girls. I had been sleeping alone for seven months and that bitch took my place with our little girls. No matter, boy number two wasn't too old to sleep with his old man yet.

Taking my spot next to the girls was not enough for her, so she decided to take the kids to Amanda's for the weekend. Not wanting to escalate things, I let her. Still, that was the last straw. I went to her that night and told her I was no longer going to be faithful to her. I had been living in a tent with a bunch of dudes for seven months and I needed a woman's affection. If she wasn't going to give it to me, I would get it somewhere else. I finished telling her my intentions and waited for a response from her. She had a chance to tell me not to, and at that point I still wanted her to. She never said a word to me and left with the kids the next day. That weekend was one of the darkest I have ever experienced. I don't think I have ever seriously considered suicide throughout this whole ordeal. I don't think I ever will. I was introduced to that little demon, though. The one that reminds you he can make it all go away. Having a top secret clearance and working for two police agencies means I've been asked about suicide a hundred times in a hundred different ways. I was always able to honestly answer no to those questions. Not sure if I could pass the polygraph now.

I sat in my empty house just crying. I didn't think I was the kind of person who could ever do that. Originally I was going to wait for a work trip to try my hand at dating for the first time ever, but I was unravelling fast. Single guys at work had always talked about one night stands with girls from dating apps so I figured I would give it a try. You need pictures for these things and I dug through my library. I have always hated posing for pictures so I don't have a lot of myself. Most pictures of me are from training trips and deployment, not the kind of pictures you share online. There were a handful of pictures of me with the kids but almost none of just me. You could delete 10 photos Maegan had taken and there wouldn't be any evidence I was part of my family. Most pictures of me were taken by my mother when we visited OR.

I managed to find a picture and used it. I got a bite and met a girl. She was an adorable half Puerto Rican, 26 year old from Florida. I didn't know how lucky I was to have that as my first experience. I don't think it was luck. She showed up just when she was needed and pulled me out of a bad place.

I have always been an honest man and I was ashamed at how easy it was for me to lie to her. I only had to lie a few times, but I did it. She made it easier by not asking those kinds of questions. We both knew we had a limited time together, so we weren't going to get too personal. I quickly realized I had never experienced a woman having a crush on me. She had worked as a bartender, so conversation came easy. It was nice to have a woman enjoy my company. The night went well, but I discovered I wasn't getting laid. She did want to see me again.

We texted back and forth and I made no effort to hide it from Maegan. She was up at Amanda's, but she could see all my texts with the magic of the internet. She could have texted the girl if she wanted to. I kind of wished she would. I still would have come running back to her if she'd asked me to. I went on a second date with the same girl and finally slept with her on the third. Remember, I was 31 years old sleeping with only my second girl ever. I knew every one of Maegan's buttons and could get her where she needed to go multiple times. To my disappointment, I realized the same tricks don't work on every woman. I gave what was probably a mediocre performance, but she blew my mind. This woman didn't love me; she barely knew me. She had passion, though, and it was directed at me. You have to understand, I had never experienced this before. Every woman I have been with since has been more of a participant than Maegan ever was. Maegan never withheld sex and would do whatever I asked her to do except want to have sex with me. I could feel that this was the first time I had slept with a woman who desired me.

We kept dating for a while. We were really enjoying our time together. The only time I had an appetite or could sleep was with her. I had orders to the east coast, so we both planned on it being a fling. I dropped down to 175 pounds. Not since high school had I been that light. My PT scores were dropping fast. With everything going on, I couldn't take the orders to the east coast. I told my command to withdraw my orders because I was in no shape to be leading a platoon. That meant I needed to tell my cute Puerto Rican. I sat down with her and told her everything. She took it well and was even about to continue with the date she thought I was picking her up for. I told her to think hard about what I had done. She reconsidered and went back inside. The next day she sent a text ending the relationship on good terms. She was the second woman I'd been with (you should have seen her face when she heard that tidbit), but I'll always think of her as my first. She was the first woman to share romantic affection with me, emotional and physical.

Despite getting a taste of Hollywood romance, I still would have stayed with Maegan. We had been in a relationship with one-sided love for 15 years. What's another 15 to get our youngest out into the world? Keep in mind, I still loved her. Some of you may roll your eyes at that, but it doesn't make it any less true. I could now talk to her without seven months of sexual frustration. I wanted to figure out how we were going to move forward. I approached her in a civil manner and explained I was willing to do what was needed to keep the family together. I made sure celibacy was not going to be one of her demands first. We tabled how we would solve that for the time being, and I focused on trying to figure out why she didn't love me anymore. She couldn't explain it to me. By her own admission, she couldn't figure it out for herself. She told me it was harder for her when I was home. She told me I was a burden. There are few words that can hurt a soldier more, especially when they haven't even been home two weeks. I snapped and yelled at her.

Maegan stormed out, taking our youngest with her. It was one of the two days a week the other kids went to school. After calming down, I walked out to the driveway. She rolled down the window and I told her to come straight home after picking up the kids; we were not finished with our discussion. She said the kids didn't get out for two more hours. I didn't ask where she was going. If she needed space, that was her right, but she wasn't going to take more time with my daughter from me. I opened the side door and unbuckled my youngest daughter. She lifted her arms to me like she always did. She knew I was hurting and hugged me tight. I told Maegan she would have to tell the children she was leaving me when she came back. I was not going to do what my father had to do all those years ago. She couldn't explain to me why she didn't love me and I wasn't going to try to explain something I didn't understand to my children. We were going to confront and deal with this now. I didn't want her skulking off to Amanda's where they could both shit on my character in front of my children to justify her tearing apart our family.

I played with my daughter for the next few hours. Some of my favorite memories are when Maegan left me home with the children. In most movies, the husband is an incompetent mess when his wife leaves him home with the kids. It's all part of that modern agenda to make men look like bumbling morons. In truth it's the opposite. When Maegan was gone, the kids knew whining would get them nothing. I would put on Heavy Metal music and chase them around the house with foam swords. This time we jumped on the trampoline and I listened to her squeal with joy as I bounced her higher and higher. She was having so much fun she had to run inside and get a drink of water. I kept jumping and I heard her yell, "Mommy's home!" I waited for the telltale clamor of three children coming home from school, but it did not come. I walked inside to find the house empty. I found the family I provided for my entire adult life outside in the driveway. Maegan was trying to get my youngest in the car with the other kids as fast as she could.

This is one of those moments I would usually say is too hard to put into words, but I have to try; you must understand, we all must understand. This is too common an evil and it ruins lives, even ends them as the male suicide rate shows. Men in general are better equipped to handle separation from their children. From the start, we had to leave our families behind to hunt prey. The most successful men were able to spend days in the field in order to provide for their family. Men like myself have to get used to spending more time apart from our families than with them. People like Maegan who have never been forced to leave their children have no fucking clue what that's like. They don't know what it's like to lay awake at night and cry for a child you can't hold. Like a child who hasn't burned her hand on a fire, she can't respect it.

Maegan thought because I could handle loneliness, I didn't care about my family. She decided it gave her the right to steal away with my children. For her entire adult life, I had taken care of her every material need; giving her the privilege of spending more time with our children than me. I was just the bank account that fed and sheltered them their whole life. Never mind all the times I got up in the middle of the night to the sound of a child calling Papa. Never mind the times my girls got so upset only I could get them to stop crying. Never mind all the things I taught my boys that she never could. She was jealous and angry. In her mind, that justified her taking children away from their father. Think of the most precious thing in your life, then imagine catching someone trying to steal that from you. Up to that point I have never felt so betrayed. If I had to pick a point where the train jumped the tracks, it was that moment.

I was furious, but I could see my children were already crying. She had taken the opportunity on the ride home to spin her narrative without me around to call her on her bullshit.

I remembered how my son had said, in front of my mother, "We don't like Papa, do we Mama?" I knew she was capable of telling the kids horrible things about me behind my back. I calmly opened the passenger door and sat down. With a level voice, I told them to come inside so their mother and I could explain to them what was happening. Maegan had obviously been explaining things the way she wanted, because the kids were terrified. Keep in mind, the last time I saw them they were happy and on their way to school. It was whatever Maegan had said that frightened them. Daughter two had just been laughing and playing with me, and was starting to figure out something was wrong. Maegan protested and panicked, but I talked the kids out of the car and into the house. We all walked of our own free will and sat in the living room. I sat in a chair farthest from the front door while Maegan stood right next to the front door with a clear path to leave whenever she wanted.

I gave her the opportunity to start, but of course she was too much of a coward. I had planned on a healthy way of breaking the news to the kids, but catching her in the act of stealing them was making that difficult. Now she didn't have the courage to tell them the real reason why. I started calm at first. Telling my children their mother didn't love me anymore tore apart my soul and I got mean; not too bad at first, but when she tried to defend herself, I called her on her bullshit and exposed her for what she is. I admit I shouldn't have been so brutal in front of the children. I wasn't cursing or insulting her, but she was looking like a terrible person the more she said. I can't remember everything, but at one point she was carrying on about how much of a burden the children and I were. I made sure the children understood that she considered them a burden; not something a child should hear, but I'm only taking 30% of the blame on that one. She's the one who said it.

At one point, daughter one cried that she just wanted things to go back to how they were. I told her I wanted the same thing and I was more than willing to try and fix it, but her mother was putting her own happiness in front of her children. I'll take 60% of the blame for that one; it was the truth, but the kids didn't need to hear it at their age. At that point I still would have come back to Maegan if she'd asked me to. It was in her power to make things go back, to give her crying child what she wanted most in the world. I don't know how she could hear that from our daughter and not sacrifice everything for her. She still couldn't explain why she was leaving me. I made more than enough money, I didn't drink, I didn't gamble, I showered her with affection, I told her she was beautiful every day, I never laid a harmful finger on her, I watched the kids so she could have ladies nights and I was always faithful. She tried to take the pressure off herself and suggested we talk about what I had been up too the last week with all the spite of a woman scorned. I looked her straight in the eye and told her to go for it. I had only just recently explained the birds and bees to our son, so good luck trying to explain I had been sleeping with another woman the last week. More importantly, she could see in my eyes I didn't feel the slightest bit of guilt. She had ripped my heart out after deployment and we had already separated when I started sleeping with another woman. She knew she had no ground to stand on so she started looking for the low blows.

She said if I didn't let them leave, she was calling the cops. I had protected this woman her entire adult life. I even stopped her from beating her own sister and prevented the cops from being called on her. Now she was threatening to call the cops on me like I was the monster. I made it absolutely clear she could leave whenever she wanted. She had been standing next to the door the entire time, and I was sitting in a chair across the room crying. I told her to leave, but she wouldn't. I knew it was heading in a bad direction, but I didn't want to risk being alone in the house after she had taken my children from me. If she tried to take the kids, I knew I could stop her physically without anyone getting hurt, but I would still be arrested when the cops showed up. Things were spiraling out of hand quickly, and I did what any good soldier does. I made a bad move now instead of a good move when it was too late.

I walked to the back room and grabbed an unloaded pistol. I walked to the front door and said, "See what happens when the cops try and take my children from me." Doubtless, a lot of you are saying *holy fuck* right now. I was thinking of that little demon who could make everything go away and I didn't want to talk to him after she left with the children. I knew if she left with the kids, she would not bring them back. I knew she would take them to a dangerous home owned by someone she had violently beaten in front of the children before. I was remembering the children screaming as I tried to separate Maegan and Amanda. People do not realize how many crimes and criminals are stopped by simply displaying a gun. I had moments before she would grab the kids and start walking out the door. In those short moments, I decided a show of force was better than exposing the kids to me physically stopping her from taking the kids from their home.

Most of you have lived sheltered lives safe in your homes while men like me try to keep the darkness as far away from your beds as possible. Understand that I've shown up at houses in the middle of the night and woken women and children up with a loaded rifle in my hands. I've stood watching them with threat while they are searched for intel their terrorist fathers hid on them. So before you gasp in horror at what I did, have a little perspective. At no point have my wife or children ever been in danger. I stood there for a maximum of ten seconds with a piece of metal (pointed at the ground) that was as dangerous as a rock in its unloaded condition. I'll never forget what boy number two cried. It wasn't, *Papa stop* or, *you're scaring me*. He cried to his mother.

"Don't take Papa away from us, we just got him back."

Even in his youthful innocence, he could see what was really happening. I'm not saying it was the best decision, but it did work for the short term. It would have been nothing but a bad memory, just like when she physically abused her sister. I walked back to my room and put the gun away. Maegan had ample time to leave, but when I came out, everyone was still there and calming down. I had showed her my resolve, and she backed down from getting the cops involved. We hugged the kids, told them it would be ok, and had them play in their rooms while we talked. When the kids couldn't see, I did something I am not proud of. I begged. I got on my knees and begged Maegan not to take the children from me. I was scared of the little demon and it takes a lot to scare me.

While all this was going on, her sister had been calling. Meagan repeatedly declined the call, so her sister took it on herself to call the cops. I suppose I shouldn't blame her, she had firsthand experience with one of us losing control and getting violent. The cops showed up in force. They had been told what I did for a living. Maegan and I walked out of the house and talked to the police separately; standard procedure. I told them everything was ok and we were going through a divorce. At that point she could have had me hauled off to jail and taken the kids. She knew that would affect her income, so she told them everything was ok. One of the cops asked what team I was at and started shooting the shit with me. Maegan finished talking with the cops and went back inside.

We watched cartoons with the kids and went to bed. In the morning, I went to work. When I came home the house was empty. Meagan would not answer her phone. She had told me boy two had an appointment, but that didn't explain why she wasn't answering her phone. I called the school and asked about my children. Surprisingly, the lady said she had just seen my wife and would have someone check on my kids. A few minutes later she said she had made a mistake and there was actually no school that day. That didn't seem like an honest mistake to me. While I was at work, earning the money to feed and shelter two adults, four kids and two cats, she had the privilege of sneaking off with my children. She had told me the night before she wouldn't take off with the children, and because I'm a man of my word, I believed her.

Chapter 19

Maegan finally called and said I couldn't see the kids, and she wanted to meet with me alone in a public place like I was some kind of threat, like I was someone who would beat their sister bloody. I reminded her which one of us had physically assaulted someone in front of the children and told her she needed to bring the children home first. She continued to play the victim and would not bring them home. She had always had complete control over our finances, and I was starting to realize she was not someone who could be trusted. I opened a new account and shifted all my money into it. I called her back and told her I emptied the account. Of course she changed her mind after that. She brought the kids down the next day, and we let them play inside while we drove to the nearby Denny's to talk. I told her I would stay at my grandma's and she could have whatever money she needed, but the kids were going to live in their home. I told her to open an account and I would put money into it. For the time being, she could use her credit card and I would pay it off. We were hammering out the logistics in a civil manner when the police called Maegan. Someone had called the police and said we were at our house and I had a gun pointed at Maegan. The cops knew it was a bullshit call and were giving us a heads up. I don't know who made that call. Maegan told the police we would meet them at the house and we stood in the driveway when they pulled up. They split us up again and we both assured them we would be ok.

I packed a bag and moved into a spare room at my grandma's about fifteen minutes away. Over the next few days, Maegan and I talked about how we would move forward with all the logistics of divorce. I told her I would pay for her to move into an apartment in the area. I did not want her moving in with her sister. Her husband drank and slept around. He wasn't a danger to the kids, but he did frighten them occasionally when he was drunk. He also had no problem bringing around the women he slept, with and I figured that would eventually blow up. All through deployment, Maegan told me how they fought all the time, and knowing how violent Maegan could get with Amanda, I did not want my children in that environment. She agreed, and I started looking at cheap studio apartments for myself.

I still wasn't eating or sleeping, the only time I could sleep or keep my crying in check was when I was with my half Puerto Rican. Maegan wanted me to give specific times when I would meet with the kids; as if she had some busy schedule to keep. Really, she was trying to make it difficult for me to see my girlfriend and the kids. She wanted to justify what she was planning by telling herself I was spending time with my girlfriend instead of my children. Conveniently, she would suggest I spend Friday night with the kids while she went to Amanda's. She felt she had the right to budget my time with the kids and if I didn't take every opportunity she gave me, then I was a bad father. It's important to note she would come up with the idea of me spending the night with the kids, and then leave them with me. She would later testify under oath that she was too afraid to leave the kids with me. When Maegan came back from Amanda's, she suggested I just stay at the house. I cannot stress enough that it was her idea I move back in. She knew I was never a threat to anyone and wanted me back at the house instead of staying the night with another woman. She wanted to tell herself she was giving me a chance to spend time with the kids, but I was off with some woman. It was never her place to give me time with my own children.

I stayed in the house I paid for with my children. A few days passed with us living together civilly. My LPO suggested I go up to Oregon for a week. I hadn't seen my parents and siblings since I got home from deployment, so I asked if Maegan would go with me.

She said I would just shit on her in front of my family and I tried to assure her I wouldn't. I figured it would be good for the kids to see their cousins and grandparents and we could tell everyone in person we were getting divorced. She wouldn't go, so I had to go by myself. I asked her how much money she needed for the week and she said $500. I wrote her a check for $1000. As I handed her the check, I asked if that was all I was to her.

She answered, "Then why do you want to be with me?" The tone was the one used to say "Duh."

Words cannot describe how hurtful it is to hear that from the woman you cared for since you were 15. I handed her the check and told her my life insurance policy was in her name. I threw all my best tactical gear in my car, and when I walked out the door, I was headed to Mexico to start killing drug lords until someone killed me. That little demon was going to have to work for it.

By the time I got to the highway, I decided I needed to go to Oregon first to get my best guns. By the time I got to Oregon, I had started to change my mind. I had thought seeing family would be good for me, but it wasn't. I couldn't be around them without my wife and children, they were part of me. I was a soldier, husband and father. I spent the week avoiding my family and chasing tail; the only thing that made me forget. I had never drank or done drugs, so it was the only vice I could lean on. It was still a very new experience. At one point, all my family were inside my mother's house having dinner, and I sat outside in my car trying to work up the courage to go inside. Eventually my brother came out and found me. It was so hard to be in the house while my siblings sat with their spouses and watched their children play. I was only feeling worse and decided I needed to go back to San Diego to spend Halloween with my kids. My old man helped me change a spark plug wire on the car before I headed down. He knew what I was going through and knew it was only going to get worse. He didn't know how much worse. My mom was a good woman. She never tried to keep my dad from his kids.

On the way down, I decided I was going to trade in our new minivan for a truck. I had always wanted a truck, and now that I was a single man, I would get one. The car I drove was the first car we bought together, a Dodge Journey. It was paid off, had a lifetime bumper to bumper warranty, fit all the kids and got great gas mileage. A perfect car for a single mother. I would still have to make payments on our brand new minivan, so I was going to be the one to keep it. Seemed fair to me.

When I reached L.A., Maegan sent me a long text. She had moved out, taken all our shit, and moved in with her sister. I say everything went downhill when Maegan tried to sneak off with the kids and that is true. I think for Maegan it was when I slept with another woman, though she won't admit it. I had come home from deployment to find my wife, the only person I had ever slept with, did not love me anymore. When I told her if she was not going to love me anymore I would try and find another woman, I did not know how easy it was going to be. I was under the impression I was an undesirable man. Come to find out, some women think I'm a catch. I hooked up with a girl and that's what really pissed Maegan off. All you women out there know its true deep down. It definitely played into her wanting to take the kids to stay at Amanda's. I can't say that being with younger, more enthusiastic women didn't fulfill a juvenile need to hurt her as bad as she'd hurt me. The difference is I was up front with her about it. I only used my own affection and other consenting adults. In response, she weaponized the children. While I was in Oregon, I was getting girls' numbers on a daily basis and Maegan could see them being saved to our contacts list. I have no doubt this heavily influenced her to empty out the house and move in with Amanda.

Where were the kids going to school now? When would I get to see them? All I knew was Maegan did the one thing I asked her not to, and moved in with her sister. I needed questions answered and I told her we needed to meet. She suggested a Starbucks near her sister's place. It was the day before Halloween, and I wanted to see the kids. I always seemed to be on a trip for Halloween, so I told her to bring them and we would switch cars, mine was full of gear.

We met at the Starbucks and I hugged all the kids. They were happy to see me. They never saw me as the monster she was trying to make me out to be. We walked to an outside table and I asked Maegan to explain. She said she didn't want to do it in front of the kids. I suggested we go back to the cars and let the kids play inside while we talked outside. This detail is important. We went to the cars so the kids wouldn't hear. I laid into her for moving in with Amanda. She was moving the kids into a rundown two bedroom home with 6 children, a dog and three adults, sometimes four when one of Amanda's friends who was also going through a divorce slept there. I called her a terrible mother and things I have never said to her before, but the kids were none the wiser as they played in the car with the windows up. She informed me they would not live in Amanda's place for long and they had already picked out a place to move into. I wanted to know how much that was going to cost me. She said $600, but she must've of thought it up on the spot. There is no way the house she got only cost $600 on her end.

At that point, there was nothing I could do but take it. I told her I wanted the kids that night and for Halloween. She said I could have them for Halloween, but I couldn't have them that night. I was sick of being told when I could see my own children and told her I was done dealing with her. I opened the driver side door to the minivan and got in with the children. At this point, they were all fine, watching cartoons on old phones. Maegan opened the side door in a panic and told them all to get out of the car. Of course they got scared and confused. I told them to stay in the car, we were leaving. Maegan jumped in the van. I told her if she wanted to come it was fine. I started to crawl slowly along with the van and Maegan grabbed the keys. They were the kind that did not need to be in the ignition. I grabbed her wrist and snatched the keys back. I started to drive off and Maegan started screaming for the children to jump out of a moving vehicle.

My son looked at me with confusion and fear. I tried to calm him down, but his mother was screaming and he opened the door. I stopped the car and Maegan grabbed all the other children out of their seats and started running across the parking lot. I pulled alongside them and yelled at Maegan to stop, she needed the keys to the Dodge so she could go back to Amanda's. Maegan stopped, reached inside the passenger side window and I handed her the keys.

I drove straight from the Starbucks and traded in the minivan for a truck. I sent her a text to make sure she got back to Amanda's safely. When I finished, I texted her that I needed all the stuff in the back of the Dodge. She told me it would be waiting where I left it. She wanted me to leave the van with the keys in it. She specifically said she did not want to see me. I told her she wouldn't and drove back to the Starbucks parking lot. I loaded the truck up and drove home, leaving the Dodge for her. I texted her that I traded in the minivan and the Dodge was now hers. The message was marked as read shortly after I sent it.

She texted me that she made a report to the police. I called the Sheriff's department to give them a statement. The Sheriff's department seemed confused as to why I was calling. I explained that I wanted my side of the story on record. They had clearly never planned on trying to get my side of the story. When I was finished, the deputy confirmed that Maegan had not wanted to press charges, and since I didn't either, it was up to a prosecutor if they wanted to do something about it. The implication was that such a small incident was not going to warrant the attention of a busy SoCal Sheriff's department. Later I would read the official report of the officer who took Maegan's statement. He had offered to help her get a temporary restraining order against me and she had declined. Why are officers suggesting one party get a restraining order that will strip the other party of rights before hearing the other party's side of the story or doing any kind of investigation? This was right after I left her at the Starbucks, so she would have been at her most emotional and fearful state, if she ever was truly afraid of me. Still she did not think she needed a restraining order against me. This was, of course, before I texted her that I had traded in the minivan.

When I got home, my house was empty. She left me maybe 10% of our belongings; mostly junk we wanted to get rid of or items too big to haul. Big screen TV, Xbox One, PlayStation 4, VR headset, all gone. The only thing of value she left was the computer and our king size mattress that was a pain in the ass to move.

Once again, I sat alone in my house with the little demon. The emptiness made his voice echo. Maegan had left the cats and they came in when they heard me crying. I cried more in the last few months of 2018 than I did my entire life. I messaged her the next morning to ask if she was bringing the kids down or if I was going to get them. She didn't reply, so I told her I was going to call the cops. She still wasn't answering, so I asked for a health and welfare check from the Sheriff's department. They never got back to me on that. She eventually replied with some vague answer implying she was too busy to talk.

The Sheriff's department said there was nothing they could do because no order was in place. I went down to the court house to see what order I could get that would allow a father to see his children. There are none. I had waited around for someone tell me nothing could be done. While I had the attention of a facilitator, I figured I'd have him walk me through how the divorce was going to work. He looked in his computer and discovered Maegan had filed for divorce. If you're not familiar with the process, she still needed to have me served with papers to make it official. He showed me the paperwork she filed and said it was fucked up and she would probably have to re-submit it. He walked me through the various ways the divorce could go down. Divorces can actually be very cheap if both parties treat each other like human beings instead of an ATM machine. Of course, the lawyers don't get fat that way.

I texted her saying she would probably need to redo her paperwork, and we needed to meet and try to button the whole thing up as cheap as possible. Why pay lawyers money that could be going to our children? She wouldn't respond, so I told her I was coming up to Amanda's for the kids. When she was trying to take the kids from me, there was nothing I could do to stop her without looking like the bad guy. Try and imagine being a father and having your children taken away from you, knowing that anything you do to stop it will get you arrested. When I tried to take the children from her, she opened the door to a moving vehicle and screamed at her children to jump out, yet I'm still the bad guy. I did not want her turning another incident into a physical altercation, so I called the Sheriff's department for an escort onto Amanda's property.

I waited for the officer in a parking lot a few blocks from Amanda's house. Dispatch said an officer was en route, but he took his sweet time coming. I know from experience cops can be very busy, but I also know cops can be very lazy. Based on the dispatchers tone and verbiage, I was guessing the officer on his way was the latter. My assumption gained merit when a patrol car finally showed up and Deputy Mark Cahill SH5858 slid his tubby ass out of the driver's seat. Just Google San Diego Sheriff's Deputy Mark Cahill. The first impression you get when you see his picture is spot on.

I explained to Cahill what was going on, and explained that I was going to try and leave with my kids. I made sure to receive confirmation in no uncertain terms that I was allowed to leave with the kids. Deputy Cahill said since there was no order in place, either of us could take the kids. I asked what would happen if she tried to physically stop me. Cahill's answer confirmed I was dealing with one of those cops on a power trip who was bullied as a kid. He said he'd have to pull his Taser and release his dog and nobody wanted that. Picture a man in a dick measuring contest, and you'll be in the ballpark of his demeanor. Despite his answer being worthless, I had confirmed I was allowed to take the kids, and made it clear that I was not going to get physical, but expected her to.

When we showed up, a moving van was parked in the driveway and the kids were nowhere in sight. I stayed near my truck while the deputy went to talk to Amanda. Cahill came back too fast to have asked any questions. He had done the bare minimum of what was required of his position and wanted to wipe his hands clean of it. He told me the kids weren't at the house in a *now fuck off* manner. I was a father who didn't know where his children were and when I would get to see them again.

I asked him, "How do I know my kids are safe?"

Cahill replied, "Oh grow up!"

There are few times I've wanted to lay someone out more. This fat piece of shit is the reason people hate cops. I thanked him for nothing and left feeling the horror I felt the day my oldest boy went missing in the woods. I didn't know where my children were. Maegan was in the process of moving to a house I didn't know the location of, and the law would do nothing to help me see the sons and daughters I had protected for a decade. If Maegan ever reads this, and I know she is too cowardly to ever attempt it, I want her to remember the day our oldest boy was lost in the woods. I want her to remember the heart strangling terror and realize that's what she put me through. That is what she's putting me through.

I parked my truck and came as close as I come to panicking while I tried to figure out what to do. Maegan wouldn't answer her phone, but the kids are always playing with our old phones. As much as I fought to keep our kids unglued from computer screens I was happy that Maegan never put in so much effort. I knew if I wasn't there to make them go outside and play, then they would be watching some blue-haired nerd play Minecraft on YouTube. I booted up the find my iPhone app. An app Maegan and I had both used to find our phones in the couch cushions. Of course there were multiple phones to choose from. All of them were named Maegan's iPhone. We always used her name on electronics because of my job.

The phone's location was at the courthouse. I figured she was fixing the divorce paperwork. The courthouse was a good place to confront her and ask the kids to come with me. If she escalated like the last time, there would be plenty of witnesses. I got to the courthouse and went through security. The place was a ghost town. The guards said everyone had left for the day. I searched what the public had access to, and couldn't find my kids. I waited in the parking lot, hoping to see them in a public place when they walked out.

The app eventually updated and showed they had already left. They stopped at a CVS pharmacy and I figured it was my last chance; if she made it to Amanda's house then they would be on private property. I pulled up as they were loading the back of their car with Halloween supplies. I parked far enough back to make sure no one could say I was blocking her car in. I stepped out of the truck, walked up to them, and knelt down with my arms wide open. The kids came running and I wrapped them all in a bear hug. Amanda, Maegan and some guy I vaguely recognized started to surround me as I hugged the kids. The guy, we'll call him Fred, got on the phone and held out some paperwork I assumed to be the divorce paperwork.

I asked the kids if they wanted to see my new truck, and of course they were all overjoyed. I stood up with my youngest daughter and walked over to my truck. I opened the driver side door so my daughter could play with the steering wheel. Amanda jumped in-between myself and the truck, pushing the door shut. This woman I had loaned money, allowed to live in my house on multiple occasions, fed and protected when my wife assaulted her, was physically stopping me from spending time with my own children. I used one hand to shove her aside. Because I was restraining myself, she bounced right back, preventing me from opening the door. Rather than risk hurting her, I went to the back passenger door.

I got inside the door, but both Amanda and Maegan were on me now. The door was slamming on me and my daughter. I managed to climb into the back seat and tried to put my daughter in her car seat. Amanda jumped into my driver's seat and started digging for the keys. Neither she nor I realized my brand new truck was a push button start. I thought she was about to take the keys to my new truck. She was hunched over and I needed to try and get to her hands without hurting her.

In that split second, I remembered my legal training on strangulation and the severity of that crime. I used a wrestling technique since chokes are illegal in that sport. I cupped her about the chin and jaw which ensured the airway and carotid artery stayed clear. I pulled her back so I could see her hands. She started to fight me, so I switched to posting technique with my hand on the back of her neck shoving her towards the center console, similar to the way you might keep a dog from jumping up on the couch. I used my free arm to control her arms until I saw she didn't have the keys. I let her go, the physical altercation being no more than 10 seconds at this point.

I turned to get out, and my wife was shoving me back into the truck and hitting me in the chest. She wasn't really trying to hurt me, it was more petulance. I gave her a hard shove to get her away from me. It wasn't enough to knock her over, but it was probably the most violent thing I've ever done to a woman; there was definitely hate in it, but it was restrained by my upbringing. My shirt had been ripped to tatters somehow. Fred had stayed on the phone with the police the entire time. Now, from what I remember, he was about the same size as me and a Marine; the kind of guy who would probably act if a friend of his was being hurt. He judged it wasn't necessary to get involved physically.

After the short spat, we commenced yelling at each other in the parking lot. My anger was directed at my wife, but of course Amanda butted in and it became mostly her and I going back and forth. I confirmed with Fred the police were on the way. I didn't want anyone doing something drastic, so I said I was going to park my truck and we should all wait for the police to arrive. I had made sure no one got hurt, so I was hoping we could all give statements and I could ask the kids if they wanted to go with me. Amanda had a little blood on her ear. I'm guessing it was from her own nails trying to claw my hand from her collar.

The deputy who showed up was none other than Deputy Cahill. We were all calmly standing there by the time he arrived. Cahill did what most out of shape, insecure cops do, and started being a dick. His disdain was directed at the entire group at first, but he quickly zeroed in on me. To be fair, I had gone to the barber nearest my house to get my deployment locks cut off. I ended up leaving with a vato cut that looked more Neo Nazi on a white guy like me. Add to that my tattooed shirtless body, and I can understand why I concerned Cahill. He made us all sit down and Amanda switched on her victim mode. Moments earlier, she was all hate and spite for me, but she turned on the water works as soon as the cops arrived.

Cahill went on about how he was the big dick now, and ended his monolog by saying he would kick my ass. Specifically, my ass. Keep in mind he hadn't asked a single question yet. Cahill was directing his spite at me, and it seemed like he was trying to get me to fight. I was sitting on the ground like everyone else, doing exactly as I was told. He kept antagonizing me. I shook my head and smirked, to say, *I'm not giving you an excuse to shoot me.* He didn't like that and kept laying into me. At one point he said "We can go five rounds right now!" Of course it wasn't a genuine offer, or else I would have taken him up on it.

Eventually Cahill got mad because I was sitting there and complying with all his commands while shrugging off his challenges to fight him. He made me stand up and put me in cuffs. Cahill heard sirens from other officers en route and slapped me in the stomach.

"That's for you!" he said with relish. Back up arrived, and he handed me off to another deputy. Apparently, he wasn't going to take this one. "That's your victim over there," he said, pointing out Amanda to the other deputies. None of us had said a single word yet and no officer had asked a single question, but this guy had already concluded his investigation and told all the other deputies his conclusion.

In the police report, Cahill says he put me in cuffs because I was not being compliant with his commands and the others said I was the primary aggressor. I don't know how that's possible, because he put me in cuffs before asking a single question. I also had complied with every one of his commands. He put me in cuffs because I couldn't help but laugh when his tubby ass challenged me to five rounds. I sat in the back of the patrol car while the scene wrapped up. I watched my kids walk back and forth, not knowing that was the last time I would be seeing them. A Deputy served me the restraining order Meagan had just gotten. *So Maegan hadn't been fixing the divorce paperwork, she had been getting back at me for trading in the car.* The Deputies booked me into jail and we shot the shit a little bit about me having been a cop. When the corrections officer put me in the holding cell, he gave me a friendly warning.

"You know what you and those two deputies were talking about?"

"Yes," I replied.

"Don't talk about it in here."

I got the point and found a spot in the cell. Later, a corrections officer pulled me out of the cell and asked if I was going to bail out. He looked very worried. As I explained earlier cops get credit for arrests whether they lead to convictions or not. All that shows up on the evaluation is the quantity and severity of the crimes. This gives cops incentive to stack on as many severe charges they can make an excuse for. My arresting officer stacked on child endangerment charges for all six children present plus an assault on Amanda. There were some mistakes and changing of how the charges were written, so I wasn't sure of which ones were felonies at that point. It would change several times after that. What mattered at that point was that my bail was $140,000. I still had a family to provide for and couldn't afford that. I would wait to go to court. Obviously someone with a clean record and four good conduct awards from the military and who never actually hurt anyone would be released, right?

The corrections officer really wanted me to bail out. I was a former cop with 6 charges of child endangerment. Your average inmate doesn't understand the wording of the law and when he hears child endangerment he interprets it as *this pig is a pedophile*, and we all know what happens to pedo's in jail. He told me to keep to myself while I was there. I spent the night sharing a cell with a very polite perpetual offender who was certain he would be released. When the check-in lady asked if he had been incarcerated before he answered, "More than I can remember." If this guy was getting out, then I would be fine.

My court day came and I got exposed to the sham of our criminal justice system. I moved to a holding cell to wait for my moment with the public defender. A pleasant mentally deranged man decided to make me his friend, and we had some polite conversation. Apparently his dad was sleeping with his wife. I got herded into a closet size room with 3 chairs and about seven other dudes. On the other side of a cage were three public defenders with stacks of case files. They would call out a name and each guy would sit down for a conversation that lasted less than a minute, no privacy whatsoever. I got my moment and tried to give the public defender something she could use. I had to slip her a note telling her I had been a police officer so the others wouldn't see. I thought even a shitty lawyer would be able to get someone with a record like mine released on their own recognizance.

I finally got shuffled into the courtroom with my mentally ill friend. His case was heard first. His fancy lawyer got up and did his damnedest. My friend was so convinced his wife was sleeping with his father, he broke down his bedroom door with a dumbbell. He had a history of such violent episodes, but his father loved him so he had shown up in the courtroom to ask the judge to release him. The judge agreed with the fancy lawyer and released my violent, mentally deranged friend with a criminal history. Obviously, my public defender couldn't fuck this up.

She got up and said I had been in the Navy and gotten some medals so I should be released. The prosecution then got up and made it sound as if the restraining order had been served before I went to get my kids and that I had knowingly violated it. He didn't bother to point out that the restraining order was served to me for the first time while I was handcuffed in the back of a patrol car. I wasn't given a chance to explain and my public defender elected to pass on her counter argument. The judge decided I was a threat to the society I had sacrificed for my entire adult life. I would stay in jail and my bail would not be reduced. I spent another few days in jail and my cell mate explained to me how bail works. I may sound stupid, but I didn't realize I only had to pay 10% of it, and because I was in the military, it would be a little less. Yeah, at least we give our service members a military discount when we fuck them. I wasn't going to defend myself in jail, so I bailed out. Police officers are all exposed to OC spray, tear gas and shot with a Taser while in the academy. The idea is if you're going to use these tools on the people you protect and serve, then you should have a personal understanding of how they feel. After my experience, I think every cop should spend a night or two in jail.

Chapter 20

I knew I was going to need a real lawyer. I did some research and settled on a firm ran by Eric Friis. I'm ashamed of how stupid I was, but I still believed the case would be dismissed if a competent lawyer gave it a little effort. All that had happened was some grabbing and shoving. Everybody was fine, and the whole thing had lasted a matter of seconds.

I met with a fella named Sam and he was a good salesman. The outfit looked legit and it wasn't ridiculously expensive. I was still thinking of providing for five mouths. I left feeling like I was in good hands. I moved out of our house and got a studio apartment. The team was very supportive, but I was useless to them. Because my wife was able to get a restraining order without me ever having a chance to defend myself, I couldn't carry a gun. Not a lot of training a SEAL can do without a gun. They moved me to a training department and let me handle my shit for the most part. They were waiting for everything to pan out in the civilian courts before they decided what they were going to do. Big Navy always wants to make an example. Double jeopardy is definitely a thing for military personnel.

The courts are a ponderous machine, so nothing would be happening soon. While I waited on the criminal justice system I was introduced to the industry that thrives off tearing families apart, Family Court. My introduction would be made by her lawyer who apparently I would be paying for, a portly little man named Robert Daniels. If you look up sleazy lawyer in the dictionary, you will find a picture of this guy. I still needed to pay all the bills, plus bail and my criminal lawyer, so I could not afford my own divorce lawyer. I would have to handle the family court side of it myself. Mr. Daniels said Maegan needed money, so I set up a Venmo account. I told him to tell me what she needed and what for and I would send her the money. He wanted me to just send her over half my paycheck every month and I told him I wasn't going to do that. She needed to send me a list of her expenses and I would pay for it. He made her sound desperate, like she was about to be thrown on the streets. She wasn't desperate enough to just tell me what she needed me to pay for. No orders were in place yet, and our hearing in family court wouldn't be for a few months, so I still had some rights to the money I earned.

This is the time period I decided to write this book. I was living in a studio apartment trying not to cry every time I saw a small child on the street, only to make it home and fall apart. In the beginning, it was a kind of therapy.

I sent her what money I could spare and told the people renting our house to send the rent payment to Maegan. I would make sure the mortgage got paid and she could use the checks for whatever she wanted. She was living with Amanda, so I knew they were fine financially. It was about time they started paying back all the free childcare Maegan gave them. Her lawyer also informed me she had traded in the Dodge for some gas guzzling SUV, so she wasn't struggling. I made it clear several times that all she had to do was ask for a specific amount for a specific purchase and I would pay for it. I tried to be civil with her lawyer at first, but try being civil with the next mosquito that sucks your blood.

My mother made plans to come down and see the kids, and at first Maegan agreed. She even said at one point my mom could act as supervisor for visits with me. She wasn't happy with the money she was getting, so she told my mother she was not going to be able to see the kids. My mom had already made hotel reservations. She told my mom it was because I wasn't cooperating with her lawyer. She wanted me to pay what her lawyer demanded for a couple months before she would let me or any of my family see the kids. Her lawyer explained that holding the kids hostage for money would not look good in court, so she changed her tune but not her decision.

My mother had given us a place to live when I was between police jobs. We would stay with her when we visited for the holidays because neither of us could stand staying with Maegan's parents. My mom had made Maegan's wedding dress. None of that matters to a person with no loyalty. Maegan was angry and taking it out on a woman who had showed her nothing but kindness. My mom tried to reason with her, but Maegan eventually cut her off completely. She asked Meagan if she wanted me prosecuted and she said no. My mom heard Amanda yell in the background that she did not press charges, either. I don't know if she was lying to my mom or Maegan, but the police report clearly stated that Amanda wanted charges pressed. My mom said if they did not want charges pressed, then to call the prosecutor and tell her that. Here is the prosecutor's account of what Amanda and Maegan told her. First, Maegan.

I called Maegan Swift to let her know we confirmed the PE date of 1/14/2019. Ms. Swift said her mother in law had called her and asked her to not file charges. Ms. Swift said her mother in law wants to know financial information. Ms. Swift told defendant's mother she did not file charges in this case, and directed the financial questions to her family law attorney.

Here is Amanda's version.

I called victim Amanda Pacheco to let her know the prelim date of 1/14/2019 confirmed, and we will be sending her a subpoena. She is nervous, because defendant's mother keeps calling Maegan Swift and telling her to call us and say they lied and made everything up. I asked Ms. Pacheco if they lied, she said no. I let her know we would be sending her a subpoena, and verified the above address.

I can't say how the conversation went between my mother and Maegan. This is also Ms. Layon's summary and not direct quotes. You can see how Amanda claims my mom told them to lie and say they made everything up. My mother would never ask anyone to lie. Maegan's statement closer reflects my mom asking her to make sure the prosecutor knows

she doesn't want charges pressed. Amanda, on the other hand fabricates a story that vili-
fies the people she doesn't like. You are going to start to notice a theme.

The next couple of months were the closest thing to purgatory. I started listening to a
lot of Five Finger Death Punch. I was always on the fence with that band, but when you've
had your heart torn out by a heartless bitch, it's kind of the soundtrack to your life. Songs
like "Wicked Ways," "Meet the Monster," and "War is the Answer" suddenly become more
relevant along with old Metallica classics like "Shortest Straw" and "Disposable Heroes."

I would go to court dates and nothing would happen. Usually, I just got more bad
news. I tried to keep myself distracted by working out and meeting women. I considered
now might be the time to start drinking, but decided against it. Spending time with a
woman was the one thing that kept my mind off my situation. I had absolutely no experience with it. Maegan had never really shown attraction to me. Women hardly acknowledged I was there when I went out with the guys. A stripper approached me on rare occasions to make money, but I would explain I was happily married and just out with the guys. I
figured I had an uphill battle with the ladies. Maegan never really even complimented me.
The closest thing was when she would say, "Everything is easy for you," implying I didn't really have to work at anything. I still took it as a compliment to my ability. It made me feel
good. I don't really like the awkwardness that accompanies a genuine compliment so I never really noticed that she never gave them to me. It came as a shock to receive them from
women I wasn't related to.

I was pleasantly surprised by my ability to talk to women. I was no player or Casano-
va, but I did fairly well. By the age of 31, I had seen more than most men will in a lifetime,
and that confidence comes through. Of course, I was in the Mecca of entitled self-centered
women that is southern California. It wasn't all success, and I made my share of missteps.

I was upfront at first, but after being with a few women I would never see again, I decided I didn't have to share all my personal baggage up front.

When I couldn't occupy my evening with a woman, I would usually cry myself to sleep. The job I had spent my whole life striving for was on hold and in jeopardy. I couldn't see or talk to the children I had protected and cared for when they were most vulnerable. I was beginning to realize the woman I had loved since the age of fifteen had never loved me, and despite being innocent until proven guilty, I was being treated like a child and spouse abuser. I have to admit, I got a childish satisfaction when the few women I explained my situation to said my ex was the dumbest woman on earth for giving me up and I should have actually strangled Amanda. Maybe the women were just telling me what I wanted to hear, but I've had a minister tell me he would have legit strangled her.

I felt my share of anger toward Maegan, but the thing that stands out the most is the absence of fear. When you have a planet separating you from the ones you love, there is a fear in the back of your head that something might happen to them. It's constant, but you learn to keep it tucked away when you have a job to do. The fear finds its way to the surface when you lay down in your rack. It keeps you company as you try to fall asleep. There were five people I worried about most when I was alone. Now there was only four. There is a tangible emptiness where someone you worried about used to be. Once the fear of losing someone shook your very soul, and then one day it's gone.

After going to a few court dates, I started to realize my lawyer sucked. He was a nice guy named Eric Orloff. Eric Friis decided to hand my case off to a lawyer who contracted for him. After our first court date, it became apparent that the prosecutor, Marnie M. Layon was on a crusade. All the charges had been dropped to misdemeanors but one. This isn't because my lawyer did anything or that Ms. Layon wanted to take it easy on me. She wanted a felony and it was the only charge she could exaggerate enough to have a chance with.

Amanda lied and said I strangled her. The charge of strangulation against Amanda was what they call a wobbler. It could be charged as a misdemeanor or felony based on Ms. Layon's discretion. Marnie M. Layon decided she wanted a felony notch on her belt.

I got to know a handful of prosecutors when I was a cop and I liked them all, but I would definitely say they are an ambitious bunch. Even the ones I liked cared more about getting juicy convictions than making sure justice was done. One common thing a prosecutor brags about is how important the person they got convicted was. Politicians, fellow lawyers, cops, and celebrities are the trophies they brag about. Ms. Layon was looking to add a decorated Navy SEAL to her conquests. My lawyer pointed out by choosing to charge it as a felony, Ms. Layon would be dropping four children from middle class to poverty if she was successful. Their mother hadn't held a job in over a decade and she wanted to make their father a convicted felon with an other-than-honorable discharge. She told my lawyer she didn't care. Ms. Layon wasn't looking to put me in jail, she knew I wasn't a threat, she just wanted another felony conviction for her resume. Children be damned.

From the start, my lawyer was trying to plant the plea deal seed in my head. I was a strong, mean-looking man with tattoos, and Amanda was a small innocent-looking woman. It was my word against Maegan, Amanda and Fred. Every time we talked he pushed for me to accept veterans' court. Veterans' court is a program offered to veterans after a felony conviction. You attend a kind of probation course with therapy and classes until a judge signs off and you can get your felony removed from your record. There are a few problems with this. First, it would require me to first be convicted of a crime. I'm sorry, but grabbing someone by the back of the neck to keep them from steeling your car keys is not a crime and is the right of anyone protecting their property. In most states, the case wouldn't have even been pursued. Nobody was ever injured or in danger of injury. The prosecutor would argue Amanda was injured, but we'll get to that.

Crimes are also never truly wiped from your record. Once you have been convicted of a felony, you lose your 2nd amendment rights regardless of the felony being wiped from your record later. So even if I accepted veterans' court, I would lose my job and the protection the second amendment offers. My lawyer tried to convince me that veterans' court didn't mean I would lose my job, but all the research I did implied it would. A competent Marine Corps JAG assured me my career would not survive any kind of felony conviction. The same JAG was convinced that Ms. Layon was overreaching and wouldn't get the conviction. The second problem was, to qualify for veterans' court I needed to be diagnosed with a job-related mental illness. I wasn't suffering from any mental illness and I made that very clear to my lawyer. He stressed that I didn't need to actually have a post traumatic stress disorder, wink wink, I just needed to be diagnosed with it. I told him in no uncertain terms that I would not fake PTSD and I would not plead guilty to a crime I did not commit. My lawyer had obviously already discussed veterans' court with the prosecutor.

During a court date, Marnie M. Layon put on a very unconvincing facade of compassion and said to the judge, "I know Daniel just returned from a combat zone, and God knows what he witnessed there or on any of his other deployments. I want to see him get the help he needs, and I would be open to veterans' court."

I don't know how someone can be so shamelessly disingenuous. It's disgusting. She was all about veterans' court because she would still get the felony conviction regardless if it was removed later. She knew I wasn't dangerous or a felon. She just wanted the notch on her belt. After that date, my lawyer met with her in private and came out to push veterans' court on me again when they were finished.

"The quickest way you're going to get to see your kids is through veterans' court," he told me. The government was holding my children hostage to get me to make a plea deal. It was abundantly clear Mr. Orloff and Ms. Layon were working together to get me to just take veterans' court. She would get a felony conviction and I would still need a lawyer while I went through the program.

To get my lawyer to drop it, I agreed to see a psych. Due to the nature of our work, NSW has pretty robust mental health support. I told the psych I was seeing him because my lawyer wanted me to be diagnosed with a disorder. I assured him I had no disorder. He said that might not be the case.

"You could have adjustment disorder."

From what I can tell, that's just a catch-all diagnosis for any problem someone has when he returns home. I was entirely honest and genuine with the psych out of respect for what he did for my brothers. It felt good to talk to him, but it didn't matter once I left. All my problems were still there when I left his office. I don't mean to talk down to anyone who sees a head doctor, but they are only helpful if your problems are in your head.

Maegan was seeing a counselor, and maybe it was helping her, because her problems were not real. Her husband never abused her, he gave her everything she had. There was no threat to her safety and she was on her way to being awarded more money than she needed. She wouldn't even need to get a job and could count on a check the rest of her life as long as she didn't get married again. She would even get a piece of my retirement. After talking to the psych, I was still standing to lose my job, be branded in a way that would make it hard to find another job, give any money I could make to a woman who did nothing for me, and I still couldn't see my children. That was the real trauma. I have been face to face with death multiple times, and it has never been more traumatic than having my children taken away from me. We've done a pretty good job taking care of our soldiers and helping them cope with the traumas of war. What we don't seem to care about is when they return home to the things they've been fighting for, only to have them ripped away by some woman who's tired of the whole wife thing. *Being married to a soldier isn't what all the romance novels make it out to be, so I'll just take all his money and leave him to suffer.* That causes PTSD, just look at the suicide rates.

I left the psych with a glowing review of my mental competency and an Adjustment Disorder diagnosis. My lawyer tucked it away while mentioning seeing more psychiatrists for second and third opinions. Lawyers are the sleaziest kind of person on earth. Sure, they can do some good sometimes, but if we could figure out a way to get rid of them entirely, it would be a huge favor to mankind. If given the choice to end poverty or get rid of lawyers, I would get rid of lawyers; it would certainly reduce poverty.

I got much closer with my mother during that time. I was always terrible about staying in touch before. She told me about all the conversations with Maegan that made her worry. Conversations my mother didn't see as her place to bring up with me before. It was hard for her to tell me. This was when she told me about when Maegan said she wished she would miscarry our daughter. It was very clear to my family that she was not looking forward to me coming home from Yemen. She had told my family I chose to spend a week in Germany partying for Oktoberfest before coming home, not that it was a mandatory one day decompression stop before returning from a combat zone. She had been developing a narrative for my family for a long time. A narrative where I was a horrible husband and she was getting ready to cash in. My mother told me about the time she and Maegan waited for me to get out of surgery my junior year. Maegan told her about Brian and how she liked him more, but chose me because I was going somewhere and she wasn't going to stay in Medford forever. I don't think she saw that for what it was, or she wouldn't have said it to my mother. In her eyes, she was complimenting me to my mother, but it revealed her nature. I was her meal ticket. She didn't choose me because she liked me.

It upset my mom at the time, but she didn't say anything because we had already butted heads over Maegan. Hearing about certain conversations cut deep. On separate occasions, Maegan talked to my sister and mother about the generous life insurance policy the military provided. She told them about how Matt Leather's widow was set for life and how great that kind of security must feel. Maegan told them she was happy I was getting back in the military because if I died as a cop, she'd be screwed. The conversations made both my mother and sister uneasy enough to talk to each other about it, but they didn't tell me at the time.

Chapter 21

It was also becoming clear my lawyer was not doing his job. I started to hound him for all the evidence the prosecution had to provide. First, I wanted to see if the CVS had a camera pointed at the parking lot. One of the claims in Amanda's statement was that I strangled her for 30 seconds. She walked that number back on the stand, but video would show how brief the entire event really was. Even if it only showed her getting in and out of my truck it would make it clear I couldn't have strangled her for 30 seconds or the 15 seconds she claimed later. Her changing her statement plus the video would show her tendency to blow everything out of proportion. I hounded my lawyer to request the video and he always assured me he was on it. I got tired of waiting and called the CVS myself. Of course they wanted me to go through legal channels. Eventually, my lawyer said there was no video. I had to remind him on a Friday we had court on Monday. The other thing I wanted was the recording of Fred's 911 call. I knew that existed. It could at least give us a time frame of the event. The other thing I wanted was the first officer on scene's body or car cam. It was post black lives matter, so most departments had body cams by that point. I was guessing he probably didn't turn his on or he wouldn't have acted the way he did. I was hoping it would at least show him telling all the officers who was guilty and who was the victim without doing any kind of investigation. I never got to see any of this. Eric assured me he had requested it, but we headed into the preliminary hearing without ever receiving full discovery. The first time I saw most of the actual documentation from the prosecution was at the prelim. The preliminary hearing is where the prosecution presents their case to a judge to see if there is enough evidence to go to trial. The defense does not present their case; Eric was adamant about this. I did try to get rid of my lawyer, but they wouldn't refund my money and I couldn't afford another one.

I finally saw police pictures from the scene. Amanda had a faint red mark on her neck that was clearly a finger print from a hand gripping the back of her neck. I was expecting more. Maegan and Amanda always bruised very easily, and I certainly didn't grip her gently. I had given Maegan worse marks during sex. Amanda did have a huge bruise on her thigh. I had no idea what it was from. The prosecution's main piece of evidence was a doctor's note. According to Amanda, she had gone trick-or-treating with the kids after, but her neck bothered her so she went to a hospital. They did an ultrasound and found minor deep tissue bruising. That sounds bad, but think about it. This bruising was so imperceptible you needed an ultrasound to find it. Bruising was all they found, no real injury. The icing on the cake was that the doctor said it was deep tissue bruising due to strangulation. I never got to see the ultrasound or find out if the doctor had any kind of qualification to make such a determination. This is how I'm guessing it went. Amanda refused treatment at the scene and said she wanted to press charges. This is stated in the police report. She went trick-or-treating, and after fuming with Maegan for a while, decided going to the doctor could help them make a case against me. When the doctor asked what happened, she said she was strangled and her neck bothered her. The doctor probably only saw faint marks, if any, so took an ultrasound. He went looking for bruising and found some. When he wrote his report, he put strangulation under cause, because that is what Amanda told him. I'm not saying I didn't cause bruising and that it wasn't the same bruising she would have gotten had she been strangled. I'm saying there's probably plenty of you walking around now with more severe versions of the same bruise from your kid yanking on your purse. I wanted my lawyer to make these points, but he said now wasn't the time. Maybe he was right, but Ms. Layon was making a big deal about the doctor writing strangulation on his diagnosis. I was screaming inside *that's because she told him she had been strangled!*

Maegan testified first, then Amanda, followed by Fred. I'm going to go over Amanda's testimony last to contrast it with the other two. For Maegan, I'll start with her first police report and restraining order. Understand the reports are police officers summarizing what the witness says. They are trained to include the key statements and actions that give them reasonable suspicion or probable cause to arrest.

First off is the initial statement given by Maegan after I tried to bring my children home. This is the Starbucks incident.

Maegan and Daniel were speaking about the kids and the divorce when Daniel became angry with Maegan. Daniel yelled insults at Maegan then got into the vehicle Maegan had driven to the Starbucks.

I don't yell insults, I force them through gritted teeth. Maegan has told multiple members in my family that I don't really yell at her. It doesn't make a lot of difference, but it shows how the Coopers like to embellish when it suits them.

Their four children were inside the vehicle. Daniel attempted to drive away with the children. As the vehicle started to move Joshua got out of the vehicle.

She left out how she was yelling at all the kids to jump out as the van was moving.

Daniel stopped the vehicle. Maegan reached inside the driver side window and attempted to grab the keys.

She was sitting in the back seat hanging a leg out the door. She reached in-between the seats to grab the keys on the center console. She'll even correct this when we get to her Prelim testimony.

Daniel grabbed Maegan's left arm and held her arm until she dropped the keys.

I peeled the keys out of her hand and let her go immediately.

While Daniel was holding Maegan's arm, all the children got out of the vehicle.

As soon as I let her go she jumped out and continued yelling at the kids to jump out. My eldest was frightened and opened his door so I stopped the car and he got out. Maegan grabbed the other kids.

Daniel drove away and threw his vehicle keys towards Maegan.

I pulled up next to her and held the keys out. She reached inside the passenger window and took them.

Maegan got into the vehicle Daniel had driven to the Starbucks and drove to her sister's house. Maegan called law enforcement.

Maegan stated she didn't want Daniel to be arrested. Maegan did not want an emergency protective order. Maegan didn't want medical care.

Note that the officer took this statement before Maegan found out I traded in the minivan and she didn't want a restraining order.

Maegan had no visible injuries. I photographed the area were Daniel grabbed Maegan. I provided Maegan with a victim resource guide and case number. Maegan provided me with information on their four kids. I conducted a welfare check of the children and photographed them. They had no injuries.

Immediately after Maegan texted me that she gave a report to the cops I called and gave this statement.

According to Daniel Swift, he traveled to Vista from Oregon to spend time with his four children for Halloween. Daniel and Maegan Swift are currently in the process of divorcing. Daniel was going to meet with his wife and pick up his children at the Starbucks Coffee, located at 1850 University Drive #100, in the city of Vista. Maegan did not want Daniel to take the children. Daniel opened the driver side door of Maegan's vehicle and got into the driver's seat.

Daniel told Maegan she could either come with him or get out of the car. Maegan opened the driver's side sliding door and grabbed the key fob from the center console. Daniel grabbed Maegan's wrist and grabbed the key out of her hand. Daniel said he let go of her wrist once he had the key in his possession. Daniel gave Maegan the keys to his vehicle and told her to take his car home. Daniel began driving away and Maegan jumped out of the vehicle. Maegan told her children to get out of the vehicle as well. Daniel saw his children get out of the vehicle so he stopped the vehicle. The children got out of the vehicle and eventually left with Maegan in her vehicle. Maegan left the location with the children and Daniel left the location by himself.

Not the best account of what I said but close enough. After she found out I traded in the car she went and got this restraining order.

I, Maegan Swift, am requesting a restraining order against my husband, Daniel Whitney Swift. Daniel and I have been married since 2005. We share four minor children in common: xxxxx, age 11, xxxxx, age 9, xxxxxx, age 6, and xxxxx, age 4.

FIREARMS: *Daniel owns two pistols and a revolver, He recently visited Oregon and I believe he brought his guns back with him to Oregon, where they are registered..*

RECENT ABUSE:

On October 30, 2018, Daniel asked me to meet him with the kids at Starbucks. While I was standing just inside of the car with all four kids inside with a window down,

We were both standing outside the car with the kids inside and all the windows up. I think she meant beside not inside. The whole reason we walked back to the car instead of staying at the Starbucks is because we didn't want the kids to hear us talk. This is a bold face lie and she knew it when she wrote it.

he started calling me a "Piece of shit" and was telling me I'm a "horrible mom," all of which the kids heard,

Again, a complete lie. They were all sitting inside the car playing and did not hear anything.

I tried to get back into the car to get away from him but he suddenly got into the driver's side and started driving away.

Another twisting of the truth to make me sound more villainous. I made the first move. I asked to take the kids for Halloween since I always missed Halloween and she said no. I said, "I'm done dealing with you," and got in the driver's seat. Then she tried to get in the car.

I managed to get the side door open and jumped inside the moving vehicle,

How can this statement and the last statement be true? If she tried to get away from me first, how did I get the vehicle moving before she jumped in? She contradicts her own statement in the very next sentence but this statement was good enough to take away my rights to my children and second amendment rights. The truth is I was trying to get away and she was trying to stop me.

at which point my 11 year old decided to jump out of the car, which caused my husband to stop the vehicle.

My 11 year old did not decide to jump out of the car. She was screaming at all of them to jump out of the vehicle as I was slowly creeping along because she was intentionally hanging halfway out of the car. I stopped because he looked scared and confused due to his mother hysterically screaming.

At this point I grabbed my purse and keys (they do not need to be put in the ignition)

They may have been her keys but I thought they were mine. Still not sure.

He suddenly grabbed me by my left arm and held me in *place, demanding I release the keys. While he was restraining me I instructed all of the kids to exit the vehicle to make sure he didn't take off with them. I released the keys and exited the vehicle at which point he drove off, He did throw his set of car keys to me, however, his vehicle lacked the car-seats needed for xxxx and xxxxx so we were still left stranded.*

I got the keys out of her hand in a matter of seconds. She did not wait until the kids got out to release them. When she failed to take the keys she started screaming at them to get out. When I drove off I realized I had both keys. I drove up to her and held out the keys which she took. The car seats wouldn't have been a problem if she let me take my own children. She was not stranded her sister lived a few blocks away. I told her before arriving I wanted to switch cars to take the kids.

I called my sister for help and we drove to her house where I contacted the police, who came and took my statement. The officer encouraged me to get a restraining order to prevent future harm,

What harm? The only dangerous thing was her telling the kids to jump out of a moving vehicle. I stopped the car once she made the situation dangerous.

On or about October 17, 2018, Daniel and I got into an argument because I told him I planned on filling for divorce,

She didn't officially say she wanted a divorce until the day after this event. She had already said she didn't love me and we had been "separated" for a week or so at this point. I was trying to get her to explain why she didn't love me and we were having an honest talk with each other in the manner we usually handled our arguments since we were fifteen. That's not to say we never got in heated arguments but they were rare and this one had not gotten to that point yet.

We were talking in private when he suddenly dragged the kids into it, telling them everything was my fault and badmouthing me to the kids,

She skipped over a lot here and combined a series of events into one. We were calmly talking in private and speaking our minds. She was talking about how much of a burden I was and that I didn't do enough. I got angry and yelled "Is it not enough to have taken care of you for 15 fucking years." Technically I've only taken care of her for 12 but we had been together for 15. Only our youngest was home and yes she heard it. Maegan left and I told her to come home once she got the other kids so she could tell them what was happening.

When she came home she tried to sneak off with the kids and I convinced them to come inside and face what was happening. I was angry she tried to steal the kids, so I made it very clear it was their mother who was leaving me and tearing apart the family. You can call it badmouthing, but it was the truth.

I told him I was going to stay elsewhere and take the kids with me. He told me I was not leaving

I never said she could not leave. I specifically told her to leave but said she was not taking the children. This was their home. She testified later that I never said she couldn't leave but when she was getting this restraining order it suited her to lie.

*and I then threatened to call the police to have them come help me leave safely. At that point he left the room and returned to the living room with his pistol in his hand. He said, "Fine call the cops. See what happens," while blocking the door with his body with **his gun in his hand.***

I did not block the door. She had plenty of room to walk past and leave.

He eventually calmed down, put the gun away, and left the room the room with the children.

This typo is how it appears in the statement.

The police arrived soon after because my sister had called them when I failed to respond to her, I chose not to disclose what had happened to the police because I did not want to damage his military career.

Because she was still planning on divorce raping me, not out of consideration for me.

We pretty much avoided each other for the following week

Again she left out a lot here. She snuck off the next day while I was earning the money that buys everything we own, so I emptied the account before she had a chance to. She came back the next day because money sways her a lot. I agreed to move out. After a few days she invited me back to stay; even leaving the kids with me overnight while she stayed at Amanda's.

until he left for Oregon on October 24th however, he intentionally emptied out our joint bank account prior to leaving town. I did not see him again until October 30th when the above incident took place.

This was out of order and vague to make me sound more villainous. As I said, I emptied out the account when she snuck off with the kids. We had been living together for a few days and I had told her I would pay off whatever charges she put on the credit card. I asked her how much money she needed before I left for a week to Oregon and she said $500. I wrote her a check for $1000.

HISTORY OF ABUSE: Daniel was deployed in Yemen for 7 months and just returned from deployment on October 1, 2018. Since his return, he has been verbally abusive, constantly calling me, "bitch" and "stupid," and telling me what a horrible parent I am, doing all of this in front of the kids,

I came home and was happy as a clam. She seemed more distant than usual but I always imagined her being happier to see me then she ever really was. Even after she said she didn't love me I wasn't angry. I was heartbroken, I still loved her. I didn't call her names until she successfully snuck off with the kids. Even when she tried to sneak off with the kids and I "badmouthed" her I didn't call her any names. I stressed it was their mother leaving me and I would do anything to keep the family together. I called her a bitch in the Starbucks parking lot but the kids were in the car playing. It wasn't until the scuffle in the CVS parking lot that I insulted her loud enough for the kids to hear. Even then they were in a car with the windows up.

On one occasion, he was screaming right in my face, calling me a "stupid fucking bitch" and being so irate that I found our four year old crying while hiding behind the couch, obviously frightened by the yelling,

This was the argument when I yelled "is it not enough that I have taken care of you for 15 fucking years," and that was it. Calling her a "stupid fucking bitch" was a classic Cooper victimhood lie. I have called her this but not in-front of the kids and not until weeks after the event she is describing. Before that I had never called her stupid or a bitch.

He also informed me that while on deployment. He was reprimanded for issues regarding his inability to control his temper.

This was a complete verifiable lie. I was never reprimanded. I got in an argument with my LT as I described earlier. I had told her about it in confidence trying to explain how hard the deployment was for me. It was my least action-packed, so she saw it as some seven month party in a war torn, famine ridden, cholera infected desert. I was trying to explain to her it's the less active deployments that are the hardest. She and the lawyer helping her were playing on the image of a soldier returning from war and being violent to his family and it is despicable.

Daniel has always struggled with anger management issues.

I'm not the one who held my sister down and punched her repeatedly until her nose bled and her eyes turned black.

About two years ago, he got angry over the cost of our child's dental appointment and left me and two of our children stranded at the dentist's office because he left us there in an angry rage.

I'm having a hard time remembering this one. She was really scraping the barrel to make me look like a villain. I'm pretty sure it was when I was a cop. I was about to head into a stint off three 12 hour shifts. One of the kiddos had a dentist appointment. It was my day off and I didn't want to go. Other appointments didn't take long, so I went anyway. I think we were going to do something after. When we got there she informed me it was going to be hours. She also informed me of how much it was going to cost. I was supporting two adults, four kids, and two cats on a rookie cop's salary. I left angry to cool off. I had hours before I would need to pick them up after all. It must have not been an important dentist appointment because she cancelled it due to my reaction to the price. I never told her to cancel it and now she needed a ride home. I'm not sure if she tried to call me or not. I could have missed it. I thought she was safely waiting at the dentist's office for the appointment. She got a ride home and the first I heard of it is when I checked to see when I needed to pick her up. They were not stranded. She cancelled the appointment and got a ride home because she didn't want to call me. I'm foggy on the details of this one, but I certainly never left her stranded.

About nine years ago he got mad at me and picked up and threw our desktop computer across the room, destroying it. He also one time threw a cubby/chalkboard across the room during an angry rage. After his rages, he always blames me,

Of course when we argued I blamed her, that's why we were arguing. It wasn't abuse, it was every marriage in history.

forces me to apologize and take the blame,

Anyone who knows me can see this is bullshit. Apologies mean nothing to me. I would never want anyone to apologize to me. The only time I've made someone apologize is when one of my kids did something mean to their mother. I don't even make them apologize to each other because I don't want them to grow up and be apology people.

and then punishes me by ignoring me.

This is called taking some space. I think most counselors call it a good coping mechanism not abuse.

Daniel's recent behavior scares me and has also frightened our children who are all afraid to be around him based on his recent temper issues. I therefore seek the Court's protection to prevent any future harm to me or my children. I declare under penalty of perjury under the laws of the State of California that the foregoing is true and correct.

So there are certainly some true statements in there. I've gotten mad enough a few times in our twelve years of marriage to throw an inanimate object in a safe direction. Any kind of property damage does count as domestic violence in some states. A large percentage of domestic protection orders are given to women who claim nothing more than a broken object or threat. It greatly inflates the battered women stats. When Carrie Underwood sings about keying her boyfriend's pretty little souped-up four wheel drive, she is singing about domestic violence in some states; that is if they ever lived with their boyfriend. Of course women rarely get prosecuted for that kind of stuff. Male privilege ensures men have their lives ruined by that kind of stuff all the time.

I've already talked about why I got my gun, but I'll say it again because that's probably where I lose most of the sheltered people reading this. Someone was trying to take my children from their home. She was going to take my children to a dangerous place. A place with two bedrooms for 6 kids and 3 adults, plus a 4th who crashed on the couch from time to time because he was going through a divorce. A place with a father who brought the women he slept with over for Thanksgiving so his wife could cook for them. A place with a person my wife had violently assaulted the last time she lived with her. A place my wife complained about my whole 7 month deployment because of how much her sister fought with her unfaithful husband. Every father has a right and a duty to do everything he can to keep his children from a place like that. Neither of us are angels, and we have both failed at being parents sometimes, but I ask you who the kids should be protected from. Someone who has broken a few inanimate objects and stood his ground with unloaded gun in hand, or someone who has held a loved one down and punched their face until it bleeds? The court didn't get to make that choice, because they made a life-changing punitive decision based on half the story.

Maegan's prelim testimony was the hardest to hear. The law allows for a spouse to refuse to testify. It recognizes marriage is supposed to be a sacred bond of trust. Maegan chose to break that trust and do it with style. She looked beautiful. It had been a while since she'd cleaned up that well for me. She took the stand with a support dog; Helix, Amanda's dog, who fucking loved me. She also had some kind of support counselor with her; the kind women who have actually been abused need. While I would not dishonor men truly suffering with PTSD, she had no such scruples. Here is her court-transcribed testimony. I'm not going to put the whole thing because it is a lot of repetition and legal proceedings. I'll make all these documents available online when I publish this.

First she was asked about the first time she tried to take the kids. This was the home incident. Ms. Layon asks.

Q:"Was he in front of the door such that you couldn't get past him?"

A: "I don't remember."

Q: "Let me ask you this, because that was probably a bad question. Was he blocking the front door?"

A: "No"

Remember when she was jealous, angry and getting a restraining order she said I blocked the door. Ms. Layon then went into the process of trying to measure how far I was from the door by using objects in the court room. Eventually she asked.

Q: "You said that you were telling Mr. Swift you wanted to take the children and leave. Why was that?"

A: "Because he wanted them to be involved in the discussion about getting a divorce and I didn't want them to be."

I did not want them involved in the discussion. I wanted her to tell them she was divorcing me. I remembered my father trying to explain why my mom didn't love him anymore and I was not going to experience both sides of such a traumatic event. It was her choice and she needed to tell them.

Q: "Where were you with Mr. Swift while you were having this conversation about calling the police since he wouldn't let you leave?"

A: "In our living room."

Meagan wouldn't say I wouldn't let her leave so Ms. Layon decided to make it up here. Ms. Layon then tried her damnedest to get Maegan to say the gun was loaded but all Maegan said was she didn't know. After failing at that she started to go into how Maegan felt. Because feelings matter more than facts.

Q: "Were you worried about your safety?"

A: "Not my safety. No."

Q: "Were you worried about the kids?"

A: "No."

Q: "Did you feel that you were free to come and go and leave the house as you pleased at that point?"

A: "No."

Q: "Why?"

A: "Because, I mean, I think he would have let me leave but not with the kids."

Q: "Okay. Was it a combination of him holding that gun and saying, "You'll see what happens if you call the cops?" Is that why you feel you could not leave with the kids, or was it something else?

A: "He said I could leave but that I couldn't leave with the kids, before that."

As you can see, she was free to leave at any time and she knew it. I wish I knew more at the time about how custody worked in California. I had every right to make the kids stay with me in their home since no custody order was in place at the time.

Ms. Layon asked about an arrangement between Maegan and Amanda to check in. It's important to see how Maegan answered it and then later how Amanda answers it.

Q: "During this period of time, did you have some kind of arrangement with your sister, Amanda, about calling to check in with her on a regular basis?"

A: "Yes."

Q: "What—tell me about that. Why did you have this arrangement with your sister?"

A: "It's not really an arrangement, but we are identical twins, so we call each other a lot, and if one of us doesn't answer after a while, we worry about each other so..."

This was how Maegan recalled the Starbucks Incident on the stand.

"The kids stayed in our van, in the Honda Odyssey, and we were talking outside the van, like, by the driver's side door. And we were talking, and he started calling me names and stuff. So I wanted to leave, but he got inside the driver's side and started to, like, drive away."

She finally gave a more accurate account. Notice she didn't stick with her lie about the window being down. She also said talking now instead of yelling. The sting of me trading in the car was fresh when she made that lie up. Now she'd had some time to calm down and was under oath. The only problem I have is that she makes it sound like she was trying to leave and I stopped her. She may have wanted to leave, but she never made any effort to. I was the first one to act. The questioning continued, and for some reason Maegan kept saying that I was backing the car up. It's not important, but when the car was moving it was crawling forward. She gave a slightly more accurate account of what happened after I got in the car.

"So I got in the—the van door slides back, so I got in and tried to dig out the keys from my purse, and he held my arm and got the keys."

I have no idea where her purse was at the time, but it never got involved. The keys were in the center console. Her purse had to be with her because I cleaned out the van when I traded it in and there was no purse. Maegan and Ms. Layon had some back and forth about penny size bruises on Maegan's arm that conveniently showed up after the cop left, so he didn't photo them. I don't doubt I left some bruises. I grabbed her arm firmly because she was stealing my keys. She bruises easily and Ms. Layon acknowledged that. I don't think grabbing someone to stop them from stealing your shit should be a crime. Here is her account of how she got the keys to the Dodge. Note how she didn't stick with her lie about me throwing them on the ground.

"Daniel was leaving, he gave me the keys to the car he had driven there."

Ms. Layon asked about when Maegan got the restraining order.

Q: "Did you make any decisions, based on this incident that happened on October 30, about restraining orders?"

A: "Yes I went and got a restraining order."

She left out the fact that she refused a restraining order right after this, as the police report shows. She didn't decide to get a restraining order until after she found out I traded the van and left her with the Dodge she hated. The restraining order was to get revenge, not to protect anyone. Here is Maegan's account of what happened at the CVS parking lot.

A: "He drove up and— so I kind of stepped back, and he was hugging the kids, but then he tried to get them in his truck."

"He picked up our four year old at the time and put her in the backseat of the truck and started to buckle her in. And so I — my sister Amanda got in the driver's seat and tried to take the keys, and I got behind him and was trying to push him so I could get XXXXX out of the Vehicle."

She skipped the part where I went for the driver's seat first so Girl 2 could play with the steering wheel. I didn't get that far, because Amanda rushed in front of me and pushed the door closed as I was opening it. I never got as far as buckling her in, because I was being swarmed by Maegan and Amanda. Here is Maegan's account of what happened between me and Amanda.

A: "He grabbed her from—Around the neck. He was, like, behind her and grabbed her around the neck, from the backseat."

Q: "Did you see him use one or two hands?"

A: "Two hands."

Q: "How long did you see your husband, Mr. Swift, with his hands around your sister's neck in the front seat?"

A: "I would say at least 20 seconds."

The whole scuffle didn't last 20 seconds. Count 20 seconds in your head and imagine a capable Marine just standing there watching his female friend be strangled. Everyone is prone to overestimate time in a stressful situation. For the rest of Ms. Layon's questioning, she tried to emphasize the emotional damage the kids went through. Emotional damage that never would have happened if Amanda didn't physically try and stop me from leaving with my own children. Regardless, I've witnessed some scuffles growing up. Sure, it's scary, but it's life. I don't think everyone who's scuffled in front of a kid should be charged with a crime.

My lawyer started his cross examination by establishing that Maegan had more access to the guns than I did. She admitted to having unregistered guns in Communist California and transporting them across state lines during trips while I was deployed. She admitted to a felony under oath. Of course she'll never be prosecuted for it. If she was a black dude she would be. My lawyer asked if I was a good father and she was about to say yes, but Ms, Layon cut in and objected. My lawyer moved on to the Starbucks incident.

Q: "Well, you were behind— you opened the back door and reached around behind the seat to grab the keys out of the center console: is that correct?"

A: "Yes."

When she was presented with events how they happened, she agreed. She wasn't given the opportunity to embellish by saying she reached into her purse for the keys or reached through the driver's side window. My lawyer then asked when she knew about me trading in the truck.

Q: "And when was the first time— when did you learn that he had bought a new truck?"

A: "When he pulled up at the CVS Pharmacy on the 31st."

I texted her right after I traded in the van and it was marked as read. She knew before the 31st. That is the reason she got the restraining order. She was lying here to cover the fact she got the order for revenge. My lawyer tried to get her to admit to hearing the kids saying they wanted to go see the truck, but she claimed she couldn't hear anything even though she was standing right next to me. Here, my lawyer called her on her bullshit.

Q: "When you say "Grabbed XXXXXX," Did XXXXXX— XXXXX run up to him, to begin with: is that correct?"

A: "Yes."

Q: "And did he pick her up, or did she jump in his arms?"

A: "Probably both."

Q: "So she appeared to be very happy to see him; is that correct?"

A: "Yes. Yes."

Q: "And he walked off with her to his new truck; is that correct?"

A: "Yes."

When she was free to tell the story her own way she said *Grabbed* and left out the part where the kids wanted to go with me. In her original statement to the police she said Girl 2 didn't want to go with me, a complete lie. When presented with the truth, she agreed with it. Remember she said I walked to the car. It becomes important later. Here she recounted how I grabbed Amanda.

"He had her, like, with one arm— I don't remember which arm—with one arm, like, around her neck, holding her head back and grabbing her with the right arm."

Just before, when being questioned by Ms. Layon, she said I grabbed her with both hands. Now it was one arm? The two hands thing was repeated in all the police reports because it is a nice textbook description of strangulation. I am a good grappler, and no good grappler is going to strangle someone with two hands unless it's a collar choke with clothing. They would do it more like Maegan was describing here: a proper choke hold. Maegan switched her story from the textbook answer she was prepped with to the way she had seen me and her son choke at jujitsu practice. Neither was how it actually happened. My lawyer asked multiple times in multiple ways if Maegan thought I was trying to deprive her of air, but Ms. Layon would not let her answer. My lawyer kept getting shut down with objections, but at least got Maegan to admit that she voluntarily stayed with me several days after the event with the gun, showing she was not imprisoned.

Next I'll go over Fred's statements. Keep in mind he was a Recon Marine who had deployed to Afghanistan from what I know. He had been in fights and most likely knew how to keep cool. He was mostly detached from the altercation, making him an ideal witness. I'm not sure if Fred and I had met before, but unlike Amanda and Maegan, he had no ill will toward me. After all the legal mumbo jumbo, Ms. Layon got into the questioning about the restraining order.

Q: *"How did Mr. Swift react to you giving him this paperwork?"*

A: *"I don't think he has ever met me before. Never met him. So he just looked at me and shrugged it off. It was more of a—Kind of, Like, "Who the hell are you," a confused look. Nothing other than that."*

Q: *"Did you see what he did with the papers after you gave them to him?"*

A: *"Once—later on, he did grab the papers."*

When he said "later on," he meant after the altercation. No state would have considered this a properly served restraining order. I was ignoring him the whole time and thought he was there to serve divorce paperwork. I didn't find out about the restraining order until I was cuffed and in the back of a police car, when it was properly served on me by a deputy. The deputy stated in his report that he served the restraining order on me after the event. Here is Fred's answer when asked about my arrival at the scene.

A: *"When he showed up, he just got out of his truck, came down, took a knee, called the kids over. And it seemed like a very nice moment. Nothing seemed too crazy at the time."*

Q: *"What happened after this interaction with the kids that seemed nice?"*

A: *"Okay. So he picks up XXXXXX to show her the—he said, "Hey, you want to see"—"look. I got a new truck." Like, "awesome." "You want me to show you the new truck?" He picks up XXXXX, his youngest daughter, and starts walking toward the back of the truck. And that's when things got a little aggressive. Amanda put herself between the truck and Dan. At that time, I believe he was still holding XXXXX and grabbed Amanda by the back of the head and, like, tried to throw her to the ground."*

The only issue I have with this is him saying I tried to throw her to the ground. I shoved her out of my way. This woman who had always hated me despite me showing her every kindness was trying to stop me from seeing my kids after a seven-month deployment, so I shoved her out of my way. Notice he heard me talking to the kids and said I walked to the truck, it will be important when we get to Amanda's testimony. He also points out everything was fine until Amanda used physical force to block me from seeing my children. That's when things got a "little aggressive," but somehow I'm the primary aggressor in all of this.

Q: *"Okay, what happened next?"*

A: *"After he pulls Amanda out of the way, he opens up the door, which is the back door, drivers side, I believe, and Amanda, like stumbles back into the door and closes the door on Daniel and XXXXX."*

What wasn't recorded in the court transcript was the look I gave him when he said I threw Amanda to the ground. It was a, *really, come on man,* kind of look. He made a look acknowledging that he might be making it sound worse than it was and changed it to pulling her out of the way. He was also covering for Amanda here by saying she stumbled into the door. In truth, she was so angry and out of control, she slammed the door on me and my daughter to keep us from getting in the truck. Here is his account of what happened between me and Amanda in the truck.

A: *"Amanda looked distraught, and I see that Dan has her by the back of the neck, squeezing her, like, kind of holding her down."*

This is exactly how it happened. Amanda was "distraught," not fighting for air. I had her clamped on the back of her neck to keep control of her with one hand while my other tried to control her wrists. Once I realized she didn't have the keys, I let her go. Maegan was hitting me in the chest as I was climbing out, so I shoved her. I walked toward her with a, *don't touch me again,* posture and this is Fred's account of how my shirt got torn off.

A: *"And that's when Amanda tried to grab Dan and pull him back, and his shirt got—tore off at that point."*

Amanda ripped off my shirt, but I'm the primary aggressor. My lawyer started off by clarifying whether the restraining order was served. It was a long winded exchange but here is the key takeaway. Remember this when we get to Amanda's testimony.

A: *"At the time, like I said, he looked at me, but it was more of a confused look, but he didn't acknowledge it, nor did he take the papers, and that is when he stood up with XXXX in his arms."*

Here is an exchange I think is important.

Q: *"Did she appear to be happy to go with him to the truck?"*

A: *"Yes."*

Q: *"And when Mr. Swift arrived in the parking lot, did the children appear to be happy to see him?"*

A: *"When he arrived?"*

Q: *"Yes."*

A: *"Absolutely."*

Here is a confusing part of the transcript, but I think you can gather that Fred was trying to say I was holding the back of Amanda's neck with one hand while the other was doing something he couldn't remember. What it did not say is that I had two hands around her neck squeezing like all the other police reports and testimonies said.

A: *"He has one arm there, and I think— and then he is—like, whatever is happening back with Mae-gan, I didn't see too much of that, so then he is—with whatever the other arm, he is doing that."*

While he was talking he was using his arms to illustrate. My lawyer didn't make sure to get his account properly recorded in the transcript like Ms, Layon did with Amanda and Maegan. Of course she didn't want Fred's account properly documented, because it contradicted Maegan and Amanda's. My lawyer did try to ask if Fred thought I was trying to control or injure Amanda, but Ms. Layon objected. I think Fred would have said I was trying to control her. The way he described the event indicated as much. He seemed like a stand up-guy that got pulled into someone else's mess.

Now we get to Amanda's testimony. Ms. Layon started off by asking about an arrangement Maegan and Amanda had the day of the first incident.

Q: *"And did you have some kind of arrangement with Maegan about remaining in contact with each other and if someone didn't answer, that the other person might become concerned? Was there some kind of arrangement?"*

A: *"Yeah. We had talked about it earlier that day, about—like, she needed to get in touch with my husband or I, like, every, like, half an hour to an hour just to make sure she was ok, because she had been really upset because her and Daniel had been fighting that morning, so we just worried about her. So when we didn't hear from her, so we called the welfare check."*

Remember when Maegan was asked this same question, she explained there was no arrangement beyond their usual habit of calling each other on a regular basis. Ms. Layon had heard this fabricated special arrangement from Amanda before and wanted to get it on record. She wanted to make it seem like I had some history of violence to warrant a special arrangement. She wanted to paint Maegan as a woman who lived in constant fear and checked in with her sister to make sure she was still alive. What she didn't expect was for Maegan to tell the truth and not reinforce Amanda's story. I don't know what conversations Maegan had with Amanda that day. I know I had given her no reason to need to check in with Amanda. We hadn't had any kind of loud argument to that point and had been giving each other the cold shoulder. That day, while we were calmly arguing, I finally snapped and yelled at her. She left to get the kids from school and she probably called Amanda. At that point the worst thing I had ever done is yell at her. Maybe they could have made an arrangement, but she was back before long so she would have missed the very first check-in during our argument, and regardless, Maegan stated herself there was no such arrangement. Ms. Layon continued her questioning and got to the event at the CVS parking lot. Here is Amanda's account.

A: *"So we got to the CVS, and we were, like, changing them all. And I had just finished putting XXXXXXX, the youngest—her costume on. And Dan drove up and, like, got out of his car really quick, and, like, all the kids, like—all my sister's kids, like, ran to him. And then he grabbed XXXXXXX, the youngest, and, like, went for the backseat of his car with her. And so—"*

Ms. Layon cut her off there, but note the difference between her account and the other two. In her version, I came running out and snatched up a child. She made no mention of me getting on my knees and hugging all the children. She also skipped over me going to the driver's side first and her physically blocking me. Ms. Lyon backed Amanda up to ask how I reacted to Fred giving me the paperwork.

A: *"I think he threw them on the ground."*

Contrast this with all the other statements. This was a fabrication Amanda came up with and you will see her double down on it later. No one else said this happened, but I think Amanda genuinely believed this. Ms. Lyon then asked her about me, *grabbing* my youngest.

A: "He just, like, picked her up and, like, ran for his truck with her."

It should be becoming clear what kind of person Amanda is. The way she is able to twist something to fit her own perception. Fred described a man walking up, taking a knee, hugging his children who were happy to see him, asking if they wanted to see his new truck then walking with his daughter to the truck. Amanda's account sounded like a drive by kidnapping. Remember she was under oath. She claimed not to remember anything between when I picked up Girl 2 and when I put her in the back of the truck. She didn't remember using physical force to stop me from opening the driver's side door. She didn't remember slamming the back door on me and my daughter. Ms. Layon moved to the part where I grabbed Amanda.

Q: "What happened next?"

A: "And then he grabbed me by, like, my face and neck."

This kind of checks out. There is a way to cup your hand around the jaw and chin in order to pull someone back and not obstruct the throat. Of course the best way, if you're not worried about hurting someone, is to simply hook around the throat. In Jiu Jitsu you can choke, so slipping the arm around someone's neck to pull them back is the best option. In wrestling, chokes are illegal, so you have to use the chin method to pull someone back. I used the chin method on Amanda, because I was specifically trying to stay away from her airway and carotid artery. However, she is still going to do what most people do in a stressful situation and forget to breathe. Ms. Layon wanted Amanda to elaborate.

A: "He had, like, both hands— like, first he had me, like, around my face (Indicating)."

Ms. Lyon: For the record, the witness has taken her right hand and held it in kind of across her mouth, just underneath her nose."

Q: "Go ahead."

A: "And then, like, he, like, pulled away and, like, ripped my earrings out, and then, like, he got, like— because I was, like, fighting with him, and, like, he had me, like, around the neck."

Notice how Ms. Layon described for the record what Amanda was doing with her hands. Notice how she did not make this clarification for the record when Fred described what happened. He had the best view as an uninvolved observer, but Ms. Layon did not want his description in the record. I don't know how her earring tore, but I'd wager it was from her trying to peel my hand away, probably when I had switched it to the back of her neck in a C clamp. That would put my fingers right by her ear. Ms. Layon had Amanda go on about seeing stars and all other kind of symptoms caused by lack of air, which she may have experienced. Most people do in stressful situations. This is what happened when Amanda started to arrive at that conclusion.

Q: "Did you have any problems with nausea?"

A: "I did, but I don't know—like, it was just, like, nerves, too, you know, because of everything that was going on."

Q: "And I'm not asking you to tell me what the source of it was; just, was this something that you noticed after this event?"

Amanda didn't realize what was going on here. She was just reciting all the trauma from the event that was all my fault. She didn't realize Ms. Layon was trying to tie as many symptoms as she could to me grabbing her neck. Amanda started to stumble onto the true cause of her symptoms and Ms. Layon quickly steered her back onto her narrative. She went on to talk about Amanda losing her voice. I don't doubt she lost her voice. We were yelling at each other until the cops arrived. She was yelling quite loudly and vigorously for someone who had just been strangled. I was trying to yell at my wife, but Amanda had so much energy and voice it ended up being between me and her. Ms. Layon asked about the bruise on Amanda's thigh.

A: "I think it, like, hit the seat belt thing when I was trying to struggle to get away. And then, when I turned around to try to get—Make sure he—like, once he had gotten off me, like, he had turned around to go after my sister and XXXXXX again. So I think when I turned, it, like, hit, like, the console or the seat belt thing."

So after being strangled, she still had enough energy to turn in the seat so hard she left a massive bruise on her thigh. This time, when she was asked about how long she was strangled, she said 10 to 15 seconds. On her initial police report she said 30. All of those are overestimates which is a common mistake for someone not used to stress. The entire interaction, from my arrival to when we started yelling, was maybe 30 seconds. I had my hands on her for 5 at the most. Ms. Layon continued to try and squeeze as much injury and emotional damage from the event as she could. Amanda's gift for embellishment made her the best option for Ms. Layon to milk. The kids were obviously scared. I could have made them all feel better if I was allowed time, with them but Maegan never let me see or talk to them after that.

My lawyer started his cross examination with the restraining order.

Q: "And did you—you saw Mr. XXXXXXX(Fred) actually hand the restraining order to Daniel, or what did you see in regard to that?"

A: "I saw him hand it to him."

Q: "And did it go from hand to hand?"

A: "No. Well, like, Dan, like, took them and threw them down on the ground."

I think she genuinely believed her own lies. She was doubling down on something no other witness saw. She had made something up because in her mind I had always been the villain. You can see how she first said *No* but it conflicted with the narrative she had made up in her own mind. My lawyer asked if she could remember what I said to my children, but she conveniently couldn't remember. My lawyer pressed her, but despite admitting to being close enough to hear, she didn't remember or didn't hear me say anything. Contrast this with Fred who was on the phone with 911, and clearly heard me ask the kids to come look at the truck and heard them happily agree. My lawyer did get her to change her narrative about me running to the truck.

Q: "And he walked with XXXXX and got in the car; is that correct?"

A: "He, like, walked quickly over to the back of his truck. Yes."

Q: "And he was walking: is that correct?"

A: "Yeah. I mean, he wasn't that far, so yeah, it was, like, walking."

Q: "So he didn't run to the truck; is that right?"

A: "It was a pretty fast walk."

See how hard it was for her to admit her own reality was false? This is the kind of woman I tried to make my sister. This is the kind of woman who drove a passive person like Maegan to violence. This is the kind of person who accused me of strangling her.

Chapter 22

Sadly I'm not the only one who has experienced this. So many women are able to play the victim and say whatever they want to a judge to take away a father's rights. The courts are all too eager to separate a father from his children despite every study and statistic showing removing a father from a child's life is one of the worst things you can do for a kid. Even as a happily married man, I was shocked to learn in the Academy that a man can lose his 2nd amendment right and the right to see his children based solely on the claims of one woman, no evidence required. The courts have a very big incentive to separate fathers from their children and extract as much money from them as possible, thanks to a little federal program called Title 4D. Restraining orders insure maximum payout, as we'll see.

Title 4D is yet another example of the government starting with good intentions then growing into a money-making beast, consuming the people it was originally supposed to protect: children. There is plenty of literature and educational material out there on Title 4D. I'll try not to bore you with legal explanations, but I encourage everyone to Google or You-Tube Title 4D (Title IV-D). There are a lot of videos breaking it down in various degrees of detestability. In simplest terms, it is a federal funding states get to process and enforce child support. Many an angry father mistakenly says it is money the state gets for every dollar of child support they order. The government is rarely so overt in its corruption. The money the state gets pays for all employees and services used in child support collection. More parents paying means more money moving. More money moving means more clerks, judges, and cops to arrest parents who can't keep up with their payments. Just like my police department didn't have a "quota," the courts don't get money for every dollar of child support they order. Lawyers are very good at polishing a turd.

California got over $500,000,000 of federal dollars in 2019 for child support processing and enforcement. This is why women are overwhelmingly awarded custody. As every feminist will tell you, women are paid less than men. More accurately, women earn less than men, but I won't go down that road. So if the government wants to maximize profit, it needs to make the most capable earner pay. If the kids' welfare was the top concern, then 50/50 custody would be standard. But if 50/50 were standard, the government couldn't make one parent pay. Each parent would be responsible for the time they spent with the kids. Parents would have one less thing to fight about and the children would see both parents equally. That is what's best for the kids, not reducing one parent to a visitor and ATM machine. Of course, if you can make a restraining order against someone without ever giving them a chance to defend themselves, then you can squeeze the maximum price out of that parent. A restraining order will be reliably followed by a divorce and child support order for maximum payout.

I tried and tried to see my kids. I asked the law to make her bring my children back to their home and let me see them, but they would do nothing. I asked them to make her comply with supervised visits at a facility with a professional supervisor I would pay for. When none of that worked, I asked if she would at least let them write me a letter. That heartless woman would not even allow that. She didn't want me using it to show the kids wanted to see me. The restraining order gave her all the power and the more time she could keep me from the kids the more money she would be awarded. When my mother suggested to the kids they should draw a picture for their father, Maegan blocked her number and my parents haven't spoken to their grandkids since. That is child cruelty; that is not what's best for the children.

I started by sending her a little less than half my paycheck every month. I subtracted bills like the last month's rent and utilities from our last apartment, the cost of her iPhone after she removed it from our plan without telling me, and the insurance for the car she was driving. She wasn't happy with this and said she would let me have supervised visits if I paid the amount she wanted for a few months. She was denying children time with their father for money. Once most of the old bills were paid for and I had been budgeting for a few months, I calculated that I could scrape by on half my paycheck. I called her lawyer and told him I was willing to pay $3,800 a month. I wanted to go in and sign it over as soon as possible so I could stop talking to him. His answer was, "I think she is entitled to more."

She was entitled to more than half of every dollar I earned? Basically, I would be working for her from now on and taking the leftovers. He knew that because I was a good husband and had provided everything for the past 12 years, he was going to get more out of me. The better a husband and provider you are during the marriage, the more you get fucked when she decides this wife stuff is too hard. *I'll just take your money and no longer have to perform any of my responsibilities.* As a lawyer, he's obligated to present the offer and I have no reason to believe he didn't. She refused and he produced a professional written offer that made absolutely no concessions to me.

I went on a date with a lawyer and she offered some free legal counsel. She looked over my paperwork and helped me with some wording for a counter offer. I sent back a counter offer requesting visitation and dismissal of her restraining order. I also specified that she could not take part in any Naval Special Warfare foundation events. One of my buddies had gone through a divorce, but was making back up with his ex when he died. She hadn't tried to fuck him over and we all knew they were trying to make it work. She was treated with honor by the community and welcomed at all the events. I wanted it to be clear to Maegan that she would not be welcome if I died.

I agreed to pay guideline child support based on my rank in the Navy. I still had not provided him any pay information but E6 military pay can be Googled. The amount would have been less than the $3,800 I originally offered. He pointed out I made combat pay, and other special pays. Yes, I made combat zone pay, during my deployment to a combat zone! I got dive pay for doing training on a regular basis that killed three of my friends. Last I checked Maegan had never been to a combat zone. She hadn't stuffed herself into a can and descended into the black of the ocean only to come back up with one less friend. How was she entitled to one cent of my special pays? The back and forth went nowhere and we had several heated conversations over the phone. I warned him if they pushed me too hard neither of them would get a cent. I told him I was a very capable person and if they thought I would just lay down and take it I would be gone and they would be left to pick up the pieces. He probably thought I was just talking a big game. He didn't know who I was. A soft man like Robert Daniels cannot comprehend men like me. We are made of entirely different stuff. I'm guessing he did not convey my warning, thinking it was just bluster. Maegan knew me though, and she probably would have taken it more seriously.

They kept on pushing and our first court date approached. It was a request by her lawyer to get interim support ordered. I had been willingly sending her a couple thousand each month to that point. I had no idea what I was doing or what I was required to provide. I finally broke down and hired a divorce lawyer. Honestly, during our short time together I really liked him, but I was supposed to. He was much more active in my case than my criminal lawyer. The lawyer I went on a date with, my divorce lawyer and every lawyer I called when I was trying to find a new lawyer gave the same response when I told them Eric Orloff was my criminal lawyer.

"Really?"

Now I understand lawyers are in competition with each other, but the woman who helped me and my divorce lawyers were in family law, not criminal. Money was tight and I couldn't hire a new criminal lawyer, but I could scrape together enough to get a divorce lawyer for the hearing. At least I would no longer have Robert Daniels calling to ruin the rare days I managed to salvage. The hearing came and she didn't even have to show up. I came in my best threads and waited for my turn at the chopping block. We were one of the last cases, so I watched man after man get up with hat in hand. Every time it was some dumbfounded guy trying to see his kids. Every time he was there by himself while his baby mama sat across with a lawyer he was paying for. All the cases were farther along in the process and these men had already run out of money to pay for their own lawyer, and probably never had enough for one in the first place. The judge berated them for not having the right forms filed, the ones a lawyer takes care of. They were sent packing with their tail between their legs, still unable to see their kid.

The one exception was an old retired man with his new wife and his own lawyer. His ex-wife from 30 years back sat across alone. He had brought his ex to court to try and get the alimony he was still paying her reduced. This guy had a new woman to take care of and he still had his ex from 30 years back leeching off him. The judge chided her for not having the right forms, but ruled they would reconvene when she had the documentation to prove she still needed the money. I don't know if this was the norm or I just showed up on the right day for God to lean down and yell at me, "You won't find justice here!"

Our turn came up and the lawyers did their thing. I don't know why they bothered, because in the end the judge just punched some numbers into a computer. Her eyes lit up with surprise. She ordered me to pay Maegan over $4,000 dollars plus $1,000 a month to her lawyer until he was paid off. I would be paying over $5,000 a month in child support, alimony, and her attorney's fees. Child support was lower than the $3,800 I had originally offered. My oldest boy was the only one who cost more than $1,000. All together they were a little over $3,000. Maegan's alimony was over $1,000. I can't remember if it was more or less than my oldest boy, but she was an able-bodied adult costing me more than two daughters and a son. I was paying the max because I had no "involvement' with the kids despite having been fighting to see them since shortly after I got home from deployment.

Even if I got free and clear of all criminal charges and the restraining order was dropped, I would be at a huge disadvantage when it came to custody. Courts want to make money and maintain status quo. If the kids haven't been seeing their father on a regular basis for months, then why start now? Plus the less we let him see his kids the more child support we can order. The more child support we order, the more employees we have to hire to handle it. The more employees we hire for child support enforcement and management, the more federal Title 4D dollars we get. And the beast keeps eating and growing.

The divorce rate has skyrocketed because why wouldn't you? It's a sweet deal! *I no longer have to cook, clean, or sleep with this guy and I get more control over his money than I had before. If he falls on hard times, the law will make sure he still pays the same amount or the police will arrest him. If I stayed married and he got laid off I would have to suffer with him and I don't want to do that.*

Maegan liked the sound of that deal and her sister talked her into it the whole time I was serving my country on the other side of the planet. Amanda was unhappy with her husband sleeping around and she wanted her sister for a shoulder to cry on and free child care. *That Dan guy has always been reliable, leave him and we can all move into a big house in a nice neighborhood and Dan will pay the rent.* I don't know how long they were planning it, so this is me making some assumptions. Some assumptions with pretty good evidence backing them up. I had made a large effort to contact her more during my last deployment, but she would give short replies and not respond for days sometimes.

When I went to the Navy JAG offices in San Diego, they wouldn't even see me after taking down my name and wouldn't say why. United States Navy lawyers, the Navy I served in, wouldn't let me talk to a lawyer. I called the Marines up in Miramar and he said it was most likely because she had gone in and seen them before. Just by contacting the Navy JAG office, it disqualified me because it created a conflict of interest. The Marines helped me out as they always do, but there wasn't much they could do but offer advice. She had obviously already gone in at some point and learned all about how much money she could get out of me to include retirement. The house she and her sister moved into was a large house in a nice SoCal neighborhood. There was no way her sister could have come close to paying the rent. They signed the agreement knowing they were going to squeeze me dry.

I hadn't seen my kids for months. I only saw them for a few weeks after a deployment. I missed Thanksgiving, Christmas, three birthdays and was on my way to missing a fourth. My incompetent lawyer was working with a crusading prosecutor to get me to fake PTSD, give up my right to bear arms, and lose my job just so I could have my record kind of clean. I was ordered to pay over $5,000 to Maegan and her lawyer every month. I was going to have to sell my truck and move in with a buddy.

I could have convinced a jury to see the truth. I was charged with PC245(a)(4) Assault by means likely to produce great bodily harm. This could have been charged as a misde- meanor, but Ms. Layon wanted a felony. I did not strangle Amanda. I was very careful not to obstruct her airway or blood flow, and I have been trained how to do that. At no point was great bodily harm a possibility. The red mark from the police photo was pretty clearly made from the thumb of a hand on the back of her neck. I think we would have had this con- firmed by Fred. I'm pretty confident we could have proven whoever made the strangulation diagnosis was not qualified to do so, and was simply putting what Amanda had told him as the cause. Maybe he was some CSI expert, but I'm even more confident that whatever bruising was present could have also been caused by rough handling and did not indicate airway or circulation was cut off. I would have liked to show the ultrasound to an analyst who knew nothing about them to see if he would even see the bruising. Neither Maegan nor Fred said I strangled Amanda in the prelim.

Ms. Layon added PC 236 False Imprisonment. False Imprisonment is when one person restrains, detains, or confines another person without his/her consent. I told Maegan to leave multiple times. During the prelim the prosecutor had to rephrase her question multiple times to get Maegan to say she *felt* like she couldn't leave the kids with me. On the way to getting that answer Maegan said she had multiple opportunities to leave and could have. I could use the transcript from the prelim if she wouldn't say it at the trial. I would also point out she suggested I come back after I left; not the actions of someone whose been imprisoned.

I was also charged with six counts of PC 273a(a) Willful Child Endangerment, which were all misdemeanors. Child Endangerment includes emotional stress. My children have had some of the most sheltered and happy lives. Amanda was the first person to use physical force to block me from opening my truck door, and is the one who willfully escalated the situation into a physical confrontation. I was trying to leave peacefully, and Amanda and Maegan were trying to stop me with force. My children were happy to see me and wanted to go with me to my truck. To date, the most traumatic thing my children have witnessed is their mother beating their aunt. Maegan is the one who told them to jump out of a moving vehicle, but she wasn't charged with anything.

The last charge was PC 243(e)(1) Domestic Battery, which is a misdemeanor version. Any offensive touching to a spouse qualifies. Most of you reading this are guilty of domestic battery by California's definition. I guarantee most women are guilty of domestic battery by this standard. Maegan certainly is, but they are never prosecuted. Every woman who has pushed or slapped her man is a domestic abuser. I was charged for pushing Maegan. I did push Maegan, but that was because she was pushing and hitting me and I was trying to get her off me, but of course she hasn't been charged with anything. The fact that my shirt had been ripped off by Maegan and Amanda should have clued any decent cop in that I was the one being defensive. Ripping someone's shirt also qualifies as domestic battery, but again, no charges against Maegan or Amanda.

Even if I was cleared of all charges, I would still have to pay Maegan over $5,000 a month. Once the initial costs of her lawyer were paid it would drop to under $5,000. After fighting for more time with my kids and paying her lawyer more money; I might get to the point where I could afford my own place. 13 years later, the kids would be over 18 and I wouldn't be paying child support, the only thing I didn't have a problem with. I would still be paying that parasite over $1,000 a month until I was put in the grave. I remembered that old guy and his new wife trying to stop paying his ex from decades back. You know, I might have been able to stand that. It was having to pay her blood sucking lawyer one cent that went too far.

I have spent countless hours submerged in water. I have slept for days in arctic weather. I have slept under the desert stars with the sound of a 105mm as a serenade. I have lived in a can under the ocean breathing recycled farts for three months. I have brushed a swarm of insects from my food in a malaria-ridden country and taken a bite. I don't need a lot to get by. Some men will roll over and take it. I am not one of those men. There are people who let their government walk all over them. Nations who have had their people persecuted, enslaved, or slaughtered en masse. Some of these people are tough, they stand there, take it, and survive. Our forefathers were not those kind of people. They started a war with the most powerful empire on earth because they thought their taxes were unfair. Some people are losers, some people are survivors, and some people are fighters. I'm not going to stand by and let people I cared for, served, and protected treat me like less than the good man, father and soldier I am.

I packed a backpack and wrote two death notes, just in case things got sketchy; I didn't know if I'd be able to send them again. And off I went, and here I am now. I'm not hard to find. I want it that way. Eventually my kids will learn the truth. Maegan has cut them off from my entire family. My children have grandparents, cousins, aunts and uncles who love them, and Maegan is depriving them of that so she can feed them her narrative. It can't last. They are smart kids. They are my kids. Maegan is her mother's daughter and they will see through her perpetual victimhood. They will come looking for me and they will find me.

To my ex. I will always take care of the kids. I will switch places with you anytime you want. I am saving as much money as I can in case something happens to the kids. Anytime you want to sign custody over, you can reach out. I will give you money, but you will never take it. I wrote this book so you can never erase me from the kids' lives. I know now how much you tried to turn the kids against me while I was gone serving my country. You will only be able to control the narrative for so long. Eventually, they will get older and discover this book. Because they are my children, they will ask questions. When they talk to those who knew me, they will discover the legacy I left. The legacy of a good man. I have walked my road with honor and those I have passed along the way will testify to it. Let my family see the kids. Every day you refuse our children that love you prove how wicked you truly are.

To Amanda's husband. You'll notice I left your name out. We knew each other since before we knew our wives. We played sports together and both served. She is going to turn on you. She will sell you out in an instant. We both know I got the nicer twin. You know I didn't strangle her. If you listed the most honest men, you know I would be at the top of that list. You know your wife is prone to exaggerate offenses against her. How many times have we listened to her describe some wrong done to her and looked at each other with knowing eye rolls? Ask yourself who is really telling the truth, not who you are duty bound to believe. Then ask yourself what kind of person lies like that. It's always been a problem of hers and we've even talked about it before. I didn't see it in Maegan soon enough. Make no mistake, Amanda talked shit about you as much as she did about her mother. Your sisters and mom were what she mostly complained about. I spent the better part of a drive to Oregon defending you to Amanda while Maegan slept in the back. That was before you started sleeping around. I know I shit on you quite a bit for that, but some of my best friends are unfaithful. I tend not to judge and have plenty of flaws of my own.

To my kids. I love you more than anything and you will understand one day. Men have left their families to sail to new worlds or fight throughout history. You are not the first and sadly not the last. You are strong and you will make it. Take care of each other. Be careful of who your mom allows around you. How well you are provided for is entirely up to your mother. You have a family that loves you and will do anything to help. If you are ever afraid, you find your grandma, grandpa or uncle. They are not hard to find. If you want to talk to me just make a Facebook page. I look. Don't bother looking for me on Facebook, you'll just find a blank page. I owe you a great debt I will never be able to pay and look forward to trying. I'm not going to pour my heart out, because I will do it in person one day.

To the boys. Long live the brotherhood.

Made in the USA
Middletown, DE
14 October 2023